CREATED *to* THRIVE

Cultivating Abuse-Free Faith Communities

General Editor
Elizabeth Beyer

FOREWORD BY
Scott Arbeiter

CBE International
www.cbeinternational.org

Created to Thrive: Cultivating Abuse-Free Faith Communities

Published by CBE International
122 W Franklin Ave, Suite 218
Minneapolis, MN 55404
www.cbeinternational.org

ISBN: 978-1-939971-90-6 (Print)
ISBN: 978-1-939971-21-0 (Hardcover)
ISBN: 978-1-939971-92-0 (MOBI)
ISBN: 978-1-939971-91-3 (EPUB)

Printed in the United States of America

Contents

What is Domestic Abuse?

Prevention and Intervention

Foreword

SCOTT ARBEITER[1]

Over the years, I have discovered two things about blind spots. The first is that I have them. The second is I cannot see them. Some of these are of small consequence (I cannot see the cowlick sticking up on the back of my head). However, others, if unattended, can have deep and enduring impact on those my life touches. For these, I need to be alerted (even disrupted) so I learn to see, confess, and change.

Blind spots also exist within our broader culture. Tragically, the evidence makes clear we are in such a place as regards the assault on the safety and dignity of women and girls around the world. We are yet blind to the depth and breadth of the assault on the *imago Dei* of over half the population of the world—women and girls who were created to thrive. Exploitation, diminishment, and abuse militate against the work of the Spirit of God both in and through these image bearers and must be confronted with hard facts, brutal honesty, and unwavering resolve.

Having worked for many years in business, pastoral ministry, and now as president of World Relief, I have been shocked to observe how widespread, debilitating, and complex abuse (in all its forms) remains. We have seen that the vitality of entire communities is directly linked to the flourishing of women. This is why in many places warring factions intentionally abuse women and girls, as they know that to destroy the soul of the woman is to destroy the soul of the community. But "warfare" sadly also takes place in bedrooms, boardrooms, and yes, congregations around the world.

Faith communities have a critical role to play in awakening our culture to the reality that nothing limits a person more than to be attacked at the very core of their identity (and especially when abuse comes at the hands of those they have trusted). Sadly, faith communities can often contribute to the problem by failing to hear and believe the cries of women, failing to confront abusers, and failing to establish the culture, systems, and accountabilities that will break this cycle. And as men are disproportionately those who abuse and those who hold the power, lasting change will come only when men become fierce allies in this cause.

For all of these reasons I am deeply encouraged that this book is now in your hands. In it you will find insight born of sound research and lived experience. You will also find wisdom and grace expressed in compelling ways. You will grieve deeply but will also be reminded of hope. And I trust your newfound insights, grief, and hope will collide in such a way as to forge a deep resolve to participate with the Spirit of God to celebrate, protect, and elevate the beauty and fullness of the *imago Dei* found in all women.

Scott Arbeiter,

President, World Relief

January 2021

Introduction

ELIZABETH BEYER

It was October and Domestic Violence Awareness Month. At the urging of some church members to provide information to the congregation about abuse, the elders of a midwestern congregation agreed to devote ten minutes of the church service to talk about domestic violence. One of the elders, a woman and a psychologist, agreed to give the presentation. She offered a brief definition of domestic abuse, quoted statistics, and listed some of the red flags that could identify potential abusers. She ended with an invitation to those who thought they might be in a relationship with an abusive person to speak with one of the elders after the service. It was a small first step, but one that had a huge impact.

After the service that day, nearly half the elders were contacted by two or more women who expressed concern that they might be in a relationship with an abusive partner. The elders were stunned and unprepared for this response. They had no idea so many women in their congregation were suffering in their marriages. Equally troubling, it was clear that none of the women realized until that day that they were being abused. In a congregation that affirmed women's gifts and equal standing in Christ, even one that appointed women elders and pastors, how could there be so much abuse? What had gone wrong? And how should they respond?

Perhaps you pastor a church or lead a Christian organization and find yourself in the same place as the leaders of that midwestern church. You work hard to foster an environment where all members can use their gifts and fulfill their callings. But you may not know the prevalence of abuse in your congregation and you may be afraid that you lack the resources or skill to respond. You may have learned of instances of abuse but don't know how to respond to that disclosure. How can leaders move from good intentions to best practices?

In the course of CBE's work, we have heard from countless women who shared their stories of abuse and marginalization in the church, of pain and disillusionment as a result of their treatment by those who claim to love them. Whether the abuse was from an intimate partner, family member, coworker, or spiritual leader, their stories made it painfully clear that there was a connection between the church's stated and implied views on women and their abuse and marginalization. This book was born out of the desire to explore the correlation between deeply held views about women's worth and the consequences of their devaluation, while also proposing solutions that can create a safe space where all members can flourish. The contributors, each highly qualified in their respective areas, tackle topics related to abuse, exposing the myths and dangers and proposing remedies.

Domestic abuse comes in many forms: physical, emotional, psychological, sexual, economic, and spiritual. Studies show that it is prevalent and occurs in all types of relationships regardless of socioeconomic status, age, education, ethnicity, religion, or sexual orientation. As you review the statistics below, consider the estimates that the rate of abuse inside the church is equal to the rate in the general population. In the United States,

- Over ten million people experience domestic violence each year.[1]
  - One in four women and one in ten men experienced intimate partner violence (IPV) and reported some form of IPV-related impact.[2]
  - An estimated forty-eight million women and thirty-seven million men experienced psychological aggression by an intimate partner during their lifetime.[3]
  - Nearly eleven million women and five million men who reported a violent incident said it happened before the age of eighteen.[4]
- Twenty-one percent of all violent crimes are domestic. Of that domestic violence, 15 percent is due to intimate partner violence.[5]
- Twenty thousand phone calls a day are made to domestic violence hotlines.[6]

- Most domestic violence is committed against females (76 percent compared to males at 24 percent).[7]
- Nearly two thousand women were murdered by men in 2018. Compared to men, women are far more likely to be killed by a spouse, intimate acquaintance, or family member, than by a stranger. Of those who knew their offenders, 63 percent were wives or intimate partners of their killers.[8]
- Nearly half of female homicide victims are killed by a current or former male intimate partner.[9]
- In general, black and indigenous women are murdered at significantly higher rates than women of other races.[10]
- Women with a disability are significantly more likely to report experiencing IPV compared to women without a disability.[11]
- Domestic violence costs the US economy $67 billion due to lost productivity, increased healthcare costs, criminal justice processes, and other costs.[12]

No form of violence or abuse is acceptable, and before you begin this book, it is important to differentiate between domestic violence and situational violence. Domestic violence is distinguished by a *pattern* of abuse. The tactics and types of abuse may vary (financial, psychological, physical, economic, or emotional), but the one constant is that each act is part of one partner's effort to exert power and control over the other. Situational violence is different from domestic violence in that (1) it usually doesn't form a pattern, (2) it occurs when one or both partners manage conflict with violence, (3) it is limited to a specific situation, and (4) it usually doesn't escalate over time. This book seeks to address only domestic and church abuse, exploring the ways that the church's theology can be complicit in perpetuating it.

The first section of *Created to Thrive* provides an overview of various facets of domestic violence. Natalie Collins looks at the language and underlying myths about abuse that are held by Christians. She then offers principles for effectively challenging abusive behavior. Chuck Derry shares insights gained from his work with batterers and offers best practices for holding them accountable while providing safety for victims. Rebecca Kotz identifies forms of sexual abuse in dating and marital relationships and outlines the dos and don'ts of supporting victims/survivors. Annette Oltmans contributes two chapters, each focused on little-discussed aspects of abuse. The first outlines psychologically aggressive acts called covert emotional abuse. The second explores Double Abuse which are actions taken by—sometimes well-meaning—individuals or groups that exacerbate a victim's trauma. Edith Johnson's chapter reveals the serious health impacts of abuse on victims, emphasizing the urgency of taking all abuse seriously.

Section two addresses prevention and intervention, helping pastors and leaders provide structures that encourage safety and flourishing for all their members. Mimi Haddad shows the link between negative ideas about women and harmful consequences that mark the lives of many women and girls in the church, demonstrating that our beliefs about women's fundamental worth matter. In her chapter on sexual integrity, Rebecca Kotz invites readers to focus on understanding what constitutes healthy sexuality in egalitarian relationships. Johnrice Newton's chapter considers both guidelines and examples for teaching and preaching about domestic violence. Jeanne Porter King contributes two chapters, one that identifies barriers to developing women's leadership and how to break them down, and another on how to recognize leadership gifts in the women of your church or organization, and find ways to make space for them. Antoinette Alvarado explores mentorship models that can be implemented to bring more women into leadership, and Ashley Easter presents two case studies of church abuse and offers guidelines for how to prevent it. Finally, in "Developing a Code of Conduct," Nicola Lock provides information and resources to help leaders create a code of conduct to safeguard all members of their church or organization.

This book is not a comprehensive treatment of domestic and church abuse. The topic is so large and complex that no single resource can adequately address the many aspects of abuse. Rather, *Created to Thrive* is an introduction to the multiple facets of domestic abuse and its prevention and is meant to be a catalyst for further study and work. To facilitate that study, you will find more resources in the appendix.

Our hope is that the information offered in this book is an impetus for transformation for you and your church or organization and that it becomes a stepping-stone to greater freedom. We welcome your feedback as your community uses this resource, which helps us improve future editions. Send your feedback to CBE@cbinternational.org.

Words Make Worlds: How We Speak About Abuse

NATALIE COLLINS

Words make worlds.[1] This wisdom of the Jewish tradition asserts that our words and the way we use them are part of forming the world. In the Genesis creation narrative, God's words speak the world into being, "Then God said, 'Let there be light,' and there was light" (Gen. 1:3, NRSV). John's gospel describes Jesus as the Word, "And the Word became flesh and lived among us, and we have seen his glory, the glory as of a father's only son, full of grace and truth" (John 1:14). We find ourselves within a Christian tradition in which words have power. Proverbs warns us that, "Death and life are in the power of the tongue" (Prov. 18:21). James asserts, "And the tongue is a fire. The tongue is placed among our members as a world of iniquity; it stains the whole body, sets on fire the cycle of nature, and is itself set on fire by hell" (Jas. 3:6).

A partner's verbal abuse can be devastating, and includes their language, tone of voice, and the wider context. Someone may call their partner awful names. Using hurtful words to describe their partner communicates to their partner that no one else would ever want them. Tone of voice and body language can turn seemingly innocuous comments into threats. Explicit threats constitute verbal violence.

For years, I ran groups with women whose partners were abusive. On one occasion I was running a group, and Anthea sat with me. She said she was confused, "This morning something weird happened. My partner lay in bed with me. He started stroking my neck. He laughed and said, 'If you ever tried to leave me, I'd have to slit your throat, wouldn't I?' And then he laughed some more. Is that weird?" Her partner's tone and general manner left her feeling confused rather than utterly terrified at the death threat she had received.

Verbal abuse is one element of the harm that words can do. Another aspect is how we speak about abuse. As we seek to raise awareness, educate others, or speak about abuse in day-to-day conversations, every word that we use in our speech or writing has the potential to either reinforce problematic beliefs and attitudes about abuse or to challenge them.

Anyone who has worked on domestic abuse issues for more than two minutes will be familiar with the questions asked by the general public: "Why doesn't she just leave?" "What about the men?" "Abuse is a private matter, why should we get involved?" "Just because he's a bad husband, doesn't make him a bad father does it?" These questions betray the deeper attitudes and beliefs about abuse that underpin societal ambivalence toward abuse, leaving many abusers free to harm with impunity.

Media reporting of men who kill their female partners or children is littered with justifications and minimizations. Men who kill are referred to variously as "jilted," "broken-hearted," and "pained by . . . separation."[2] The women they kill are often blamed. She left him, had an affair, denied him access to the children, or found a new partner. In everyday conversation this reporting could sound like, "Oh how awful for him, his wife left him, so he killed her. He's such a nice man! How hard it must have been for him."

Philosopher Kate Manne coined the term *himpathy* to describe "the excessive or inappropriate sympathy extended to a male agent or wrongdoer over his female victim."[3] As the #MeToo movement has risen across the Western world, so have levels of himpathy. Many lines of print and personal conversations are focused on how hard it is for men to live in a context where they might be accused of rape. Outrage for men whose flirting might be interfered with seems to outweigh the horror of a world in which no woman or girl can guarantee that a man will not rape them.

Within this context, the concept of words making worlds is an important one. Every verbalization of victim blaming, celebration of harmful masculinity, and minimization or justification of abuse contributes to a society in which domestic abuse is perpetrated and those who are harmed are at least as likely to be shamed as they are to be supported by many people in their lives and communities. Within churches, it is sadly the case that shame and ignorance are even more prevalent. Christian leaders and others who are preaching and offering pastoral support do not always need to be experts in understanding abuse, but they do need to consider how they use language. This chapter will look at some of the language and underlying myths about abuse that Christians (and the wider society) hold and offer a few basic principles that can increase the potential for effectively responding to abuse and challenging abusive behavior.

Language and Myths

Women are just as likely to be abusive as men.

Throughout this chapter I have referred to abusers as male and those they abuse as female. This is because the data evidences this to be the case. In the US, 86.1 percent of offenders in spousal abuse were male (82.4 percent of dating violence offenders were male).[4] 84.3 percent of spousal abuse victims were female (85.9 percent of dating violence victims were female). In the UK, 92.1 percent of defendants were male, 7.9 percent were female; 83.3 percent of victims were female and 16.7 percent were male.[5] Often it is argued that men are less likely to report abuse than women. However, UK research found that women were three times more likely than men to get arrested for domestic violence, regardless of who called the police.[6] There are groups of women who are less likely to report abuse, including disabled women and those within Muslim communities. Yet, we know that rates of male violence toward women are high in both communities. UK murder rates also echo men as the minority of victims; six percent of men murdered are killed by a partner, whereas 44 percent of women murdered are killed by a partner.[7]

In recent years there are those who would assert that men are almost as likely to be victims of abuse as women, with women almost as likely to be perpetrators of abuse as men. Research that has sought to assert this has not engaged with the wider aspects of coercive control and doesn't take into account women acting in self-defense. Men are generally the perpetrators and women are generally the victims. This does not invalidate men who are subjected to abuse any more than breast cancer campaigns that focus on women seek to invalidate male breast cancer sufferers or that women's experiences of suicide are invalidated in suicide campaigns that focus on men. This is about proportionality according to the facts. Abuse is never acceptable and always harmful, whoever is perpetrating it and whoever is subjected to it, but we must always be mindful that domestic abuse is a gendered issue.

Real abuse is bad, but these days nearly anything counts as abuse.

The public conversation about abuse has escalated dramatically in the wake of the #MeToo movement. While many people view this as a profound and important moment in history, some people are concerned that it diminishes "real abuse," with others sure that the issue is being blown out of all proportion. This is not the first time such arguments have been put forward.

In 1896 Freud published *The Aetiology of Hysteria*, arguing that women's mental health issues were generally a result of men sexually abusing them. He subsequently withdrew his analysis in disbelief that men were sexually abusing girls and women on such a massive scale. Instead, he concluded women had subconscious sexual desire for their fathers. Reports about Jimmy Saville and other famous men abusing children were ignored because it was too extraordinary to believe.

There will always be people who do not want to believe the world is a dangerous place for women. As psychiatrist and trauma specialist Judith Herman explains, "Women quickly learn that rape is a crime only in theory; in practice the standard for what constitutes rape is set not at the level of women's violation but just above the level of coercion acceptable to men."[8] Rather than seeing #MeToo as an unfounded "moral panic" leaving women with a "victimhood mentality," perhaps it is time for us to accept (where Freud could not) that there is a society-wide issue with a significant proportion of men believing they are entitled to sexual access to female bodies.

It's a private/family matter, we shouldn't be getting involved.

The false dichotomy of public and private stems from the Enlightenment, during which women were relegated to the private sphere of the home and childrearing and excluded from the public sphere of politics, government, and civic life. As integrated human beings, what takes place in the home affects the marketplace and vice versa. Second wave feminism's cry that "the personal is political" came about in recognition that the violence and oppression that men subjected women to was political. In 2008, it was estimated that domestic violence cost the UK economy £15.7 billion; in the US, that cost is estimated at $3.6 trillion.[9] This cost is not private but public. Christian arguments viewing domestic abuse as a private matter ring rather hollow when those same Christians generally oppose abortion and pornography—both of which could be argued to be private matters.

But he's such a nice man!

There is a presumption that if we haven't experienced someone as abusive, then they couldn't be abusive. Abusers are generally only abusive toward their partner (or an ex-partner) and their children. He needs to ensure that his partner will not be believed if she does speak out, and so he seeks to turn others into his allies.

There is a human tendency to make abusers into "monsters." We all want to believe that we are safe from abuse. Presuming that abusers are easily identifiable is a strategy for maintaining that belief. It can seriously threaten someone's sense of psychological safety if their character judgement does not enable them to recognize an abuser. However, in reality the only way to protect ourselves from abusers is to presume that they are likely to be people who are average, ordinary, and often very likeable.

She's not that sort of woman, though.

Alongside the monstering of abusers, another strategy that operates in maintaining psychological safety is the stereotype of the "abused woman." She is usually poor, uneducated, already struggling with low self-esteem, and lacking in confidence. It is presumed that only those with some form of moral or other deficit would begin or maintain a relationship with an abuser.

After the First World War, the traditionalist view was that "the soldier who developed a traumatic neurosis was at best a constitutionally inferior human being, at worst a malingerer and a coward."[10] Society now understands that war is inherently traumatic, but when it comes to domestic abuse, entrenched attitudes remain about those who "allow themselves to be abused." This is utterly contradictory. The nature of abuse means the person is *not* allowing it, but they are being subjected to it. The only commonality among those who have been abused is the misfortune of meeting an abuser.

Why doesn't she just leave?

Leading from the presumed flawed character of the person who is being abused is the question of why someone doesn't simply leave an abuser. It is understandable that people cannot fathom why someone remains in a relationship with an abuser, but the question betrays numerous misunderstandings about abuse.

Nobody asks, "Why doesn't he just stop?" The abuser is the one perpetrating the harm, committing illegal offenses, and destroying lives, yet the public focus is on what his partner should do. Male violence is presumed to be static; we cannot even begin to imagine an abuser changing, and so we focus solely on what his partner should (or should not) be doing. Yet, it is only in abusers stopping their abuse that we can truly effect change.

The primary reason that someone does not leave an abusive partner is because the abuser's behavior makes such action impossible. Through isolating her, devaluing her, degrading her, making her financially dependent on him, and convincing her that he will kill her/the children/her family/pets/friends if she leaves, she is forced to stay with him. It can feel like the safest option, particularly as an abuser is most likely to kill his partner within the first year of her separating from him.[11]

Alongside the abuser's behavior is his partner's physiology. Both psychology and theology recognize that humans have a basic need to maintain attachment. In situations of trauma this is particularly pronounced. Where it is assumed that someone would automatically move away from a perpetrator, the victim's physiological response is to maintain the attachment if the abuser is a primary object of attachment for the victim.[12] A domestic abuser will isolate his partner from other attachment objects (friends, family, colleagues, etc.), and upon traumatizing her, she will find that the only person left to attach to is the abuser. I describe this process as "traumatic attachment."[13] It is also known as trauma bonding, Stockholm syndrome, and the betrayal bond.

Added to this is the social context where a woman will be judged a failure for not working at her marriage or for leaving her children fatherless. Within the church this social context is particularly pronounced with Christian leaders bemoaning the "fatherless wastelands of social deprivation."[14] Certain teachings on divorce and forgiveness can leave women feeling like God wants them to endure the abuse.

Well, those women who are abused often end up with more than one abusive partner in their lifetime. It's obvious that they have a personality that attracts abusers.

There have been psychological theories put forward about women's "learned helplessness," or their sadomasochism, when a woman repeatedly has abusive partners. Such theories are incredibly damaging. In my experience working with women who have been subjected to abuse, only a minority of women have more than one abusive partner. For those who do have more than one abusive partner, each abuser looks different from the previous one. One abuser will demand his partner not work and remain at home with the children, another abuser will demand his partner work long hours and refuse her access to the children. These tactics appear very different but are in fact different ways of achieving a single goal—controlling a partner.

Women are socialized to be kind and caring, surrounded by messages that they are a failure without a partner. Disney, the *Fifty Shades* series, romantic films, and magazines all give women (and men) very distorted ideas about love and romance, which may leave women unable to identify an abuser, particularly if he is tall, dark, handsome, and rich. Building literacy about abuse and toxic cultural messages can help women and girls to recognize abusers before they have already invested themselves in a relationship with one.

Traumatic attachment is often experienced as a feeling of intense love. If a woman manages to leave an abuser successfully (without him murdering her), she will often discover that non-abusive partners do not provide that same feeling of intense love. Until women in this situation understand traumatic attachment, women who have pursued intense relationships that defy logic and sense can seem aligned with cultural understandings of love and romance.

It's an abusive relationship.

The term *abusive relationship* has become very pervasive. However, it is not an abusive *relationship* that is the problem, but rather an abusive *person* who abuses his partner within the context of a relationship. By using the term *abusive relationship,* we suggest that it is a relationship issue, which could be responded to with relationship-based solutions. We also infer that if the relationship ends, then the abuse will end. This is not the case. Many abusers continue to harm their partner and any children after the relationship ends. This may include stalking and harassment, using child contact to undermine his ex-partner's parenting, denying financial support, threats, violence, and murder.

They both need to be working at the relationship. It can't all be his fault.

Generally, when a couple has issues, both parties have responsibility for the issues (and for the solutions). This is not the case when one partner is abusive. The abuser holds the power and maintains control over his partner, and resources like marriage counseling, marriage enrichment courses, or books about resolving conflict will not be helpful. In most cases they will make the situation worse. The abuser will use couple's counseling to manipulate the counselor into being his ally and will use relationship resources to further blame and berate his partner.

He didn't mean to hurt her.

Disputing the abuser's intention is a way of minimizing his behavior. Intention is not the same as impact, and so regardless of his intention, if he has hurt his partner, then her experience of the harm should be validated and taken seriously. The majority of abusers are entirely intentional in their behavior. Their violence and abuse serve to get them what they want—a partner who is controlled and serves the abuser's needs, wants, and whims.

It was only a little push.

Abuser's ubiquitously use minimization, denial, and blame to avoid responsibility for their choices and behavior. Others around them may tend to repeat these minimizations (including their partner). "Only" and "little" within this sentence are intended to minimize his behavior. In response, we could ask the abuser why he only pushed her, why he didn't punch her in the face. The answer would likely be that punching is too severe. However, if an abuser can choose what level of violence to use, he is clearly able to choose not to use violence. Alongside pushing his partner, an abuser will likely have also called her names, thrown things, isolated her from family and friends, and controlled other aspects of her life. By focusing only on the act of physical violence, we are blinded to the wider elements of coercive control, which are used by an abuser to maintain power and control over his partner (and children).

Abuse is always about physical violence.

Control rather than physical violence is the primary element of abuse. In maintaining control, the *threat* of violence can often be more effective than the physical assault itself. Some abusers do regularly use violence, but many use it either occasionally or not at all. One act of physical violence by an abuser can be enough to keep someone controlled for twenty years, while another abuser's efforts to degrade, demean, or devalue their partner can be as effective as violence in maintaining control.

Abuse is nearly always the fault of drugs and alcohol. If we deal with those dependencies, abuse will stop.

As anti-abuse specialist Lundy Bancroft explains, "Alcohol cannot create an abuser, and sobriety cannot cure one."[15] He explains that substances do not alter a person's *value system* and although substances may lower an abuser's inhibitions and might increase the severity of violence, they will not cause a non-abusive person to become violent. An abuser's other controlling and coercive behaviors will remain present even when he is not under the influence of substances. And addiction recovery can be used by an abuser to further control his partner. A threatened relapse may leave the abuser's partner feeling she has to do what he wants, "If you don't give me sex when I want it, I'll turn back to drink."

Hurt people hurt people. Abusers are hurting, and we need to help them heal.

The majority of abusers have not been abused themselves, with research suggesting that "men who are violent toward other *men* are often victims of child abuse—but the connection is much less clear for men who assault women."[16] Most abusers are male, but most of those who are abused are female, which suggests that the issue is not that "hurt people hurt people," but rather "some hurt men, hurt people (mostly women)." While trauma can affect people in lots of different ways, it is hugely problematic to attribute abusive behavior to trauma. An abuser makes choices to behave abusively, and his behavior stems from beliefs of ownership and entitlement ("I own my partner and am therefore entitled to get what I want"). Addressing abusive behavior requires abusers to identify and overcome these beliefs. Counseling and other therapeutic interventions will not only be unhelpful for the abuser, they may put the abuser's partner at greater risk of harm, as the abuser feels supported and is potentially given more justifications for his behavior from well-meaning supporters.

Abusers just need a chance to be listened to and heard. It's mainly about a struggle to express their emotions.

When a female politician expresses emotion, she is seen to be unfit for leadership, when a male politician does the same, he is described as passionate. Appealing to emotional literacy for abusers infantilizes the abuser and misunderstands the skills he has, generally. Most abusers are very able to manage their emotions, including hiding their behavior from others and targeting their partner and children. Abusers are not emotionally unskilled; they just choose to use their emotional skill to abuse their partner rather than to build a healthy, respectful relationship. In choosing to make space to listen to and hear people, our primary focus should be on listening to those who have been subjected to abuse, and their experiences should shape all of our listening to an abuser.

I've heard that pregnancy is a high-risk factor for an abuser; that's because his partner's pregnancy hormones make her less agreeable, and she won't be giving him enough sex.

An abuser's behavior may escalate during pregnancy, with one English survey finding that 17 percent of pregnant women are subjected to abuse.[17] The increase in abuse is never rooted in his partner's behavior. Many abusers engage in reproductive coercion, manipulating or forcing their partner into pregnancy by pricking holes in condoms, hiding her contraceptive pills, or secretly removing the condom during sex. By impregnating his partner, the abuser increases the potential for control and reduces the likelihood that his partner will leave him. However, paradoxically, the abuser's beliefs of ownership and entitlement may be threatened when his partner acts to protect her unborn child. This paradox means she is both less likely to leave (women generally do not want to leave their baby's father), but more likely to resist the abuser's control. And the abuser's behavior escalates.

Our church is starting an anger management course to help abusers.

It is more palatable to see abusers as out of control, but their choices and behaviors are a result of their need to be in control. Anger management, like couple's counseling, can do more harm than good and collude with the idea that an abuser is not responsible or in control of his actions. The most appropriate intervention for abusers is an accredited perpetrator program. Within the UK, a church could work with the national perpetrator accreditation body, called Respect, to develop a program for working with men who use abusive behavior.

An abuser's behavior will stop if he is supported by his church to repent.

Knowing abuse is rooted in beliefs of ownership and entitlement enables us to understand that the work of deconstructing abusive behavior is slow and gradual. God can do miraculous transformation in people's lives, but an over reliance on immediate transformation through repentance is dangerous for women and children and can be taken advantage of by abusers. Churches should always prioritize the safety and wellbeing of women and children by directing abusers to specialist services that will help them take responsibility for their behavior. If an abuser is authentic in his repentance, he will not object to measures that will make his family safer or to attending a program that will help ascertain that he has changed.

When an abuser repents, his partner must forgive him and reestablish the relationship.

Abusive behavior has long-term consequences. Very often it is only once an abuser begins to change that his partner feels safe enough to leave him. While forgiveness and reconciliation are part of the Christian tradition, neither of these nullify the consequences of someone's behavior. The prodigal son in Jesus's parable did not inherit further money; it all went to the older brother who remained faithful to the father (Luke 15:31). If either the abuser's expectation or the community's expectation requires the abuser's partner to remain in the relationship, he remains in control of the situation. She must have *free* choice to leave him. If he has repented and fully recognized the impact of his behavior, he will be supportive of her flourishing, even if it means she ends the relationship.

What's happened is bad, but we can't be seen to be supporting divorce.

Many Christians are reluctant to address abuse because it appears to offer acceptance of divorce; however, as Bible scholar David Instone-Brewer has found, Jesus's teaching on divorce came within a context where a husband's abuse of his wife was grounds for divorce under Levitical law.[18] Divorce is the public breaking of a covenant just as a marriage ceremony is the public making of a covenant. The abuser will have repeatedly broken the marriage covenant privately through his abusive behavior, and her filing for divorce is making public his abuse and covenant breaking. It is not a moral failure on her part. The Bible explains that, "Religion that is pure and undefiled before God, the Father, is this: to care for orphans and widows in their distress, and to keep oneself unstained by the world" (Jas. 1:27). If we do not prioritize the needs of women and children who have been abused, we cannot call our religion pure and undefiled.

Women who leave a husband who has been abusive clearly do not take their marriage vows seriously.

To get to the stage of acknowledging that a partner is abusive is extremely difficult for most women and taking steps to leave—particularly for women of faith—is not done lightly or without needing to process a great deal of extreme loss. One of the fears that keeps religious women in a relationship with an abuser is fear that she will be judged not to have cared about her marriage. If we want to build communities of faith that are safe for women and children, we must trust that women who leave their husbands do so as a last resort. Sadly, it is often an extremely radical approach to presume that we can trust women.

He's a wonderful father; he just isn't a good husband.

A core element of being a wonderful father is being a good co-parent. Raising children cannot be separated from the co-parent relationship. A father must be supportive and caring towards his children's mother if he is to care for his children effectively. In a household with children, a domestic abuser always abuses the children as well as his partner. No matter how many ways their mother seeks to protect them, the children will be harmed by the tension, violence, destruction of property, irate behavior at mealtimes, controlling attitudes, and the abuser's general demeanor of entitlement. Both during the relationship and if the relationship ends, the children become a weapon to abuse, rather than human beings with needs, feelings, hopes, and dreams.

Children need their father in their lives, or it will cause them untold damage.

The impact of domestic abusers on children is well documented. UNICEF explains, "Personality and behavioral problems among children exposed to violence in the home can take the forms of psychosomatic illnesses, depression, suicidal tendencies, and bed-wetting. . . . Some studies suggest social development is also damaged."[19] Many abusers engage in maternal alienation—turning the children against their mother—either during the relationship or after it has ended. While having an absent father may lead to identity issues, and the value of positive fathering cannot be overstated, the tangible and lasting damage of having an abusive father must also be recognized. Children need protecting from harm by informed adults, rather than the amorphous concept of fatherlessness being used as a weapon to prevent women and children from accessing safety away from abusive men.

Christian culture regularly bemoans fatherlessness. In his book *A Better Story*, psychiatrist Glynn Harrison explains, "Marriage creates a culture that binds men to their responsibilities for the children they bring into the world."[20] Divorce does not cause motherlessness. Mothers stick around in their children's lives even after divorce. Perhaps we could consider fatherhood itself as not properly focused on children if a relationship breakdown with the children's mother is enough to make men absent from their children's lives.

Disabled women are less likely to be abused because men who remain in relationships with them are obviously very committed to them.

Some abusers will deliberately target vulnerable women (although, many abusers do not). If a woman is more likely to become dependent on their partner, this enables the abuser to quickly increase his control. Women with disabilities are 40 percent more likely to be abused by a partner,[21] and sadly their disability will often leave them being disbelieved and not trusted. Their partner will often be celebrated for "taking on" someone with additional needs and women's capacity to seek help is then diminished further.

Principles in Addressing How We Speak About Abuse

1. The situation may not present as domestic abuse.

    Often when someone is subjected to abuse, denial is a survival strategy. Someone may seek help from the church for marital issues, parenting advice, mental health struggles, or general support, but underlying these support needs may be an abusive partner. Taking the time to ask questions and reserving judgement is helpful. Until you are certain, presume that the situation could involve an abuser, regardless of whether the woman's partner is a church leader, businessman, police officer, or respected in any other way.

2. Name the abuser.

    When we talk about abuse, we will often ignore the agent of the abuse. If we are discussing a situation where the perpetrator's name is known, his name should be used throughout the conversation. If his name is not known, ensure that we are including considerations about him and that our language places the responsibility onto him.

3. Avoid minimization, denial, and blame-shifting.

    Minimization includes using qualifiers, like "just" or "only," and in suggestions that it could have been worse. Someone can deny either the abuse itself ("I can't believe that he would do that") or deny the intention of the abuser ("I'm sure he didn't mean it"). Blame-shifting involves redirecting responsibility for the abuse elsewhere. "Had he been drinking?" "What did you do to let things get this bad?" "He has been under a lot of stress at work hasn't he?" Avoiding these will help us ensure we place the responsibility on the abuser.

4. Do not engage in himpathy.

 Himpathy is "the excessive or inappropriate sympathy extended to a male agent or wrongdoer over his female victim."[22] When thinking about, discussing, or supporting someone through abuse, be aware of the tendency to himpathize. In both your language and thought processes reflect on whether you are more understanding of the abuser or his partner. Do you find yourself more shocked about his violence or about her staying with him?

5. Trust women.

 The blaming of Eve across Christian tradition evidences how distrust of women spans the centuries. Patriarchal culture conditions both men and women to disbelieve and distrust women. Legal expert Helena Kennedy's books, *Eve Was Framed* and *Eve was Shamed*, provide stark evidence of the distrust of women that remains deeply entrenched across society, while Riet Bons Storm's book, *The Incredible Woman*, documents the ways Christian pastoral care views women as not credible. In understanding and speaking about abuse, we may question whether women are exaggerating, being alarmist, or maintaining a "victim mentality," or we can choose to communicate that we trust women and their experiences.

Conclusion

The myths and language identified in this chapter are relevant to us all. We all have believed many of these myths at one time, and many people still do. Taking the time to identify this enables us to begin deconstructing and rejecting the myths and problematic usage of language. We need to consider how we can build church communities and cultures in which these myths are dismantled by developing a vocabulary that challenges, rather than colludes, with abusers. The five principles listed are a good start, but there is much more to be done. We must all grapple with the ways we are part of the problem in order that we become part of the solution.

Why Men Batter

CHUCK DERRY

In this chapter, I will be using gender-specific terms when referring to victims and perpetrators, identifying the man as the abuser and the woman as the victim. This language reflects the vast majority of domestic-violence-related cases where there is an ongoing dynamic of power and control. The examples of men who batter, that I use in this chapter below, are also only in the context of heterosexual relationships.

In cases where women use violence in heterosexual relationships, "the context of that violence tends to differ from men. Many women who do use violence against their male partners are being battered. Their violence is primarily used to respond to and resist the controlling violence being used against them".[1]

While men can also be the victims of battering, that victimization is most common in same-sex relationships.[2] Likewise, in violent relationships where the woman is the batterer, those also occur most commonly in same-sex relationships.[3] Many of the references in this chapter related to men's tactics to control women also correspond with the tactics and intents of those who batter within same-sex relationships.

The Power and Control System

Before we dive into who batters and why, it is essential to understand what battering is. I use the term "battering" because it puts the physical violence aspect of abuse into a broader context of power and control. Intimate partner violence is not just one person hitting another. It is one partner, usually the man who is bigger and stronger, using violence to control "his" woman. Once the act of physical and/or sexual violence has occurred, the woman now knows that he is willing to hurt her to get his way. This experience and the ongoing threat of violence becomes the foundation, the "rubber on the wheel," so to speak, of a system of power and control that the offender establishes.

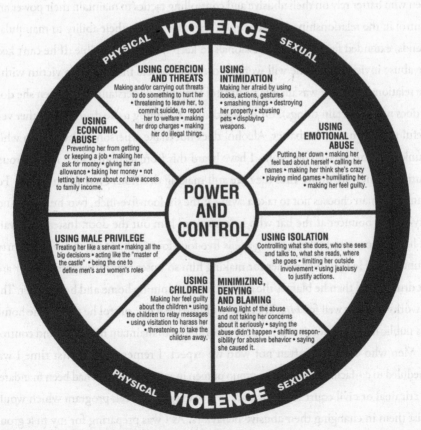

Power and Control Wheel, used with permission of DAIP

The Power and Control Wheel identifies the system of battering as a sophisticated strategy where the batterer utilizes multiple methods to abuse: intimidation; emotional and psychological abuse; isolation from family, friends, and colleagues; minimizing and denying of violence or blaming the victim for his behavior; using and/or abusing the children to control them, and their mother; exercising cultural norms of male privilege to assert his power and dominance in the family and relationships; controlling money and all family assets; verbal and nonverbal coercion and threats; and often presents himself in public as a very nice, respectful, and caring man to hide his abuse. This all makes it very difficult for her and her children to live safely inside or outside of the relationship.

Who Are These Guys? And How Do They Get Away With it?

Men who batter rely on their abusive and controlling tactics to maintain their power and control in the relationship and the family. They also rely on their ability to manipulate friends, extended family, and professionals to keep the abuse invisible. If he can't keep the abuse invisible, then he will work to convince others that he is the victim within the relationship, or he was unable to control himself ("understandably" when she does or does not do certain things). Or he was drunk. Claiming to be drunk is another very useful tool for men who batter. Alcohol does not make a person violent. Even while drunk, men are making decisions. I have heard this from alcoholic men in my groups routinely. They are aware that they are still making decisions even when drunk. For example, a man chooses not to take a swing at the six-foot-five-inch, two-hundred-and-fifty-pound bouncer at the bar who is "escorting" him out the door. Instead, he waits till he gets home and takes a swing at his five-foot-four-inch, one-hundred-and-forty-pound wife. He then blames her for making him so upset that he went to the bar and got drunk. And then he blames the alcohol for him coming home and beating her. This all works out very well for *him*. Together with the coercive control he uses in the home, this public manipulation is a key aspect of his ability to maintain his power and control.

Men who batter are often not who we expect. I remember the first time I was scheduled to co-facilitate a batterers group of men in 1983. These men had been mandated by criminal or civil court to participate in a twenty-four-week program which would assist them in changing their abusive behaviors. As I was preparing for my first group session, I thought to myself, "This will be really interesting. I wonder how these guys will be different from me?"—since I had never been abusive to women. But that is not what was interesting. What was interesting was how much I was like the men who batter and sexually assault their wives and girlfriends, not how I was different from them. For example, in one of the first sessions I co-facilitated, a group member told a very sexist joke and we all laughed, including me. Then the female co-facilitator said "Hey, let's put the brakes on this and back up a little. What was that joke really about?" And I thought to myself, "Oh damn, I just laughed at this nasty joke." And I got called out on it, along with the other men in the room. This was just the tip of the iceberg. As time went on, the similarities between us were notable and quite pervasive.

After facilitating and coordinating the batterers intervention program for over ten years and working with over two thousand men, I can count on both hands the number of men I actually disliked. The vast majority of the men were very likeable—to such a degree that I had to go back and look at their files to remind myself what they were like in private, at home. So again, men who batter do not often fit the stereotype we have in our heads. And that, of course, is to their advantage. If he can convince you that he is a good man, he can also convince you that it is his wife or the relationship that is the problem, not him. This is a key strategy of men who batter: divert attention from their behaviors, and when that does not work, present themselves as the victim of those they are actually victimizing.

I have had multiple conversations with men who identified the various tactics they used with law enforcement officers and other helping professionals, including counselors, to shift the focus to the woman and escape any responsibility and subsequent accountability for their behavior. This was all effectively done at the expense of their wife/partner and children, who live with constant fear of retribution and abuse.

In the 1980s, the court systems and other professionals were suggesting or mandating marriage counseling when violence was involved in a relationship. At that time, they believed the violence was a symptom of a bad relationship, rather than understanding that the bad relationship was a symptom of the violence. I heard multiple stories from women who had been forced or coerced into these marital counseling sessions or were motivated to go by a desperate hope for change. They reported how they did not even get out of the parking lot after their first session without being back handed across the face in the car, and hearing their husband/partner say something like, "See, even the therapist says it's your fault. I've been telling you that for years, but would you listen to me? No way. Well now you know. So, don't try to put this all on me!" This was simply due to the therapist or counselor treating this as a relationship problem, where both parties bear responsibility for the issues that come forward.

Not in this case! When men batter their partners, it is about the individual conscious decision to hurt someone in an attempt to get what they want. That may include wanting their partner to shut up, wanting their partner to admit to things they did not do, wanting to spend the money as they please, wanting to win an argument, or wanting to make the process of maintaining power and control easier and easier as time goes on. Once his use and threat of violence is made clear, even a simple look can produce the results he wants.

Men in batterers groups routinely talked about their "look." Often it only took a "look" to get his wife to start or stop doing something. One man told a story of being at an event in a large community center. He was talking to someone on one side of the hall and his wife was talking to someone on the other side of the hall. He did not want her talking to that person, so he caught her eye and gave her his "look". Within forty-five seconds she was standing right next to him. No one around them realized what had happened. The person he was talking to had no idea this was happening, and the person she was talking to had no idea this was happening. But, he said, she knew by his look that "if she did not get her butt over here right now, there was going to be trouble." She knew she was going to get hurt. This control, intimidation and isolation becomes so sophisticated that it simply takes one look in a crowded room to let her know she must submit to his wishes now.

Understanding the consciousness of this behavior becomes key in providing effective responses to assist both the adult and child victims, and to hold the perpetrator accountable for his abuse. Understanding that this is a *choice*, not a mental health problem, or a psychological issue, or some type of "anger problem," guides helping professionals in providing the necessary response to heal the wounds and provide the needed safety for victims, and perhaps impact the decision-making process of the man who batters.

When you begin to understand this is a conscious decision, you begin to wonder how you can make it stop. How do you impact his behavior? His decisions?

The Benefits of Violence

When I started facilitating mandated groups for men who batter in the early to mid-80s, we were concentrating on building skills for having healthy relationships, emotional identification and self-control, anger management, etc. Then battered women in Duluth, Minnesota got together to discuss the impact of the violence on their lives and created the Power and Control Wheel. What emerged from their discussions was a more complex picture of battering. The men who beat women, not only beat them, but controlled where they went, who they talked to, what they wore, if and where they worked, how the money was spent, when, with whom, and how they had sex, how the children were raised, how the domestic labor was done in the household, and on and on. Basically, the men controlled the women to get what they wanted; the threat and use of violence was the tool that made that happen. Violence is powerful.

At that time, I was training men in weekly groups to use assertiveness skills when in conflict with their wives or girlfriends, teaching them how to access and express their feelings appropriately. Then I would send them home to practice. The next week they would come back and report that their new assertiveness "skills" weren't working. I asked them why and they would say "Because she still did A, B, C, and D and would not do E, F, and G"—which is what *he* wanted. I then began to slowly understand that I was teaching men multiple personal life skills and they were simply using those skills in attempts to control their partner even more effectively. I was actually helping to develop more sophisticated batterers. When I began to listen, believe, and understand women's experiences, I began to understand that men who batter could not be this effective in their abusive and controlling behaviors unless they were fully aware of what they were doing, and the subsequent impacts it would have on those they abused. It was just too sophisticated!

So, what was the point? Why was he so invested in this controlling and abusive behavior? Finally, I asked the men in the group.

One night I started the group by asking the men what they thought the *benefits* were of their violence. At first, they all looked at each other (notably) and said, "There are no benefits." This did not surprise me, as men who batter routinely deny their actions *and* deny their intentions as well. So I said, "Well, there must be some benefits from the violence. Otherwise, why would you do it?" They looked at each other again, and one guy started admitting to the benefits. Then they all chimed in until the four by eight-foot blackboard I was writing their responses on was full, and we ran out of space.

(Please take a moment to consider the implications of each of these benefits.)

- **Get your way**
- Respect
- She won't argue
- Feeling superior
- She's accountable to me about being on time
- **I decide**
- Keeps the relationship going—she's too scared to leave
- Get the money
- Get sex
- **Total control** in decision making
- Use money for drugs
- Don't have to change for her
- Power Decide where we go
- Decide who she can see
- Decide what she can wear
- If she's late, she won't be again
- Intimidation
- She's scared and can't confront me
- Control the children
- Can convince her she's screwing up
- She feels less worthy, so she defers to my needs and wants
- She will look up to me and accept my decisions without an argument
- So she won't get help against me for past beatings because she has no friends to support her and she is confused by my lies
- Convince her she's nuts
- Convince her she's unattractive
- Convince her she's to blame
- Convince her she's the problem
- I can dump on her

- Can use kids to "spy" on mom
- Kids won't tell mom what I did
- Kids won't disagree with me
- Don't have to talk to her
- **I'm king of the castle**
- Have someone to unload on
- Have someone to bitch at
- She won't call police
- Tell kids they don't have to listen to mom
- Get her to drop charges
- Get her to support me to her family, my family, cops, prosecutors, other authorities, etc.
- Get her to admit it's her fault
- Win all the arguments
- She's to blame for the battering
- She's an object
- **I get a robot babysitter, maid, sex, food**
- She tells me I'm great
- Bragging rights
- If she works, I get her money
- Get her to quit job so she can take care of house
- Isolate her so friends can't confront me
- Decide how money is spent
- "I'm the breadwinner"
- Buy the toys I want
- Take time for myself
- She has to depend on me if I break her stuff
- **I get to know everything**
- She's a nursemaid
- She comforts me
- Supper on the table
- Invite friends over without her knowing equals more work for her
- No compromise equals more freedom. Don't have to listen

- to her complaints for not letting her know stuff
- She works for me
- I don't have to help out
- I don't have to hang out with her or kids
- Determine what values kids have—who they play with, what school they go to, or getting to ignore the process—dictating what they "need" in terms of food, clothes, recreation, etc.
- **Dictate reality, etc.**
- Kids on my side against her
- Kids do what I say
- Mold kids/her so that they will help do what I should do
- Keeps kids quiet about abuse
- Don't have to get up, take out garbage, watch kids, do dishes, get up at night with kids, do laundry, change diapers, clean house, bring kids to appointments or activities, mop floors, clean refrigerator, etc.
- **Answer to nobody**
- She's scared and won't go out and spend money
- **Do what you want, when you want to**
- Get to ignore/deny your history of violence and other irresponsible behavior
- Choose battles and what it will cost her
- **Don't have to listen to her wishes, complaints, anger, fears, etc.**
- Proves your superiority
- Make the rules, then break them when you want

The first time I did this exercise I looked at the blackboard and I thought to myself, "Oh my God, why give it up?" I then decided to ask the men. Why give it up? They filled a two-by-two-foot space on the black board with things like, "getting arrested," "divorce," "civil protection orders against you," "not being invited to adult kids' weddings," "having to go to groups like this," and that was about it. These men clearly understood the benefits of violence and how much they gained from this abuse, and that is why they did not want to stop. Violence is functional!

This was the first time I fully comprehended the necessity of a consistent, coordinated community response through the criminal, civil, and family court systems to levy safe and effective interventions that hold men who batter accountable, while preserving the safety of the women and children they abuse. It was on that day that I realized if I had to choose between providing batterers groups for men who batter *or* a consistently effective and accountable criminal, civil, and family court response to domestic violence, I would choose the latter every time. There are just too many benefits gained from this behavior.

Once I considered the "cost-benefit analysis" of their use of violence, I began to be much more effective in my work. It was astounding how dramatically the groups changed once I acknowledged and remembered that the violence was *functional* and that is why they used it.

Making Change

The "cost-benefit analysis" is evident in research which indicates that the more intrusive the interventions are by the courts for abusive behavior, the more likely the individual will change.[4] The following is an example of how we implemented the research into our batterer's groups in conjunction with the courts to provide consistent and meaningful parameters to those in batterer programs.

If a man in my program continued to blame his wife or partner or children for his abuse, or continued to deny his behavior into week sixteen of a twenty-four-week program, he would be terminated from the program and sent back to court for a violation of his probation. We recommended that he serve three to ten days in jail, and then return to the same group to start the program over. We were able to terminate men from the group under these circumstances because we were part of a broader

Coordinated Community Response (CCR) which focused criminal justice and other provider policies and procedures on victim safety and offender accountability. We knew the court had our backs.

We always suggested consequences such as partial jail time served and/or further restrictions on his criminal or civil court order. We also requested he return to the same group, so he did not have the opportunity to manipulate a new facilitator. He had to come back to the group where the facilitator knew of his manipulations, minimizing, denial, and blame, and he knew now that that behavior would not be tolerated.

Often, I would notice after men had returned to the group, usually about three months after being terminated, that they had changed. At week four or five, I would mention to him that I was noticing he was taking more responsibility for his abuse and not blaming his partner like he had before. Then I would ask him why. And man after man, through the years, would say the same thing, "Because I don't want to go to jail. I know I can't get away with it anymore." That was the primary motivator for change. The group sessions simply provided the challenge, a critical analysis of his actions, intents, and beliefs, support for change, and occasionally, a significantly new perspective. This new perspective, along with the consistent consequences, resulted in a change in his behavior.

It is critical to place parameters around an abusive man's behaviors and then stick to those parameters. This cannot be done by the victim herself, because she will be harmed. It can be done, however, when she has the support of the court system, other helping professionals, advocacy programs, family, friends, faith communities, and other social structures. Understanding that she bears no responsibility for his behavior begins the process of change and assistance.

Faith communities can be a foundation for safety, support, and care for women and children who are abused. They can also be used by the man who batters to manipulate their partner, their children, the courts, child protection services, and others in the community. I have worked with many Christian men who present themselves as God-fearing, moral, biblically-faithful individuals. Several times men brought their Bibles to group and actually waved the Bible saying it was God's will that men be in charge and have the right to punish their wives if she does not obey his wishes. Religion can be a very powerful social tool used by men to harm those they profess to love.

Men who batter will try to slip past the parameters and expectations required of them, irrespective of whether the parameters come from the criminal, civil, and family court system, from organizational practices in the workplace, other professional interventions, or congregational expectations. They will do so in very sophisticated ways. Once the intervention boundaries are set, it is critical that the batterer adheres to them consistently. As we maintain those boundaries and expectations, it lets men know they "can't get away with it anymore."

Faith communities have the power to assist victims and hold batterers accountable. Whether or not a church, synagogue, temple, or mosque becomes a tool of manipulation by the batterer is determined by that faith community. It is critical that comprehensive protocols be developed and implemented, and local advocacy programs assist in this development. Safe Havens Interfaith Partnership Against Domestic Violence is a national resource to assist communities in providing the support and assistance necessary in these dangerous and complicated circumstances. You can find their resources at www. interfaithpartners.org.

When developing protocols, in addition to providing support and safety, other factors should be considered. For instance, if the pastor, minister, or faith counselor is engaged in marital counseling with a couple and it becomes clear that domestic violence is occurring, how will the counselor attend to that reality? Under these circumstances, marriage and relationship counseling is dangerous for women and children.

As faith communities provide the needed support by understanding and articulating that the victim is not at fault for the abuse in any way, other factors come into play. For instance, what if they are separated and she has obtained a civil protection order that denies him access to her and restricts him from being within the same building, a park, or on a country road within one mile of her home? What does the faith community do about the couple's involvement in services, especially in communities where there is only one congregation of their faith? Who leaves that congregation, him or her?

In most cases where there are no protocols, there seems to be a default position. He simply continues going to services and she stops going because his presence there makes it too dangerous for her to attend. Or she must now drive thirty miles to the next town to go to services where it is safe. Either way, she loses her faith community. This can add a substantial burden to all the other complications she is currently juggling. Now she is a stranger in a new congregation while going through a separation or divorce (which is one of the most dangerous times for a woman), seeking housing and a new job, navigating legal obstacles, and attempting to keep herself and her children safe. What does the congregation do?

And what does a congregation do if she has *not* separated from him? Some women choose to say with their partner because it may be the safer option. How can effective assistance be provided for her and appropriate responses to his behavior be expressed to him? Is there a way to utilize the power of the community to influence him and stop his abuse?

Victim safety and *offender accountability* is the foundation of response protocols. Accountability begins with acknowledging that the man who was abusive is responsible for the harms he has created, and consequently responsible for mitigating those harms to the extent that he can. Accepting responsibility for creating harm and responsibility to mitigate that harm is not a common reaction from men who batter. Rather, when their violence and abuse is publicly recognized, often their response is to further isolate and blame their partner for their behavior and seek community support as they do so. So, he will turn to his congregation for "help," as he portrays himself as a victim going through this traumatic separation and false allegations his wife has made "in her effort to get the kids." So how might his congregation truly help him?

The best response is to clarify that you believe the woman, and encourage him to accept full responsibility for his violence and coercive control. Often, when his behavior is made public, especially through an arrest or civil protection order, a man will say, "Okay, I may be 99 percent responsible, but she needs to be responsible for her behavior too. She's not perfect." Which is another very successful tactic men attempt to use, because we all know none of us is perfect. But the point is that it doesn't matter what she does, because he does not have the right to beat, rape, and abuse her in a sophisticated system of coercive control (which he is attempting to facilitate at that very moment with the congregation, by shifting the focus away from himself and on to her). So, as you clarify again that you believe the woman who has shared these painful and traumatic experiences she (and her children) have been living through, and you believe he is 100 percent responsible for the decisions *he* makes, you begin to dismantle his system of power and control. This steadfast understanding and articulation then leads to action by the congregation. In this case, understanding that he is 100 percent responsible for his actions and subsequently 100 percent responsible for mitigating the harm he has created over the years, the congregation should ask him to leave at this time. This provides a safe and supportive space for her. In the event he accepts full responsibility for his actions and attends to appropriate accountability measures to mend the harm he has created, then he may return. This is totally dependent on his future decision making and subsequent behaviors. It's up to him!

What Does Accountability Look Like?

Accountability is the key indicator of change. To be accountable, a man must fully acknowledge his harmful behavior. He must dismantle the system of coercive power and control he has established and make amends for the harm he has created. What does this look like? First, he will listen to, accept, and abide by the wishes of the woman he abused. If they are still together, he will accept her independent opinions and her behaviors that he previously attempted to control. He will listen authentically to her anger, pain, and fear—without refuting or interrupting her. He will simply listen. And if he says anything, he should say, "Tell me more about that." He will support her parenting. He will share access to all bank accounts, assets, and financial resources. He will support her relationships with friends and colleagues, releasing her from his entrapment. He will honor her in stories to family and friends. He will fully acknowledge his abuse and replace that behavior with dignity and respect.

If they are separated or divorced, accountability may mean no contact with her in any way. If that is her wish, this may mean not being in the same building or space as her. For example, if he comes into a grocery store and notices his ex-wife/partner in the store, then he will leave. If he is at the park in town and his ex-wife and their children arrive not knowing he is there, he will be the one that leaves the park, since he is the one that is the cause of the pain and fear they will experience if they see him.

An accountable man will accept the consequences of his behavior, even if that means jail time, loss of a job, removal from a congregation, or less time with his children. He will abide by court orders and stop his abusive behavior, including all aspects of the Power and Control Wheel. He will then continue to make amends for the harm he has created. If those he has victimized require medical or mental health care due to his behavior, then he will accept the responsibility of paying for that care if the people he abused are willing to let him do so. This activity can also be dangerous. Men can present themselves as mending harm but instead are motivated to entrap those they have victimized in new ways. Those who have experienced his abuse are best able to assess their safety. When they have the support and expertise of effective advocacy programs and others in their life, those determinations are more easily made and that safety is more likely to expand.

If he has kept her from working or going to school in the past, then he should assist her by providing the economic support necessary for her to regain her life. This may occur either directly or through a third party, if she wishes no direct contact. This assistance could be as simple as providing the damage deposit for a new apartment if they have separated. Again, this would need to be something the victims of his abuse would feel comfortable accepting. In many cases, if separated, they do not want any connection with the man who abused them because of his history of manipulation, false promises, false apologies, and more. In another example, suppose he is in the middle of a custody battle and his attorney is telling him to utilize the fact that she has been in therapy in the past or has mental health issues, in an attempt to win custody of the children? An accountable man will refuse that strategy! Instead, he will accept a custody arrangement that works best for her and their children, and he will respect the boundaries that have been established. While this may be an incredibly difficult thing to do, it is also a clear indicator that he is willing to bear the brunt of his past choices and heal the wounds he has created as much as possible. He will do so by supporting his childrens' mother, expressing his respect for her to his children, and providing them the consistency, structure, and loving care necessary for them to heal.

Lastly, he will approach all those in his family, those at work, those in his faith community, helping professionals, and all others that he has manipulated by providing false information about his wife/partner, and will acknowledge and take full responsibility for his behavior. He will then apologize for his manipulations and the impact those manipulations have had on their lives. He will fully accept the consequences of these revelations. Those consequences may include the end of professional or private relationships, and a change in his public reputation.

These are just a few examples of accountability. These behaviors would need to occur consistently, over months and years, to be proven genuine. To determine real change in the individual, you will need to speak to the woman he has abused in the past, and the woman he is currently in relationship with, if it is safe to do so. This is where truly reliable information can be found.

This is a significant challenge. These are not small requests to ask of these men. However, compared to the trauma and lifelong impact he has had on his wife/partner and the children, it is still minimal.

Not all men will make this change. Many will simply move away and find another relationship, another job, another faith community, and simply bring the abusive behaviors with them. But I have seen some men make remarkable progress toward healing. I have seen them take the steps honestly and authentically, which takes inner strength, determination, and refined principles and beliefs. Consequently, I have seen many of these men years later, walking down the street with their wife and children, together again, because his change was determined to be real, as he sought a different kind of benefit from his behavior than the ones he sought while abusing his family.

Primary Prevention: "Stop it Before it Starts"

The Culture Wheel is a representation of how cultural norms and values influence institutions and a society's use of power and control. By examining the ways society reinforces the use of power and control, those using the wheel can identify actions that might be taken on a personal, cultural, and institutional level to end the tolerance of abuse.

One in three women are physically assaulted in their lifetime by a man they have an intimate relationship with. That is not just a statistic, that is one in three women you know: sisters, mothers, aunts, nieces, daughters, wives, girlfriends, friends, colleagues, etc. As you walk down the street, or through the mall, or look around you at work, or look to those in your congregation, count the women. One, two, three (abused). One, two, three (abused). One, two, three (abused). Every third woman you pass or encounter has experienced domestic violence. To add to this, one in three women will be sexually assaulted in her lifetime.

How is this possible? This many men and boys could not be beating and raping this many women and girls (and boys) without widespread cultural support! So where is that support coming from, and how do we change it?

It is all around us. When I was a small boy, the worst thing I could be is the kind of person at least half of the people reading this chapter are—a girl! "Don't run like

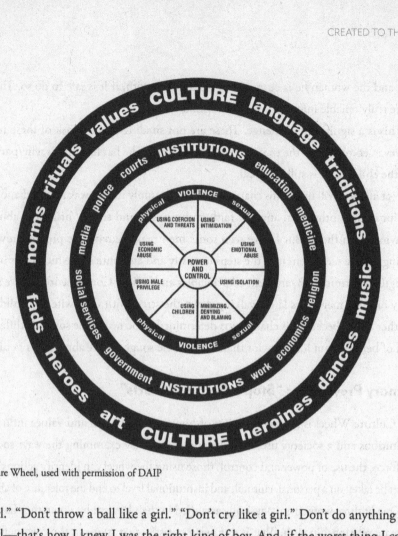

Culture Wheel, used with permission of DAIP

a girl." "Don't throw a ball like a girl." "Don't cry like a girl." Don't do anything like a girl—that's how I knew I was the right kind of boy. And, if the worst thing I could be is a girl, then obviously boys are better than girls! As I looked around in my world, men were in charge everywhere, especially white men. Now, this dynamic is changing, but even today if you look at the highest levels of power in our local, state, and national governments, private corporations, and faith communities, you will still see that the majority of those in control are men. And women are still marginalized, with limited status, and making anywhere from 60 to 80 cents on the dollar compared to men, depending on their race or ethnicity. So, these social norms we take for granted contribute to this sense of male superiority and subsequently a perceived "right" to control women and others we consider inferior.

The power men hold in society is routinely highlighted, respected, and acknowledged. Women's accomplishments, opinions, and expertise are routinely ignored. Some of this is changing due to the astounding courage, strength, brilliance, and resiliency women have brought to the public and private sectors of our society, while challenging sexist notions of male domination and privilege.

Some men are beginning to listen and acknowledge their own participation in a sexist culture of male privilege, both directly or indirectly through their silence. But more men who recognize this patriarchy are needed to reshape our culture.

Historically we know that any time one group of people believes they are better than another group of people, attendant hostility becomes a cultural norm. We have seen this with racism, anti-Semitism, heterosexism, classism, etc. This is so "normal" that it becomes invisible right before our eyes. So "woman hating" became a part of a sexist male culture. Sexist comments and jokes, and the sexual objectification of women has become so common that we hardly notice it anymore. The simplest example of this cultural misogynistic norm is the language men routinely use when speaking with each other about women. Men use offensive, demeaning, coarse, and objectifying language to refer to and describe women all the time. And it seems that men don't make the connection between this common language and the fact that one in three women is being abused. This is the same language men use as they are beating and raping women. And we use this language routinely in our everyday lives to make jokes, express disgust, or just talking in general about women and girls. It is, in fact, a way that men bond with each other.

If you are a man reading this and have never noticed this, start paying attention to how often anti-woman or sexually-objectifying comments occur when you are in the company of other men. Comments such as "I'd like to hit that" as the waitress walks away from the table after delivering the drinks. This is a regular part of male culture. So how do we change this? And how do we answer the question, "Do we care about women's lives?"

Men's silence supports men's violence! This many men could not be assaulting this many women if the men who were not abusive stood up and said "No! No more!" So how do we do this? How do we stop it before it starts? Because if sexual and domestic violence is going stop, men are going to have to stop it. Men need to play a key role, in partnership with women, in reshaping these social norms and holding men who batter, sexually assault, and abuse women accountable. This is another chapter to be written, but there are solutions. Here are a few examples of what men can do to help.

LEVEL OF SPECTRUM	DEFINITION OF LEVEL
6. Influencing Policy and Legislation	Developing strategies to change laws and policies to influence outcomes
5. Changing Organizational Practices	Adopting regulations and shaping norms to improve health and safety
4. Fostering Coalitions and Networks	Convening groups and individuals for broader goals and greater impact
3. Educating Providers	Informing providers who will transmit skills and knowledge to others
2. Promoting Community Education	Reaching groups of people with information and resources to promote health and safety
1. Strengthening Individual Knowledge and Skills	Enhancing an individual's capability of preventing injury or illness and promoting safety

Spectrum of Prevention, used with permission of Prevention Institute

This graphic is based on public health initiatives used to address social norms which harm individuals and those around them. Often people think that to prevent societal problems we just need to raise awareness. But we know from experience that raising awareness or providing education about an issue alone does not change social norms. As the Spectrum of Prevention demonstrates, the most effective method of prevention is through organizational practice and public policy change. So, we use education and community awareness to build the social capital and political will to change organizational practice and public policy. That is what reshapes social norms.

A good example of this is smoking. We knew for years that smoking was harmful to our health, but it wasn't until we made changes to workplace policies and legislation that the level of tobacco use started to decrease. Remember when we could smoke in a movie theater, the waiting room at the hospital, at work, at school, anywhere? It was the norm, "just the way it is." If you had told someone in Minnesota in 1997 that in ten years it would be illegal to smoke in a bar, they would have laughed and said "No way. Are you kidding? That would never happen!" Ten years later it did. People think changing social norms is impossible. But it is possible and essential!

So, how do we as men join women in partnership, to identify and reshape these social norms leading to sexual and domestic violence?

How do we use our influence at work, at home, at school, with friends and family, in our congregations, to support women's equality, honor their historical and contemporary achievements, and produce organizational practices and public policies that provide the gender equity and respect due to every individual? In my work and in my faith community, do I highlight and acknowledge women's successes? Are they a key part of my workplace's or congregation's leadership? Are women honored at events? How are women portrayed in your faith community or workplace: as a subordinate or equal to men? These are questions that begin the work of engaging, evaluating, and reshaping social norms within organizations and society.

Conclusion

As we begin to make these institutional changes in policy and practice, we will see the changes that we want. It will no longer be a wish, but a reality! The end to endemic levels of physical and sexual abuse, the end to the sexual exploitation and the objectification of women and girls. Equal pay, social support, leadership, and ultimately, gender justice will happen.

In making this change, we will contribute to making the world we envision a place where all people are respected and provided the equal rights and privileges due every human being—the opportunity to live in peace, joy, and safety, fulfilling our dreams and those of our children.

Sexual Abuse in Dating and Marital Relationships: The Ultimate Betrayal

REBECCA KOTZ

When you are raped by a stranger, you have to live with a frightening nightmare.
When you are raped by your husband, you have to live with your rapist.[1]

Sexual violence can happen to anyone, regardless of sex, age, race, religion, sexual orientation, ethnicity, ability, or socioeconomic status. Oppressed and marginalized communities are targeted and assaulted at higher rates—particularly women who are Indigenous, homeless, and/or disabled. However, this chapter will focus on the sexual abuse in heterosexual relationships where the male partner is the abuser and the female partner is the victim. Although females can be sexual abusers as well, this is far less common.

Sexual violation by a person one trusts is the ultimate betrayal. Unfortunately, the most likely perpetrator of sexual violence *is* someone the victim trusts. The commonly-used media scenario of the stranger-perpetrator in the dark alley does happen but is quite rare in comparison to the diverse spectrum of sexual violence in which most female victims are assaulted by someone they know, often very well. The most dangerous place for a female is not the streets; it is her own home. The closer women/girls are to men (physically and emotionally), the more at risk for abuse they become. Sexual abuse by a spouse, date, partner, or ex (SDPE) has been described by survivors as an "unending nightmare," "terrorism," and "sexual slavery."

It is hard to imagine how a man could abuse the very person he claims to love. It is just as confusing for non-abusers as it is for victims. But popular clichés such as "it's hard to hate up close" obscure the nature of domestic violence. This distorted perception is why we see even some anti-violence advocates attempt to encourage men to *stop* other men's abuse by appealing to patriarchal relationships. *What if she was your daughter? Your wife?* Ironically, these are the two female groups men are *most* likely to abuse in their personal lives.

There are no statistics that can accurately quantify the pervasiveness of sexual abuse in SDPE relationships because many victims/survivors do not self-identify as victims of sexual violence, and most data relies on self-reporting. People will usually not know someone has experienced sexual victimization unless the victim discloses. Victims of physical battering may have the marks of abuse on their bodies. However, there may be no physical sexual trauma signs (such as bleeding or tearing) that can be used as "evidence" of victimization.

In my professional work, I often find individuals do not recognize themselves as victims of sexual violence. I see this to be true particularly when the victim's experience does not fit popular stereotypes or portrayals of rape. Others may not recognize it for what it is because this abuse is so normalized. However, just because something is common, this does not make it less traumatizing. If anything, the compounded impact makes it more so.

Forms of Sexual Coercion

Sexual coercion in SDPE relationships is not uncommon. All sexual coercion *is* sexual assault, but it can be hard to recognize. These are some ways in which an abusive partner might manipulate and coerce a victim into sex:

- Pressuring, badgering, whining, pouting, "wearing you down."
- Guilt-tripping about being "owed" sex.

- Tricking, fraud.
- Using power inequality, authority, status, or influence to demand sex.
- Obligation, e.g., "I've done so much for you, can't you do this one thing for me? You've already turned me on. Finish what you started."
- Blackmail: revenge porn, threatening to embarrass victim.
- Ultimatums, e.g., "If you don't have sex with me, I will leave you, cheat, or use porn."
- Bribery, e.g., gift-giving, shopping, or giving money in exchange for sex.
- Male privilege/sexism, e.g., "This is your duty as my girlfriend/wife."
- Spiritual abuse, e.g., "God says you must submit to me."
- Verbal abuse, e.g., name-calling (prude, frigid, whore), criticism of a partner's body, sexist or degrading comments/jokes, belittling, spreading rumors, speaking with others about intimate details of sex life without partner's consent.
- Threats to sabotage victim's job, school, or family, threats to harm victim or others, threats of self-destruction or suicide.
- Force, e.g., physical violence, restraint, torture.
- Alcohol or drug-facilitated coercion.

Other forms of coercive and sexually abusive behavior include:

- Controlling a partner's appearance, criticizing a partner's body, using gender-based or sexually shaming slurs (e.g., slut, whore, prostitute, prude, frigid, damaged goods, uptight, etc.).
- Requesting sexual acts after battering, emotional, or verbal aggression.
- Sexual acts that hurt your partner. Painful sex is a serious problem. At least a third of women report pain during vaginal sex and almost three-fourths report pain during anal sex.[2] If a partner continues to push for sexual acts that are painful for the other partner, is apathetic to a partner's pain, or intentionally causes pain, this is abusive. Women must be aroused and (naturally or artificially) lubricated for intercourse to be pleasurable. For some women, intercourse is never pleasurable. Penetrative sexual acts (the act most likely to cause pain for women) are *not* necessary for a thriving sex life. Respectful, non-abusive partners adjust or avoid sex acts that are painful for the other person.
- Sexual words/acts that humiliate or degrade. If one partner is uncomfortable and feels a sexual act is demeaning or degrading, neither partner should partake.

- Reproductive coercion involves going against a partner's wishes or pressuring a partner to become pregnant, have children, adopt, or abort against their will. Some examples of this include: removing a condom during sex without the partner's knowledge, refusal to wear a condom if the partner requests it, intentionally getting partner pregnant who does not wish to become pregnant, purposefully sabotaging birth control methods, forced abortion, or lying about contraceptive use.

- Intimate Partner pimping/trafficking is when a partner profits, facilitates, aids, or recruits the other partner into prostitution-related activity, sex-trading, or legal sex industries such as strip/exotic dance clubs and pornography. *The most common trafficker/pimp is a boyfriend, husband, or relative of the victim—not a stranger.*

- Voyeurism, pressuring a partner to have sex with someone else, coercing group sex or risky sexual situations, having sex in front of children, or photographing/video-taping a partner while changing, naked, or having sex without their knowledge and/or agreement.

- Coercing a partner to watch or imitate pornography, coercing a partner into creating porn or taking nude or sexual pictures/videos.

- Dissemination of private sexual images by sharing or distributing naked/sexual pictures, videos, or explicit written material/texts from a partner. Abusers distribute these images/videos to humiliate, blackmail, or to maintain control inside or outside the relationship. Some SDPEs initially agree to take these photos/videos, but only with the understanding that they will *not* be shared. Abusers violate their SDPE's boundaries by sharing these images/videos with others. Abusers are known to use *sextortion*, a control tactic to coerce a victim into doing what the abuser wants through threatening to release the image/video if the victim attempts to leave or to get revenge after the partner has already ended the relationship.

- Demanding or withholding any sexual act in order to "manage" other forms of abuse. A victim's compliance with an abuser's demands may deescalate abuse temporarily. Abusers purposefully set up this system to offer the victim incentives—they use their power over the victim to coerce submission. After abusers get their way, they may "reward" the victim by using (manipulative) kindness, gift-giving, favors, or by temporarily lessening other forms of abuse to provide the victim a false sense of relief.

- Using bodily responses to justify sexual assault. The body is wired to respond to sexual stimulus. A man can have an erection, or a woman can have a lubricated vagina and still not want to have sex. In some cases, victims have been aroused, felt pleasure, and even orgasmed during a sexual assault. Partners should respect the partner's expressed wishes and never hold the partner's bodily responses as "evidence" that their partner wanted sex.

- Having sex when SDPE is unable to consent, such as when they are sleeping, highly intoxicated, incapacitated, or passed out.
- Sexual-spiritual abuse and ritual abuse most often perpetrated in cults, but also in families, churches, religious communities, organized crime, trafficking.
- Forced marriage.
- Genital mutilation.
- Other privacy or sexual boundary violations.

How Survivors Cope with Sexual Violence in SDPE

Survivors cope in unique ways. Here are just a few examples:

- Denial, e.g., blocking sexual assault from memory, not admitting she has been assaulted, convincing herself that she wanted it, thinking, "He's such a good guy; it was just a misunderstanding."
- Minimization, e.g., "It's not a big deal; it's not that bad; at least he doesn't . . ."
- Rationalization/justification, e.g., "All women have sex when they don't want to; if I would just have sex more often or do the things he wants he wouldn't have done this; he only does this when he drinks/uses; he has 'needs'; he'll cheat or use porn if I don't."
- Dissociation, e.g., thinking about something else during an assault, out-of-body experiences, substance abuse
- Avoidance, e.g., faking illness, purposefully deescalating a partner's arousal, sleeping in a child's room or staying away from home to avoid sexual assault
- Spiritualization, e.g., "I am suffering for Christ; I do not own my body; I am called to submit to my husband; I will lead him to sin if I don't have sex with him."

As a result of the trauma of sexual violence, survivors may develop an utter disdain for their body and intimacy. They may respond in extremes—becoming hypersexual or entirely avoiding sex. They may self-mutilate and self-destruct.

Survivors may feel confused and betrayed, especially because many victims have had positive, consensual sexual experiences in the past with the same partner that is abusing them now.

Supporting Survivors of Sexual Violence in SDPE Relationships: Dos & Don'ts

How do we support survivors of sexual abuse in SDPE relationships? In a society that often blames the victim and supports the perpetrator, we can counter rape culture by maintaining the default position of believing the *victim*. Recognize the enormous courage it takes to disclose sexual violence. SDPE perpetrators may convince the victim that this is a secret she must keep—that she is disloyal, "gossiping," or betraying him by bringing to the light what he has done. If/when the abusive SDPE discovers that the victim has disclosed his abuse, he may deny it completely, discredit her ("she's crazy/mentally ill"), become defensive, enraged, or violent, and escalate the abuse. Knowing this, a listener/witness to a victim's disclosure has a responsibility to respond with extreme caution and care. In some of the most severe cases of abuse, a perpetrator convinces a victim that her disclosure is a death sentence. Some abusers use this to threaten and intimidate a victim into silence. Others carry out the threat and murder the victim or someone close to them. Outsiders do not know how abusers will respond (sometimes the victim doesn't know either!), which is why it is crucial we do not share an adult victim's information without her permission (child abuse, obviously, must be reported immediately). Disclosures should be handled in a way that is sensitive, validating, compassionate, empowering, and above all else, *centers the needs of the victim*.

Do's

Do ask how you can be supportive. All victims/survivors are individuals; there is no one-size-fits-all approach. Avoid assuming you know what they need or know better than they do about their own situation. Instead, allow the victim/survivor to guide you on how best to respond. When in doubt, ask! "How can I support you? What do you need from me right now? What would support look like for you? What would you like to see happen?"

Simple questions like these help caring individuals and communities tailor their support in a way that truly benefits the survivor. These questions honor and respect a survivor's unique needs and considers impact (not simply good intentions).

Do validate their experience. Helpful, validating response statements may sound like the following: "I believe you. This is not your fault. You are not to blame. Your reaction is normal. You're not crazy. I'm here to support you. I'm sorry that happened to you. That must've been really scary/uncomfortable/frightening/invasive. No one deserves to be treated that way. Everyone deserves to have their boundaries respected. There is no excuse for assault. How you responded or whatever you did to survive was the right thing to do. I'm here to listen if you need to talk. Thank you for telling me, I know that must've been difficult. I won't share what you told me with anyone unless you want me to. How can I support you?"

Many survivors will appreciate you simply listening and validating their experiences. An active listener bears witness, shares the burden, avoids the "righting reflex" and quick fixes, and supports the victim in their pain.

Do your best to control your reaction. An extreme emotional response (though valid) shifts the focus onto the listener rather than the survivor's needs. The survivor may hold back in the future, worry they are a burden, or think that people can't handle what they are sharing.

Secondary survivors (partners, parents, friends, and those close to the survivor) can also experience post-traumatic stress symptoms. Because of this, secondary victims need support and deserve a place to process their feelings too. If you are someone close to a survivor, instead of processing with the survivor herself/himself, choose to process with someone more removed from the situation.

Do recognize your stereotypes and biases surrounding victims' responses to trauma and avoid comparison. How people respond to and cope with trauma is as varied as their experiences. Survivors may feel angry, sad, numb, relieved, fearful, anxious, depressed, enraged, betrayed, distrustful, guilty, emotionless, or sorry for the perpetrator. They may seek revenge, withdraw, cling, blame themselves, or even joke about the assault. None of these responses indicate the severity or level of trauma they have experienced. There is no one reaction.

Recognize the victim did what they needed to do at that moment to survive, and did so successfully. It's not fair to judge or critique how victims survived at that moment. Most people assume victims will respond in "fight or flight," but the more common responses to sexual abuse—especially when one feels trapped (which is almost always the case in SDPE relationships)—are freezing or fawning (pleasing or complying with what the abuser wants, asks, or does).

Do keep the victim's confidentiality. When someone takes the risk to share personal information with you, keep it confidential. Ask the victim if there is anyone they would like you to share/not share this information with. Never gossip or break their trust by sharing with someone else unless they give explicit consent.

Do encourage the victim to seek medical attention. A victim's choice to seek medical care at a hospital or doctor's office is critical to assess and treat injuries, give medication for pregnancy or sexually transmitted infection prevention, and check the overall wellness of the survivor. Many hospitals employ Sexual Assault Nurse Examiners (SANE) who have specialized training in sexual violence and collecting evidence for a potential forensic investigation.

A note on sexual assault kits: nurses can collect evidence for sexual assault kits up to 120 hours (five days) after the assault. To collect the optimal amount of evidence, nurses recommend getting a kit done as soon as possible and to avoid showering, brushing teeth, eating, drinking, urinating, or defecating. Evidence can still be collected even if these actions have already been taken. Collect clothing, sheets, or anything that could possibly have evidence, and place in a paper bag to give to police.

In some places, kits can be stored anonymously if the victim is unsure about wanting to make a report. The evidence can then be preserved if the victim changes their mind and would like to make a report later. Kits are often free-of-charge to the victim and costs are usually covered by the county—but consult with your local sexual assault advocacy agency and medical provider first to inquire about cost and kit storage. Sexual assault kits do not guarantee usable evidence. Even evidence such as DNA and semen may not prove sexual assault.

Do affirm a victim's/survivor's unique healing journey. Healing looks different and unique to each individual. Avoid pressuring a survivor to "forgive and forget." Traumatic experiences are life-altering and induce neurological changes. Victims cannot simply "forget." Biologically, both the brain and the body store and record trauma, even if we try to fight, block, or repress it. Trauma responses can manifest in chronic physical health issues, mental health issues, and/or chemical dependency. Human beings do not simply "get over" trauma.

Healing is not a linear path; it has many highs and lows. Those in community with the victim should never place their own comfort above the healing of the victim. Often victims are pressured and expected to "move on" because their community is tired of dealing with the emotions or pain of the survivors. This communicates to the survivor that their pain is a burden and "inconvenience" to others. Forgiveness can happen only on the survivor's timeline, not someone else's. Forgiveness may look different for everyone. A victim can forgive an abuser, yet still set firm boundaries, hold the abuser accountable for their actions, and report them.

Don'ts

Don't blame the victim. No choice the survivor makes, no matter how dangerous or risky, means they asked to be, or deserved to be, assaulted. The definition of sexual assault and rape indicates the act was unwanted. The abuser makes the choice to violate the boundaries of the victim. The victim should never be held responsible, even partially, for the abuse against them. Victim-blaming is often an attempt to grasp control in a situation that was intrinsically out of the victim's control. If a person can point to a "reason" or justification for the assault, they may also falsely believe the illusion that they can protect themselves in the future by avoiding certain people, places, or behaviors. Patriarchal cultures side with perpetrators and blame victims, either because it is too difficult to confront the reality that a beloved or well-respected man is capable of abuse, or because it is too difficult to confront our own vulnerability or the vulnerability of the women and children we care about. While anyone can face victim-blaming, oppression and identity play a significant role in who is believed vs. who is blamed. For example, whiteness is a protective factor due to the historical links of whiteness tied to innocence and purity. Black, Indigenous, and other victims of color are often adultified in their youth, hypersexualized, and stereotyped negatively. In addition, victims who are poor, homeless, disabled, have mental health struggles, are using drugs or alcohol, have a criminal background, have had many sexual partners, have been in the sex industry, identify as LGBT+, or do not conform to gender stereotypes, are far less likely to be believed or they are outright blamed.

There is no such thing as a "perfect victim." As a community, we recognize our biases that lead us to only believe victims who fit in neat boxes of "innocence." We should also recognize biases that lead us to question the validity of a victim's disclosure simply because the victim responded differently than what we feel is the most "correct" or appropriate response.

Victim-blaming may look differently depending on the victim's relationship with the perpetrator.

- Victim-blaming when the abuser is a dating partner: "Why were you alone with him? Why'd you sleep over at his house? You must be giving off an impression that you want to have sex. Why did you turn him on? Maybe if you dressed more modestly, he wouldn't have 'stumbled.' Why didn't you fight back or scream? He's a boy/man, they struggle more with sexual temptation. You were irresponsible and caused him to sin."

- Victim-blaming when the abuser is a spouse: "He is your husband and has needs! Sex (and submission) is your duty as a wife. If you don't give it to him, someone else will. A husband can't rape his own wife. Why did you tempt him? You turned him on, don't be a 'tease.' Men need sexual release in a way you can't understand as a woman. Marriage is for sex. He will cheat or use porn if you don't have sex. For him to feel loved, he needs sex. Don't use sex as a punishment. You chose to marry him, now you have to deal with it." And, only if the sexual assaults are considered "brutal enough": "Why don't you leave him?"

- Victim-blaming when the victim is male: If the perpetrator was a man, people often question the victim's sexuality. If the perpetrator was a woman, the assault often is reframed as a sexual experience he should have "enjoyed" or felt "lucky" to have. "Men/boys can't be assaulted. He must have liked it. He got lucky! What man turns down sex? Something must be wrong with him! Is he cheating? Is he gay? Why didn't he fight back? He must be weak. I wish my wife/girlfriend would take advantage/dominate me!"

Don't feel like you need to have answers. Sometimes there aren't solutions, quick fixes, or any good reasons for why some people experience horrific pain and struggle in their lives and others don't. Sometimes when people try to pursue meaning and answers to these tough questions, they perpetuate victim-blaming or promote damaging or invalidating clichés (e.g., *everything happens for a reason, God won't give you more than* *you can handle, this is a temporary cross to bear for Christ, love your enemies, hurt people hurt people, he's suffering just as much as you are, God is using this for his glory).*

Don't attempt to take control, tell the victim what to do, or pressure them in any way. It is important to recognize that a victim/survivor of sexual abuse has already experienced the feeling of being coerced, controlled, or powerless. Don't imitate the abuser by doing the same.

Don't take on the role of an investigator. Don't ask for details about the assault. Don't question, critique, or scrutinize the victim's experience or responses. Check your motives when asking victims/survivors questions about their experiences of trauma. You don't need to know any details to appropriately support and respond to the victim's needs. Only ask necessary questions if it would help you assist them—not questions for your own knowledge or out of curiosity. Do not be a voyeur to others' trauma.

Don't report *for* the victim or pressure them to report. This is critical for the reasons listed above. A victim's family, friends, partner, and/or community may have many strong beliefs about how the survivor should move forward. Most survivors feel immense pressure to engage the criminal justice system against their will. While some victims find reporting and going through the court process empowering, many find it extremely difficult, even unbearable. Some survivors have said the criminal court system felt like a "second rape" or even worse than the sexual assault itself. In the criminal system, victims are forced to relive and publicly state all the details of the assault, are asked intrusive questions, and have their every action scrutinized, blamed, publicly shamed, humiliated, and retaliated against. Because of this, it is crucial that the victim makes the choice about what action they would like to take (if any). Avoiding victim-blaming also means not further burdening victims or making them feel responsible for the safety of *others* (e.g., "If you don't report, he'll do it to someone else").

A note on reporting to law enforcement: Each state has different statutes of limitations. Reports are made to either the city law enforcement department or the county sheriff's department in the city/county *where the assault occurred*. Once a report is made to law enforcement, victims usually do not have control over the ongoing process. Victims have a right to request a victim advocate to be present during the reporting and court process.

A note on the legal system: Victims themselves do not have the power to "press charges" against the perpetrator. After law enforcement investigates, the county attorney's office will review the case and decide if they will move forward. If a case is accepted by the county attorney's office, the county attorney/state makes a formal charge against the perpetrator. Attorneys typically do not take on cases unless they believe they can win and successfully prove the case to the standard needed in criminal court.

The majority of perpetrators are never charged, and sexual assault cases rarely reach court at all. For those that do, most cases will not go to trial. For the minute percentage of cases that do go to trial, most perpetrators are not convicted. To reiterate, even when a perpetrator is found "not guilty," this *does not mean the assault did not occur*, it simply means there was not enough evidence to prove it beyond a reasonable doubt. Faith communities must recognize that because so few victims come forward, and because so few perpetrators will have convictions on their criminal background, there are many abusers in our churches that we know nothing about. Background checks are still necessary as a bare minimum, but are also unreliable and tell little about a person's boundaries or capability for abuse.

A note on mandated reporting: Dating abuse by similar-aged victims (even youth) or abuse by an adult against another adult is usually not a mandated report, however it is important to check your state's statutes as all states have different laws. Usually, mandated reporting requirements involve adult abusers in a position of authority/care over a child or someone living in the home of the victim.

A note on recanted reports: Victims recant reports and disclosures for many reasons. Recanting does not mean the assault didn't occur. Oftentimes, victims recant because of pressure from others, harassment, threats, doxxing, stalking, blackmail, mental health, bullying, suicidal ideation, victim-blaming, guilt about consequences for the abuser, pressure from faith communities not to "ruin a man's life" or "ruin Christianity's witness," and/or because the process is so exhausting that victims don't want to move further or hope it will just "go away."

A Safe Haven for Abusers

Many victims of sexual abuse feel isolated, alone, misunderstood, invalidated, and silenced. The 2017 revival of #MeToo and sexual violence awareness was a catalyst for the #ChurchToo movement. Victims/survivors felt emboldened to speak the truth regarding their experiences—some for the first time.

No one wants to believe a Christ-follower is capable of sexual violence. If a well-respected, supposedly honorable "man of God" could be capable of this, couldn't anyone? The answer is yes, anyone can be an abuser. To acknowledge this reality threatens people's trust in the absolute goodness of the church. As a result, some people prefer denial.

When this is a church-wide response, it is not surprising that so many victims have expressed they feel the church has not only enabled abuse, but is one of the safest places *for abusers*. The church has historically failed to protect victims, and instead chosen to protect the institution's image, reputation, power, and credibility.

Faith communities have improved in acknowledging the reality of physical violence and battery. However, faith communities often struggle to acknowledge or understand the severity of other forms of abuse that do not leave physical evidence or obvious scars and bruises: sexual, emotional, financial, and spiritual abuse.

Why Do People Abuse?

Why would someone violate the person they claim to love? In the framework of complementarian/patriarchal theology, men are the leaders, pursuers, initiators, and aggressors. Men may be encouraged not to take "no" for an answer right away. Eventually, if he "pursues" her enough ("pursue" is often spiritualized language for men's boundary-pushing), she may change her mind, be convinced, or give in. Complementarian writers often perpetuate stereotypes that women/girls don't mean what they say or know what is best for them; a woman will act coy or say "no" when she really means "yes." For example, Kris Vallotton's blog post on why men delay marriage advises men to "not give up" on a woman they'd like to date because her failure to reciprocate does not necessarily mean she doesn't like him. He instead says this is a "misunderstanding" of women and that women want to be chased. He makes clear that men must respect a "hard no," but still sends a dangerous message.[3] In a patriarchal world, it is the man, not the woman, who decides if her *no* is "hard" or "soft."

Men who sexually assault their SPDE use the same rationalization: her *no* didn't really mean *no*. *He* knows what she *really* wants. These messages form the psyche of *all* men, religious or not, who sexually abuse women. The same messages are sent in romance movies: *"no"* doesn't really mean no—it means *try harder, convince her, she doesn't know what she wants, wear her down, she'll eventually submit.* Men are promised that women will eventually give in with enough pressure—whether for a date or sex. And some do. Sexual abusers use pressure and coercion because it *works.*

While many men would never physically assault their partner, these same men may abuse their SPDE in other ways. Abusers see coercion not as abuse, but simply a *method* to get what they want.

Chuck Derry, the author of the second chapter of this book and a colleague with whom I facilitate a program for male offenders, worked with abusive men in batterers programs for decades. He uncovered the functional nature of their violence by asking a simple question: *What are the benefits to your violence/abuse?* Their answers showed that they used violence and coercion to control their partners because they understood that their chosen tactics would result in getting whatever they wanted.[4]

Abusers aren't confused or misunderstood. An abuser carefully calculates and controls others and their interactions to work out positively for himself. Abusers clearly see the outcome of their manipulation—benefits, privileges, and rewards. *In the eyes of an abuser, coercion is simply the solution to a problem.* Abusers often try a wide variety of tactics and adapt their methodology based on what most effectively provides him the outcome he wishes. The reward of power and control in the relationship is why he abuses and why he continues to abuse—and why most abusers are not willing to change/give up these behaviors.

Abusers hardly ever see themselves as abusers; it's *those* men over there. His own stereotype of an abuser (formed and affirmed by society) is a brutal, monstrous batterer that ruthlessly beats his wife. He feels like he is a "good man" because he would never do *that.* Because he would never do that, he may feel even more sexually entitled. If he considers himself to be the "good guy," he may feel he deserves to be rewarded sexually for not treating her like *those* men. His idea of his own "goodness" is not genuine—he uses it manipulatively as a pawn to get favors. If he can be better than the next guy, the spectrum of abuse works in his favor. He will always come out looking better.

Sexual abuse, as with all other forms of abuse, is always a choice made by the abuser—it is never due to a loss of control. No one ever owes their partner sex. There is no such thing as a "point of no return" in sex. Although most people don't enjoy halting sexual activity while they are highly aroused, non-abusers make a choice to respect their SDPE and recognize their own sexual interests and pleasure is not more important than their SDPE's sense of safety, trust, and comfort. On the other hand, abusers think their desires are more important than their SDPE's needs.

There are different "reasons" abusers push their partner's sexual boundaries. For many, it is purely sexual selfishness and attitudes of sexual entitlement. Some men feel their partner is responsible for meeting all their sexual desires, or even exists to do so. Male abusers may feel they are owed, as if sex is a right to which they are entitled.

Other abusers use sexual means to assert power, establish dominance, or seek revenge. They may use tactics of sadistic punishment or intentional degradation. Abusers may justify this sadistic abuse by telling themselves that it is for their partner's own good. The abuser takes on a distorted parental role instead of a partnered role. They believe they must "punish" or discipline their SDPE for not doing what they want. Abusers don't feel responsible for the abuse they inflict. Instead, they blame their partner for not meeting their expectations or "causing" them to react this way. *Look what you made me do.*

Violence has long been used to force submission. Violence has long been used to coercively control, intimidate, and punish resistance on the micro level, in interpersonal relationships (such as sexual, emotional, and physical abuse). Violence and coercive control are also used on the macro level as a tool of the state. State-sanctioned violence includes torture, war, police brutality, militarism, the prison industrial complex, genocide, white supremacy, male supremacy, concentration camps, border violence, nationalism, ethnocentrism, authoritarian governments, human rights violations, and all forms of systemic and structural oppressions such as sexism, racism, classism, ableism, poverty, colonialism, and environmental destruction. To stop violence and abuse, Christians are called to denounce violence at all levels. One cannot be stopped without the other, as state and interpersonal violence are entwined. Both reinforce and feed each other.

Victims/survivors of violence may find comfort, validation, and solidarity with Jesus, as he was a victim of both interpersonal and state-sanctioned violence. Crucifixions served political ends as public displays of domination to incite fear and manufacture submission. In David Tombs' illuminating article, he highlights the sexual nature of the state-sanctioned abuse in crucifixion:

Crucifixion was intended to be more than the ending of life; prior to actual death it sought to reduce the victim to something less than human in the eyes of society. Victims were crucified naked in what amounted to a ritualized form of public sexual humiliation. In a patriarchal society in which men competed against each other to display virility in terms of sexual power over others, the public display of the naked victim by the "victors" in front of onlookers and passers-by carried the message of sexual domination. The cross held up the victim for display as someone who had been—at least metaphorically—emasculated.[5]

Sexual passivity is part of what society associates with femininity. Sexual violence magnifies the stereotype by forcing a woman, man, or child victim into an explicitly powerless position, and this is gendered. Sexual violence against another, regardless of the sex of the victim, aims to "feminize" the victim. For female victims, this subjugation is a brutal reminder and extension of what they already experience as their "place" in the world. For male victims, it is an introduction to the experience of being a woman in a male supremacist culture—a position of powerlessness and subordination. Jesus's experience of being stripped, crucified naked (there was no dignified loincloth), and possibly sexually assaulted (as was common practice), reveals a God who can truly and intimately identify with the suffering of victims of all violence—including sexual violence and patriarchal abuse.[6]

Violence + Objectification

A rape culture is a culture that normalizes sexual violence, fails to hold perpetrators accountable, and/or blames/disbelieves victims. To be clear, abusers and rapists alone are responsible for sexual violence. However, cultural norms do play a significant role in sexual socialization and the foundational attitudes that make violence and abuse seem acceptable, even to victims.

How often in the media do we hear respectful, medically accurate, and informed discussion about sex? How often do we see sex as a mutual expression of love, connection, and faithful commitment? How often do we see people treated as whole persons, not a collection of body parts to use and dispose of? This is a rare portrayal. This type of sexuality is an act of resistance and rebellion, whereas perpetrating sexual violence, in a culture that normalizes sexual violence, is conformity. As a result, the high rates of sexual violence should not be surprising.

The media surrounds us with eroticized language and imagery of violence—graphic depictions of rape in TV shows/movies, jokes about rape and prostitution, horror/slasher films that sexualize women before murdering them, rampant pornography use, sexist comments, objectifying the use of women in advertising, and terms such as *bang, screw, nail,* or *destroy* to routinely describe the act of sex. Women are objects to be used, tick marks on a scorecard, and trophies to be won by men.

Sexist attitudes and objectification always precede an act of sexual violence. Pastors and leaders have significant power to reinforce or resist these toxic attitudes. One of the most common ways pastors send objectifying messages is through preaching on women's/girls' dress. Nate Pyle, pastor and author of *Man Enough: How Jesus Redefines Manhood*, wrote an excellent blog on reshifting "modesty" to male responsibility:

> It is a woman's responsibility to dress herself in the morning. It is your [men's] responsibility to look at her like a human being regardless of what she is wearing. You will feel the temptation to blame her for your wandering eyes because of what she is wearing—or not wearing. But don't. Don't play the victim. You are not a helpless victim when it comes to your eyes. You have full control over them. . . . [W]e've been taught a woman's body will cause men to sin. We're told that if a woman shows too much of her body men will do stupid things. Let's be clear: a woman's body is not dangerous to you. Her body will not cause you harm. It will not make you do stupid things. If you do stupid things it is because you chose to do stupid things. . . . I'm not telling you to not look at women. Just the opposite. I'm telling you to see women. Really see them. Not just with your eyes, but with your heart.[7]

Pyle recognizes the path of least resistance for men/boys in a patriarchal culture *is* to objectify women. However, we are called to choose the road less traveled. The role of the church is to resist, not reaffirm objectification. In Matthew 5:28, Jesus says, "But I say to you that every man who looks at a woman lustfully has already committed adultery in his heart." Jesus took objectification very seriously—not even the most extreme feminists advocate men gouge out and throw away their own eyeballs (Matt. 5:29)! Jesus continually held the men who leered and lusted responsible and refused to blame women for men's sin. Women were fully covered, yet men still objectified and sexually assaulted them. This reveals that objectification and sexual violence have nothing to do with clothing and showing skin, but are due to men's sense of power and entitlement.

Objectification is not simply women in bikinis being used to sell products on TV. Objectification also includes women being told they must hide their God-given bodies to prevent men's sexualization of them. Part of this objectification process is to see women in narrow categories: "good girls" worthy of respect or "bad girls" who are "asking for it," women as romantic interests or potential temptresses, woman as human or woman as object.

Objectification is not limited to presentation or dress: it includes reducing a human being's value to their use by another. In this objectification process, her identity is no longer fixed and unchangeable in Christ, but is instead shaped and validated by external sources—men's use of her sexually, domestically, emotionally, and reproductively. Her personhood is denied, and her value is reduced to how she conforms to traditional roles of taking care of men and children. Objectification of women in the church can come down to this: if I can't *use* her, I ignore her.

Objectifying attitudes of sex see women not as mutual active agents, but passive receptacles. Patriarchalists agree on this belief: sex is something *men* do *to women* and is intrinsically hierarchical. Jared Wilson, a writer for The Gospel Coalition, quotes Doug Wilson (in a blog, later removed, critiquing *Fifty Shades of Grey*), "A man penetrates, conquers, colonizes, plants. A woman receives, surrenders, accepts." Wilson even goes so far as to say that power inequality is an "erotic necessity."[8] The Gospel Coalition, in their dozens of blogs critiquing *Fifty Shades*, ironically aligns with the same sexual messaging. Though most complementarians would not condone the physical abuse, bondage, or overt sexual violence in the books and movies, complementarianism provides the belief system that precedes it. Male authority and female subservience are the foundational beliefs of both complementarians and abusers. To achieve it, complementarians rely on a theology of spiritual coercion. Abusers, like the man in *Fifty Shades*, rely on other, non-spiritual forms of coercion—psychological, physical, and sexual.

Eroticized inequality is a tired, regressive script that has become so accepted and pervasive that many people struggle to believe two people can be sexually aroused *without* sexism and hierarchal power-plays. What is often naturalized as innate sexual preferences, turn-ons, and arousal associations are actually socialized and molded by environment, social norms, and experience. In C.K. Egbert's article, "Why Consent is Not Enough," she talks about the phenomena of "adaptive preferences":

> Adaptive preferences pose a particular problem for the idea that pursuing whatever preference we have expresses our status as free and equal human beings. Adaptive preferences result when we unconsciously change our preferences to adapt to our circumstances. Women often do not feel entitled to equality with men, bodily integrity, sexual pleasure, or even basic necessities such as sufficient food, because they have been placed in a situation where these are not available to them or these are systematically denied them. But there is another, and even more pernicious psychological fact: women are often not aware of the abuse they suffer at the hands of men as abuse . . . because he/she does not have the option of withdrawal or confrontation. If we add to this that women are invalidated or subject to various degrees of social violence when they do not comply with gender norms, we have a serious problem for "individual choice." . . . Consent relies upon the presumption that people will choose in their own self-interest, or at least in ways that do not fundamentally violate their humanity. As demonstrated in the case of adaptive preference, that is simply false.[9]

Nevertheless, there is another way. Biblical egalitarians aim to bring us back to God's original intention for cooperative relationships that do not rely on oppressive systems of dominance and subjugation. Egalitarians consistently uplift the values of mutuality, power-sharing, safe vulnerability, pleasure, joy, and connection that existed before sin destroyed what God called "good." These values should be applied both inside and outside the bedroom.

A Patriarchal Power Trip

Sexual violence can inflict trauma, humiliation, pain, powerlessness, loss of control, and feelings of worthlessness to a different degree from other forms of abuse. Sex is already so vulnerable and intimate; sexual abuse is, therefore, callous, cruel, and vile.

> It's a popular mantra that "rape is not about sex, but about power." This mantra tells only half the truth. Rape is about sex, too, because the power-hungry who seek to dominate know that sex is more deeply personal, more private, than almost any other

human sphere, and that to enter into and manipulate this realm is a power-trip like no other. Power and sex are connected. . . . men—already physically stronger, and biologically consequence-free—are able to back up sexual aggression with religious power. Religion should not have power of this sort, especially a religion that follows Christ, who told us that we must be last if we are to be first, and who rejected the pomp of earthly kingship.[10]

In a patriarchal culture, male *sexual* power over women provides a unique reward that differentiates it from physical violence. When an abuser has an orgasm during his act of violation, he receives pleasure and sexual satisfaction as a direct result of his violence, coercion, and boundary-pushing. His pleasure is a result of her pain.

In a patriarchal culture, men's sexual conquering of women is encouraged and applauded. The interpersonal sex lives between men and women are the clearest depiction of the patriarchal political system. Men's sexual dominance, aggression, conquest, and control are eroticized. Female powerlessness, submission, and vulnerability are eroticized. To the victim, rape is violence, rape is power over another, rape is terrorism. To the perpetrator, rape might just feel like "ordinary" sex—normal and inconsequential to him.

Pornography and Sadism

Pornography incarnates male supremacy. It is the DNA of male dominance. Every rule of sexual abuse, every nuance of sexual sadism, every highway and byway of sexual exploitation, is encoded in it. It's what men want us to be, think we are, make us into; how men use us; not because biologically they are men but because this is how their social power is organized.[11]

The effects of porn are far-reaching, as Andrea Dworkin describes in her book, *Pornography: Men Possessing Women*. She argues pornography is a "blueprint" for abuse that introduces and affirms male dominance and sadism for viewers to internalize.

Sadists take pleasure in intentionally causing others pain. They may do this through rough penetration, forcing victims to do sexually degrading and humiliating acts, causing sexual injury, prostitution/trafficking, rape with objects, or BDSM (Bondage Discipline/Dominance Submission/Sadism Masochism)—a euphemism for sexual torture. BDSM is inherently anti-egalitarian, even when it is desired by both partners, as it replicates the abusive patriarchal system (regardless of the gender of the partner who is dominating or inflicting pain) that has eroticized power inequality and violence since its existence. In addition, legally, a person cannot "consent" to violence.

Long before a boy becomes an abuser, he is likely to have been groomed by porn. Porn is the most potent patriarchal propaganda tool that ties women's subordination to sexual arousal. Everything depicted in porn reinforces sexist roles. In porn, like the patriarchal social system, men are on top, women are on the bottom. Decades of research has exposed the shift in attitudes as people continue to use porn. A 2016 Barna study found that 56 percent of porn users see nothing wrong with "someone depicted in a demeaning way" and 46 percent see nothing wrong with "sexual acts that may be forced or painful."[12]

Pornography severs the emotional and spiritual connective power of sex. Most pornography does not depict intimacy, affection, sensual touch, connection, or care. In a presentation I attended, Gail Dines described porn as "making *hate* to women" rather than "making love." Pornography is filmed sexual violence and trafficking, not a depiction of sex.

When a man develops abusive attitudes reinforced by his porn use, he may begin to pressure his partner into imitating the acts he sees in porn. Girls and women I speak with tell me they feel they must act like porn stars. They feel they must endure violent sex. They have partners reach for their neck to strangle them, ejaculate on their faces, pressure them into painful anal sex, or shove their heads down to force aggressive oral assault. Women tell me men get sexually excited when women say "no" or resist. Pornified men may either expect total sexual submission of women or eroticize her resistance.

All women, regardless of whether they have used porn themselves, become secondary victims of it. In the church, a woman's sense of betrayal, trauma, and pain associated with the discovery of her partner's porn use is often minimized. She may be pressured to "have grace" and tolerate her partner's use in a way never expected if he was cheating. She may be dismissed and told that "all men struggle with porn." She may feel unrealistic or prudish to expect a partner to be faithful to her sexually.

Pornography not only hurts the partner and family of the user, it is an act of violence against all women. Women in porn video/images are abused and trafficked, even in the legal porn industry. All women suffer the ripple effect of living in a porn culture where their naked bodies are always on display, their vulnerability and submission sexualized, and their worth dictated by more powerful men. The crucifixion of Jesus and the pornography of women—are both patriarchal, public displays of humiliation, powerlessness, and degraded subhuman status for political ends. Pornography and the culture that promotes it are incompatible with equality, justice, mutuality, love, respect, and the end of oppression.

Conclusion

Sexual abuse in SDPE relationships must be taken seriously in the church. The good news is that sexual violence is preventable! When our faith communities are educated on healthy sexuality and relationships, we can help reduce the risk of abuse. When our faith communities decide to resist sinful patriarchal attitudes, coercive control, and selfishness, we make way for respect and mutuality and lay a solid foundation for sexually ethical decisions.

We can believe women and support survivors—especially when it is inconvenient. We can side with the abused and marginalized. We can fight for justice for the oppressed. We can confront hard truths and confront our complicity and/or perpetration of harm. We can hold abusers and oppressors accountable. We can create an environment that is truly safe and supportive for survivors to disclose "me too" and be the church that declares, "never again."

Covert Emotional Abuse

ANNETTE OLTMANS

"Abuse is a learned behavior . . .
Abuse is a choice, and it's not one that anyone has to make."[1]

"There was no punch on the very first date with my ex-husband. That's not normally how abusive marriages start.

In fact, my first date was probably pretty similar to yours: he was charming, he paid attention to me, and he flattered me. . . . Emotional abuse in a relationship takes time to build. It's slow and methodical and incessant, much like a dripping kitchen faucet.

It begins like a little drip you don't even notice—an off-hand remark that is 'just a joke.' I'm told I'm too sensitive and the remark was no big deal. It seems so small and insignificant at the time. I probably am a little too sensitive.

DRIP, DRIP.

I occasionally notice the drip but it's no big deal. A public joke made at my expense is just my partner being the usual life of the party. When he asks if I'm wearing this dress out or whom I'm going with, it only means he loves me and cares about me.

When he tells me he doesn't like my new friend, I agree. Yes, I can see where she can be bossy. My husband is more important than a friend, so I pull away and don't continue the friendship.

DRIP, DRIP.

The drip is getting annoying, but you don't sell your house over a leaky faucet.

When a playful push was a little more than playful, I tell myself he didn't really mean it.

He forgets he's stronger than me. When I confront him in yet another lie he's told, he tells me

I'm crazy for not believing him. Maybe I'm crazy. . . . I'm beginning to feel a little crazy."[2]

According to the Centers for Disease Control and Prevention (CDC), the standardized term *Psychological Aggression* within Intimate Partner Violence (IPV) categorizes multiple forms of emotional abuse.[3] While *psychologically* aggressive acts are not *physical* acts of violence, and may not be perceived as aggressive, psychological aggression is an essential component of IPV. Research suggests that the impact of psychological aggression by an intimate partner is every bit as significant as that of physical violence.[4] You may find it helpful to break down psychological aggression into two separate categories, overt emotional abuse and covert emotional abuse (CEA). Overt emotional abuse consists of the verbal assaults or concrete manipulations that are much more obvious to the victim and those around them. These include, but are not limited to, name calling, put downs, or angry outbursts. By comparison, when facing CEA alone, the victim experiences a bewildering inability to sort out their traumatic feelings, ineffective communication, or a way to escape the abuse. CEA confuses, keeping the victim off-balance cognitively and emotionally, and causes the victim to doubt their own perceptions of what transpires between the victim and their abuser. Covert emotional abuse is one of the most damaging and pervasive forms of domestic violence. Yet, of all the forms of abuse, it is the least understood and, therefore, the least confronted.

Why Is This?

Covert emotional abuse is hard to identify, even though it is present in every type of abuse, because CEA significantly confuses a victim's perceptions, memories, ability to think, and their sense of sanity by causing them to question reality and doubt themselves profoundly. These repercussions are only the beginning. For the victim, prolonged states of stressful confusion take hold, leading to anxiety, depression, post-traumatic stress disorder (PTSD), complex post-traumatic stress disorder (C-PTSD), and physiological illness. Mostly, victims do not realize they are interacting with someone who is abusive and speaking an entirely different "emotional" language, one that is rooted in three pillars: entitlement, faulty belief systems, and image management.

CEA is often undetectable to those outside the intimate partner relationship. In public and with extended family members and friends, abusers may be charming, confident, witty, and successful. The insidious nature of CEA comes from the abuser denying their manipulative tactics, confusing the victim. The motive for doing so is usually to avoid responsibility and accountability. This is often done through defensive tactics which dismantle the victim's perspective and position, causing harm. These character traits are often accompanied by the abuser's drive to appear to others that they are better than they really are.

Whether we are talking about bullying, cyberbullying, harassment, molestation, child abuse, workplace sabotage, or IPV, each have CEA running through them. CEA is the common thread found in *all* abuse cases. Damaging repercussions are the end result.

So, What Is CEA?

Covert emotional abuse is a combination of disguised tactics used by the abuser to control the victim while confounding them at the same time. These tactics run the gamut from disavowal to undermining, from blame shifting to subtle (and at times overt) forms of retaliation. Throughout the spectrum of CEA, each of these tactics has one goal at its center: to throw the victim off balance and thus strip them of personal identity and power.[5] Victims of recurring CEA are held in prolonged states of stress and confusion, resulting in the PTSD and C-PTSD that comes from hopelessness and despair often caused by Double Abuse (for an explanation, please see page 83). If a victim cannot name what they are experiencing, they cannot acquire proper interventions or therapeutic help. Clarity is the first necessary step toward healing.

There are, of course, other factors at play, but first, to understand the scope and depth of CEA, we'll name and examine the many characteristics of the abuser's defensive or aggressive actions that aim to maintain control, avoid responsibility, or maintain a sense of stature.

The Categories of CEA Behaviors

Clarity is the archenemy of CEA. To be successful, the abuse needs to remain as undetected as possible. To bring the experience into full light, this chapter focuses on four categories of CEA and the associated behaviors: gaslighting, hiding, shifting responsibility, and entitlement.

#1 – Gaslighting

The most affecting manipulation of CEA is known as gaslighting, a term originating from the 1938 play, *Gas Light* by British playwright, Patrick Hamilton. When gaslighting, an abuser corrupts information or data specifically to make the victim question their own sanity. Abusers alter or deny what should be a shared reality so that victims feel they are incorrect in their perceptions and wrong in their experience. The abuser communicates verbally or behaviorally to the victim that the victim's sense of reality is imagined or inaccurate, that no one will believe them or give any credence to their stories. This tactic inspires the victim's feelings of confusion, "craziness," isolation, and hopelessness.

As is true for all four categories, there are several forms of gaslighting:

- *Crazy-making behaviors*: A cousin of gaslighting, crazy-making behaviors are intentional distortions of reality for the purpose of making the victim feel confused or "crazy." Naming the abuser's crazy-making behaviors is often met with feigned disbelief, distractions, or concrete denials from the abuser.
- *Creating a cloud of confusion*: The abuser weaves a spell of sorts telling false stories to third or extended parties to undermine collateral objectivity by others and manipulate the end result.
- *Deflection*: Deflection is a result of an abuser's refusal to authentically communicate. Instead, they establish what can be discussed, withhold information, change the topic, invent false arguments in another area, all of which severely bewilders the victim. This tactic undermines the victim's surety and prevents any resolution of uncertainty. Using deflection, abusers can directly or indirectly thwart all possibility of solving conflicts through blocking and diverting.
- *Denial*: Dr. David Hawkins of the Marriage Recovery Center states that denial is the abuser's refusal to accept responsibility by living in a state of D-E-N-I-A-L:

<u>D</u>on't <u>E</u>ven <u>N</u>otice <u>I</u> <u>A</u>m <u>L</u>ying to myself. While this activity can be a dissocia-tive defense, when CEA is involved, the abuser uses manipulation to deny that the abuse is happening.[6]

- *Faux confusion/abusive forgetting*: A form of manipulation that allows abusers to absolve themselves of responsibility and accountability by claiming forgetfulness of their actions or any remedies they promised. They may appear confused or angry about the details of their actions to put the victim off balance and avoid taking responsibility.

- *Lying*: This type of abuse is due to the blatant disregard of reality and is enacted by omitting facts or altering the truth. While such lying is often conscious and may be a serious sign of sociopathy, it can become pathologically unconscious, with the abusers convincing themselves of their own lies.

- *Undermining*: This act of withholding emotional support to erode a partner's confi-dence and determination is a sneaky way to squelch joy, effort, creativity, and ideas, reducing the value of anything that could bring their partner positive attention or joy. This devastating tactic can be done overtly through verbal condemnation and criticism or covertly through a lack of acknowledgement or enthusiasm.

#2–Hiding

Hiding is another category of CEA. Its purpose is to ensure that the abuser is not "caught." This abusive "game" is set up to disarm the victim and continue the abuse in concealed ways so that accountability is difficult to apply.

- *Cover-ups*: Doing a molehill of good to cover up a mountain of bad is often the road taken by an abuser living a double life, who cannot, or refuses to, come to terms with his own abusive enactments. Abusers may seek opportunities to serve the community or church through volunteerism or service leadership as a cover-up so their abusive actions can still play out behind closed doors. An example of this is the Pharisees and Sadducees praying in the streets to make people believe they were good, all the while masking their true evil intentions (Matt. 6:5).

- *Dismissing*: With a wave of the hand, the abuser disregards the value of whatever the victim holds dear, arrogantly removing responsibility and absolving themselves in order to not show respect, or care and to avoid accountability.

- *Rationalization/excuse making*: In this type of action, the abuser crafts justifications for their abuse. This goes hand in hand with scapegoating and blame shifting.
- *Minimization*: This behavior occurs through abusive belittling of the victim's perspective. The result is intended to make what the victim values unimportant, and therefore, kills the victim's sense of confidence and individuality.
- *Reductionism*: An abuser degrades the value of a partner's ideas, expressions, creativity, or accomplishments. This may also take the form of the abuser minimizing their own culpability.
- *Shunning*: One of the most painful forms of abuse, under the guise of deserved punishment, is the individual or group act of rejecting someone and keeping them at a distance or acting as though they don't exist. In a group situation, the painful exercise of withdrawing or shunning may be used as a method of coercing and enforcing compliance. "In a religious context, shunning is a formal decision by a denomination or a congregation to cease interaction with an individual or a group."[7] The popular word today for this action is "ghosting," a Double Abuse form of punishment.
- *Withholding*: In one of the most toxic and habitual forms of abuse, the alleged abuser refuses to listen to their partner or honor the victim's experience. They may also refuse to communicate for extended periods of time or share themselves or their good fortune with their partner, putting themselves first in all circumstances. They are stingy with affection, respect, and energy, and go out of their way to simultaneously disregard their partner's feelings, views, individuality, and personhood.

#3–Shifting responsibility

Shifting responsibility is a form of blaming used *against* the victim to disable them and free the abuser from accountability. This tactic is not done casually but purposefully moves guilt onto the victim.

- *All or nothing*: This black and white thinking is designed to disarm the victim, while making whatever they do look bad and whatever the abuser does look all good.
- *Catastrophizing*: Catastrophizing exaggerates situations and potential outcomes. This allows the abuser to react to situations as if they were "pie-in-the-sky worst case scenarios" in order to instigate fear and negative dependence in the victim.

Catastrophizing is also used to avoid healthy communication and resolutions or to exaggerate reasons to blame the victim.

- *Disavowal*: Belittling and devaluing the importance of one's abusive behavior is a very effective tactic to undermine the victim's thoughts, feelings, and credibility. It works to repress the victim's story and helps the abuser avoid responsibility.

- *False accusations*: The abuser engages in telling negative lies to or about the victim. These unexpected attacks are most often based on fictional conversations, problems, or arguments. Even if they may contain an isolated grain of truth, such truth is completely distorted to serve the abuser's ends. These lies can be very persuasive to others, and feel shocking, especially to the victim, since they seem to come out of the blue. But there is always a dark purpose within the lies—shifting responsibility to the victim to make the abuser appear innocent. False accusations often lead to scapegoating and gaslighting.

  We see an example of this in Matthew 12:22–33. Jesus is casting out a demon by the power of God, but the Pharisees accuse Jesus of casting out demons by Satan, the prince of demons. They are inventing a false argument or false accusation meant to vilify Jesus and confuse others. Jesus, a masterful communicator who was not deceived by the Pharisees, firmly rebukes them using sophisticated arguments that reveal their evil thoughts and manipulations. But imagine the experience of an unsuspecting victim who believes their intimate partner has their best interests at heart. You begin to get an idea of how difficult it is for a lessor skilled or traumatized victim to overcome false accusations.

- *Pathologizing*: There is an intricate and insidious pattern to pathologizing. The abuser initiates a problem or conflict, then labels the victim's normal reaction or response as the problem.

- *Blame shifting*: While blaming is a form of overt emotional abuse, in which the abuser makes sure that the victim is the one held responsible, blame shifting occurs when the abuser accuses the victim of being responsible in some way or finding something new to blame the victim for, obscuring their own bad behavior and placing the victim on the defense.

- *Powerplay/power over*: The abuser powers over or uses power plays to suppress the victim by exerting control over the victim. This causes the victim to feel weakened and emotionally and mentally impotent in their actions. For example, the abuser does not allow the victim to have access to bank accounts or personal earnings or to determine the focus of the conversation.

- *Scapegoating*: Scapegoating often plays out publicly. The abuser uses endless opportunities to create scenarios, arrange situations, or turn consequences against the victim so the victim is viewed to be at fault or forced to take responsibility for the problem. This results in the victim being abused twice, first by being made the brunt of the situation and second by being made to bear resulting undue shame and punishment.

#4—Entitlement

When an emotional abuser carries the conviction that they are deserving of privilege, special treatment, or double standards—regardless of merit or at the expense of the victim—the abuser places unrealistic demands upon the victim. At the core fueling this dynamic is the desire of the abuser to diminish or strip the victim's sense of value, while inflating their own sense of value.

We see this process playing out in Scripture again and again. Cain killed his brother Abel because he believed he was entitled to God's blessing over his sacrifice. David believed he was entitled to Bathsheba because he was King. In the New Testament, the Pharisees are the epitome of entitlement and abuse against the poor. In Matthew, Jesus said, "The teachers of the law and the Pharisees sit in Moses' seat. So, you must obey them and do everything they tell you. But do not do what they do, for they do not practice what they preach" (23:2, NIV).

- *Broken promises*: With this tactic, the abuser makes promises to do certain things or to change, but then never keeps them. They may deny ever making the promises, or give justifications for not keeping them, or say they forgot, without apology, all to placate the victim while stalling or never following through.
- *Grandiosity*: The abuser excessively inflates their own sense of hierarchical stature and diminishes the other person. Alternatively, they blow circumstances out of proportion to intensify the negative impact of those circumstances upon the victim.
- *Joking*: "That was just a joke" can be the first sign of an abusive relationship. This type of abuse takes the shape of backhanded compliments, making fun of a partner, their appearance, or something they say. The abuser may "joke" about

the partner's intelligence, talents, or accomplishments in front of friends and family, then put an arm around them saying, "Just teasing, honey." The abuser may laugh at what the victim holds dear or discredit the victim. They might also make disparaging comments disguised as jokes about their partner's gender, their intellectual abilities, or their competency. This hostile ridicule is always at the other person's expense. Proverbs states, "Like a madman who throws firebrands, arrows and death, is the man who deceives his neighbor and says, "I was only joking" (26:18-19, NKJV).

- *Magical thinking*: The abuser encourages the victim to believe that their perception of the abuser's behaviors is incorrect, or the abuser offers a faux apology, leading the victim to believe the abuser's behaviors will go away. Victims demonstrate magical thinking when they wrongly believe that an apology by the abuser means that positive change is imminent.

- *Partial confessions*: Partial confessions are a manipulation intended to gain undeserved favor from the victim, an accountability partner, or a person of authority in order to protect the abuser by distracting from the real issue. This partial or false apology staves off consequences and inflates an empty promise to change. It's important to note that *any* apology by an abuser requires it be accompanied by much hard work.

- *Playing the victim*: The abuser uses defeatist postures, such as feigned hurt or pouting, and/or artful language, acting as if they are the one being harmed. The purpose of this ploy is to avoid accountability and responsibility while aiming to gain sympathy at the same time.

- *Refusing to take responsibility*: Almost all abusive strategies are a measure for the abuser to avoid responsibility and to continue the abusive behavior. Negating any responsibility for one's actions is a way to divert accountability and avoid the hard work of changing.

- *Retaliation*: This form of emotional abuse occurs when the abuser feels entitled to deliberately harm another as "payback." This device concerns image management: the perpetrator's pathologically narcissistic sense of self has been offended in some way, so the victim must pay for the abuser's pain. Retaliation, expressed in aggressive or passive-aggressive behaviors, is at its worst when the victim attempts to separate or bring their concerns out in the open. This may include physical violence or public slander by the abuser, and it is a most dangerous time for victims.

- *Sanitization*: This occurs when an abuser normalizes their behavior or artificially portrays the behavior as good. Victims tend to inflate the sincerity and character of their abuser before they have gained a full understanding of how pervasive and insidious the abuse really is.

Understanding the Emotions of Those Who Emotionally Abuse

The nature of CEA relationships is rooted in an abuser's faulty capacity to process thoughts, access and manage emotions, and take responsibility for one's actions.

American psychologist Daniel Goleman popularized the capacity of emotional intelligence, postulating that emotional intelligence is as important to success as IQ. Elaborating on the work of Salovey and Mayer[8], Goleman offers five key elements: self-awareness, self-regulation, motivation, empathy, and social skills.[9] The following summaries of these terms can help us understand how emotional intelligence influences an abuser's actions:[10]

- *Self-awareness*: In general, individuals with high emotional intelligence are very self-aware. They are willing to look at themselves and assess their strengths and weaknesses, and then work on these areas in order to perform better. Understanding their own emotions and trusting their intuition enables them to not be ruled by their feelings. "Many people believe that this self-awareness is the most important part of emotional intelligence."[11]
- *Self-regulation*: Self-regulation is the ability to manage emotions and impulses. Those who self-regulate are characteristically thoughtful, comfortable with change, demonstrate integrity, and have mastered the ability to say "no." Individuals who self-regulate do not often make impulsive, careless decisions or allow themselves to become too angry or jealous.
- *Motivation*: Being highly motivated is another element of individuals with high emotional intelligence. "They're willing to defer immediate results for long-term success. They're highly productive, love a challenge, and are very effective in whatever they do."[12]

- *Empathy*: Possibly the second most important element of emotional intelligence, Goleman defines empathy as the ability to identify with and understand the wants, needs, and viewpoints of others. Empathetic people excel at identifying the feelings of others. Consequently, they can relate to others, are good listeners, and in general, just manage relationships well. They tend to be open and honest in how they live their own lives and hold off on judging and stereotyping others prematurely.
- *Social skills*: Another element of high emotional intelligence is strong interpersonal skills. Individuals with strong social skills communicate well, skillfully manage disputes, and excel at building and maintaining relationships. Overall, they are great team players who help others to shine.

A covert emotional abuser's emotional IQ is not at a level that allows them to authentically engage in healthy and productive levels of these traits, although they may have a grounded social circle and appear gifted to others. They are also deficient in two of the seven types of intelligence, described by Goleman as comprising emotional IQ:

- Interpersonal intelligence: the ability to make healthy connections with others
- Intrapersonal intelligence: the ability to deeply connect with oneself[13]

As with any of the seven intelligences identified by Dr. Howard Gardner, (linguistic, logical-mathematical, bodily-kinesthetic, visual-spatial, musical, interpersonal, intrapersonal) each person's emotional IQ falls at a specific point on a wide-ranging continuum.[14] With practice, each of these aspects and the totality of one's emotional IQ has the potential to improve. Gardner states, "Only if we expand and reformulate our view of what counts as human intellect will we be able to devise more appropriate ways of assessing it and more effective ways of educating it."[15]

Societal influences affect gender development and behavioral patterns. Although the following information makes a distinction between traditional male and female gender roles, each human being has an emotional IQ and capacity for emotional intelligence. The freedom to explore and improve emotional development and communication can be exercised at will. Dr. Gardner even proposes that a sense of self be considered the eighth form of intelligence.[16] This freedom is a gift to victims *and* abusers to improve and bring meaning to their lives and the relationships they hold dear.

Many people possess underdeveloped emotional IQs. Cultural ideas about acceptable expressions of emotion by men and women can contribute to the seeming undeveloped emotional IQ. Many men, when faced with emotionally provocative interpersonal interactions, often turn to anger and manipulation because they are socially acceptable. Meanwhile, women are mainly, but not always, trained to be attentive and responsive to others. This often leaves men and women consulting opposite emotional playbooks in life, particularly in intimate partner relationships. In some cultures, men are raised to believe they are to be dominant and women are to be submissive; men are more powerful and "know more" and women are weaker and "overly emotional" and therefore "know less." Cultural forces create blind spots, such as a failure to see an accepted practice that is causing harm. In such a situation, not only is the victim being abused but also additional harm is inflicted upon many men when their culture fails to inspire or compel them to develop their emotional IQs.

Patriarchy can cause a harmful way of thinking. Even the most benevolent forms can inadvertently foster abuse. Some men believe that simply going to work and earning money gives them the authority to be in *complete* control over anyone residing in the home. Someone needs to be in charge, so they think it must be the man. They view themselves as the person who takes care of things, fulfilling their self-imposed obligations and responsibilities within the patriarchy. Unfortunately, their thinking frequently evolves into the belief that, in return, the male deserves preferential treatment over his wife, partner, or children. Soon, double standards become the acceptable norm. In some families it is the opposite. The matriarch dominates or defines others and the ways in which others are allowed to move about interpersonally within the family relationship.

Most often, those with faulty belief systems have never examined their own thinking, nor do they realize they need to be confronted, because they are unhealthy, oppress others, and behave harmfully. A healthy relationship that allows both people to thrive cannot exist if one person repeatedly has their ideas, gifts, individuality, and creativity stifled. Although various situations call for leadership, that does not mean that one person in the relationship is guaranteed that slot while the other automatically relinquishes it. Nor does it mean that providing leadership automatically gives an individual the right to exercise "power over" their partner. Individuals bring different gifts to a relationship that make the relationship stronger, emotionally fulfilling, and spiritually rewarding. Shared leadership roles maximize the benefit of the gifts bestowed upon each person. Where hierarchy exists, equality and mutual respect are denied, which is at the heart of CEA.

As we examined each of the terms and descriptions of abusive behaviors described earlier in this chapter (blaming and blame shifting, broken promises, creating clouds of confusion, false accusations, and gaslighting), it is apparent they share common attributes: low levels of one, two, three, four, or all five of the key elements of emotional intelligence.

Daniel Goleman's work can be extended to show that if a person improves their self-awareness, self-regulation, motivation, empathy, and social skills, their emotional IQs improve. While there are additional contributing forces at work in CEA, improving an abuser's emotional IQ could lessen CEA in a relationship. This deep and exacting introspective work is worth doing.

These same key elements can be applicable to institutions. When a church, community, family, or workplace improves their group-awareness (groupthink), group regulation, motivation, empathy, and social skills, their group emotional IQ might improve. It is up to all of us. The responsibility of every church, community, family, workplace, and institution is to no longer allow covertly abusive behaviors and traumas to occur without consequence. Stigmas and taboos will begin to break away when members of these groups open the discussions. Victims will be set free. And, many abusers who are not of the pathological nature would be set free as well. Knowing this and being keenly aware that so many victims are currently enduring covert emotional abuse continues to inspire me to push for enlightenment and change.

Responding to Disclosures of Abuse

At The M3ND Project, there are three key points we keep in mind upon disclosure of abuse:

1. We accept that the person is telling the truth because 90 percent to 98 percent of victims are telling the truth.[17] Refraining from immediately judging, distrusting, or minimizing a potential victim prevents Double Abuse, unless over time adequate information proves otherwise.

2. Neither my team at The M3ND Project nor I debate or take sides with complementarian or egalitarian church cultures because abuse exists in every culture. However, we acknowledge that the responsibility to recognize our cultural biases and blind spots belongs to all of us. We have a responsibility to challenge ourselves and consider how our environment may be inadvertently or intentionally fostering abuse.

3. If we notice that we are at all defensive by the topics we discuss, that feeling needs to serve as a signal to explore the message inherent in the discussion rather than to shut it down.

We have an important role to play, therefore it is important to find it in ourselves to care about the issue of CEA, because emotional trauma is treacherous and intensely damaging. Those who inflict emotional abuse cause harm. Until we are able to keenly identify this extremely destructive form of abuse, lives will continue to be damaged. Abusers may feel hurt when confronted about their behaviors, however, we are not talking about a simple case of hurt feelings. Henry Cloud says, "There is a big difference between hurt and *harm*. We all hurt sometimes in facing hard truths, but it makes us grow. That is not harmful. Harm is when you *damage* someone. Facing reality is usually not a damaging experience even though it can hurt"[18]

Hurt vs. Harm

As stated earlier, overt emotional abuse is more evident, which helps the victim discern that they may be experiencing abuse. It may lead to earlier identification and interventions. In contrast, CEA is much more damaging because it is very difficult to decipher. A single covert behavior in a repeated pattern is enough to be destructive to an individual or relationship. But multiple patterns are exponentially harmful to a victim in terms of their ability to understand what is occurring: the victim becomes unable to identify their experience, find support, confront the abuser, or free themselves of these insidious manipulations. Even worse, prolonged confusion and stress not only compromise the victim's ability to think clearly and function, but greatly impact their physical health. Stress over taxes the adrenal glands causing cortisol spikes, both of which can severely weaken the immune system, making the victim vulnerable to disease and physical, emotional, and spiritual collapse.[19]

These traumatic responses can manifest differently from person to person and situation to situation: one woman may become suicidal due to her constant state of anxiety and hopelessness or break out in rashes; another may begin fainting from drops in blood pressure; and another may end up in the ER with a dangerously low white blood count, to name a few examples. These symptoms are expressions of the impact CEA has upon one's endocrine, immunological, and nervous systems. If these symptoms are not taken seriously or are minimized by the religious, therapeutic, or medical community, the consequences can be life threatening. This is especially true when persons of authority confront the victim and minimize the truth and severity of the victim's experience. These responders are contributing to an escalation of the victim's decline.

It is vital to understand that a healthy portion of individuals who, when confronted and told their behaviors are harmful, immediately analyze their actions and the consequences of them and seek to stop the behavior. They are open to gaining a level of self-awareness to understand why they are doing what they are doing, how it is harmful, and what they need to do to alter their behavior. They have an internal wellspring of desire to grow, which doesn't come from outside pressure, but from an intrinsic sense and desire within themselves to be their best selves. We can make the case that it is important for pastors to educate about abuse from the pulpit. Healthy individuals who display abusive behaviors will likely seek to change.

By contrast, psychologically entrenched abusers do and say things that demonstrate their failure to take responsibility for the harm they cause. They say things like, "That's the way I am, take it or leave it. My family has always been that way, and I grew up fine." These kinds of statements are accompanied by defensive posturing and minimizing their impact on the victim. "Well, I see that. All right, well, I'll try not to do that." Unfortunately, this response does not demonstrate any true ownership for their actions nor is it followed by tangible change. If change is not immediately forthcoming, the abuser is entrenched. Being in a relationship with someone who is unaware, and resists change versus someone who is self-aware and actually changes means the difference between a relationship that is ingrained and doomed for failure and one that is an ultimately healthy relationship.

How Do Conversations Become a Toxic Maze?

A substantial part of a relationship consists of the conversations that occur between the partners. I like to use the metaphor of a maze to demonstrate the differences between healthy conversations and toxic ones. A healthy conversation has a beginning, an entrance point, there are twists and turns of building upon what the other says, and then there is an exit. There is a pathway of least resistance that transports each partner to a solutions-oriented exit. Therefore, a healthy conversation that follows the pathway of least resistance to a successful conclusion will include reciprocal listening, a mutual desire to understand, validation of one another, and identification of a reasonable solution. They may not agree exactly, but there is mutual respect for the thinking and feelings of the partner.

Conversely, a conversation with someone who is a covert emotional abuser is full of dead ends. Mutual responsibility does not exist. The victim is forced to take responsibility for just about everything. The abuser stonewalls conversation through various methods, including all the ways noted above.

The following graphic illustrates what happens during conversations with a covert abuser:

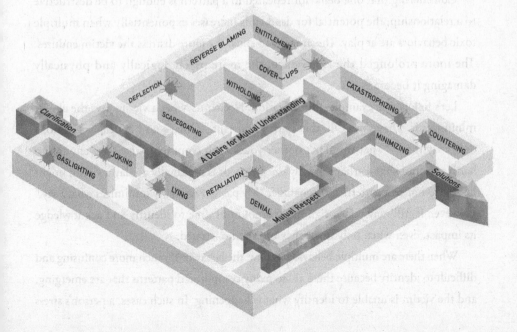

The gray line through the maze line indicates a healthy conversation. Imagine, instead, that the conversation line takes turns toward the end-stops of the walls identified with covert emotionally abusive behaviors. This CEA maze is where all covert emotional abuse resides, blocking and stonewalling the victim from finding any way through or out.

As you look at all the dead ends that are created, the visual conveys what it is like to be in a conversation with a covert abuser. One can begin to grasp how confusing and stressful it is to be a victim in the clutches of a covert emotionally abusive person. Imagine being lost in a maze and repeatedly finding dead ends. Imagine being stuck in it with someone who is constantly working against you. Every day is a different pattern and a new toxic experience. Every conversation includes a different stonewalling technique, a different deflection, and a different defensive posture. You don't know where you are. You cannot identify the patterns. You become disoriented and start to panic. You may call for help. When you are finally out of it, by some seemingly magical way, relief washes over you. If reading this description elicits feelings of being trapped, then you have a sense of the reality that so many victims of CEA face on a daily basis. The maze provides an effective graphic representation of what causes prolonged states of stressful confusion that lead to recurring trauma and PTSD.

Considering that one behavior repeated in a pattern is enough to be destructive to a relationship, the potential for dead ends increases exponentially when multiple toxic behaviors are at play. The more dead ends, the more distress the victim endures. The more prolonged the experience, the more psychologically and physically damaging it becomes.

Let's follow one example: minimization. No matter what a victim says the abuser minimizes it. They say, "Oh, that's not important." "That's no big deal." "Oh no, I didn't say that." "That shouldn't bother you." Such comments alone are enough to harm a relationship. Perhaps, if only one behavior is repeatedly at play a victim might be able to notice a pattern and conclude, "My partner regularly minimizes what I say." However, it still may take a significant amount of time to identify and acknowledge its impact, even when only one behavior is demonstrated.

When there are multiple behaviors at play, the behavior is much more confusing and difficult to identify because there are so many complicated patterns that are emerging, and the victim is unable to identify what is happening. In such cases, a person's stress increases exponentially. Prolonged states of stress and confusion like this, accompanied by unresolved problems, are extremely traumatic and damaging. Clarity often provides the beginning steps for relief as well as validation.

This is why we at The M3ND Project say that clarity is the first necessary step for healing. Even if a person is being abused, if they are able to look at the definitions of terms to identify their experience, they may be able to say, "Oh my gosh! I didn't realize it, but this is exactly what I've been trying to describe, but I didn't have the words." The newfound clarity they didn't have reduces their confusion and stress. Prior to that, they desperately searched for answers as to why communication was so difficult. They are likely carrying all the responsibility for the relationship falling apart, even believing that they are the one who has poor communication skills.

When I interviewed victims, they shared things like, "Maybe I'm not saying it right. There must be something wrong with me. I must be unlovable." They couldn't articulate why their relationship was so dysfunctional and toxic. They thought it was their fault. I remember thinking this myself. "Why can't I solve our communication problems? There must be something wrong with the way I convey my points. I need to try harder. Maybe something is wrong with me. Maybe I'm unlovable." Negative garbage was being projected onto me by my husband and by my own thoughts as well. I tried to make sense of situations and interactions that were being purposefully manipulated by my husband not to make sense. I was stuck in the CEA maze and didn't realize it, over and over and over.

Sadly, many victims of abuse are in these states for years—not because they like it, or they are weak, or they are "stupid," but because they don't know what is wrong with their relationship. If someone simply gives them the words to describe their experiences, they will know almost instantly that they are in an abusive situation. They can then choose to confront the condition of their relationship or leave.

Unfortunately, when prolonged stress and confusion are inflicted and endured, the effects of C-PTSD take hold. This type of trauma diminishes both one's sense of selfhood and one's ability to think clearly, causing fragmented thinking and communication, which further complicates attempts to find resolution. Removing oneself from the CEA maze once and for all seems improbable, but luckily it is not impossible, as my husband and I discovered.

Therapeutic Assessment of Appropriate Use of Couple's Therapy in Cases of Covert Emotional Abuse

Often, referrals for couple's therapy are made by local churches with little information attached. Since well-trained therapists know that when physical or emotional abuse is suspected or confirmed to be present, couple's therapy can create an environment where traumatic experience repeats itself for the victim. Because of this, a telephonic consultation with the referred therapist is initially helpful when making the determination of whether couple's therapy is appropriate. In its absence, the therapist would be wise in first seeing each member of the couple separately for consultation. Following these two individual appointments, the therapist may decide to see the couple together for one additional session. When the therapist or pastoral counselor understands abusive behaviors in its many forms and knows the protocols applicable to treating such abuse, they will use their observations of each partner's narrative, emotional responses, and body language to assess the dynamics playing out between the partners.

In this process, they listen on many levels to the stories while verifying examples of CEA by the victim and a number of blaming statements by the abuser, which are evidenced in the physiological and psychological difficulties being experienced by the victim. The therapist's main concern at this point needs to be the victim's safety and ultimate wellbeing. If the therapist determines that CEA is actively present, they will uphold both their recognition of abuse and their protocols by referring each partner to individual therapists, postponing any couple's therapy until other necessary requirements have been fulfilled.

As the therapist completes the consultation, they offer three names of pre-screened viable therapists who specialize in the areas of concern to both the apparent abuser and victim, and informs each that with written permission, the therapist can consult with and provide preliminary information to the individual therapists selected. The consultations are ended with advisement that although couple's therapy in strictly contraindicated, individual therapy may help to provide meaningful interventions. Leslie Vernick, clinical social worker and author, describes it this way, "All research on domestic violence indicated that marital counseling is contraindicated. The victim will not be free to be honest and the abuser will continue to intimidate and control, even in the counseling. Without specialized training in abusive relationship patterns, it is unwise to tackle these issues in a counseling relationship."[20]

Any future decisions regarding subsequent couple's therapy will be determined by consensus between the individual therapists, a chosen couple's therapist, and the couple. This therapist is always mindful of what they need to know:

- Know the protocol for attending to victims of abuse and when to apply it
- Know when to refer the client elsewhere. If the client's needs are outside the therapist's level of training and expertise, refer to someone qualified to meet the client's needs
- Know how to assess for and identify original, covert, and Double Abuse
- Research where to go to learn more and/or become a specialist in abuse
- Connect with therapists who are experts in abuse and develop a working relationship to hold consultations when necessary

While the alleged abuser is encouraged to contact a therapist suited to confront their behaviors and support them in their efforts to change, the consulting therapist understands the abuser may not follow through on their recommendations or may not be fully truthful in therapy to avoid confrontation and accountability. Regardless, the therapist will focus on the immediate needs of the victim. The abuser's feelings need to be secondary until their emotional and thinking processes can be assessed, identified, and worked through. My words cannot truly capture the depth of despair I was in during my journey not only due to my marital challenges, but to the misguided or failed therapeutic work we endured for too long. I have worked extremely hard with exceptional therapists to get where I am today; my husband has as well. Seeking information through hundreds of interviews with victims, therapists, pastors, and higher learning educators, while gathering resources assisted my process and resulted in developing the teachings of The M3ND Project. With the training and materials provided to first responders, I am confident that therapists will be more equipped to accurately address the needs of their clients and stop Double Abuse in their practices. The same can be said for church leaders, educational staff and administrators, medical and law enforcement personnel, and so many more.

As you know by now, one of my goals is to provide tools to others so they can effectively respond to victims, preventing further harm to victims and their abusers. I have developed a two-pronged approach: While we educate and equip first responders, it's important for victims to be diligent about finding the path toward clarity and gathering the courage to implement clear and firm boundaries. Through the information provided by M3ND, victims are able to understand what makes a situation abusive. We equip them with a conceptual understanding of covert emotional abuse and the words to use when processing their situation in order to effectively reach out for help. This clarity can offer life-saving avenues toward healing, not only for victims and their families, but ultimately, if abusers are willing to work hard, for abusers too. Without clarity, the need for help is nearly impossible to assess and provide. All those who have experienced abuse, and those who are responding to them, require this crucial and meaningful knowledge.

Double Abuse[1]

ANNETTE OLTMANS

"Being heard and being loved are so close that for
the average person they are almost indistinguishable."
David Augsburger, *Caring Enough to Hear and Be Heard*

Anyone who looked at me could tell there was something terribly wrong. I was a shell
of my former self, thirty pounds lighter than my frame should hold. While appearances
broadcasted an obvious crisis due to my PTSD symptoms, they paled in comparison to
the physiological collapse happening internally, and also, spiritually. The desperation I
felt was profound when meeting with the female leader of my Bible study group who
taught marriage classes in the community. I hoped to discuss an imminent separation
from my husband. I was shocked however when my tearful appeal for understanding
was met with her pointed inquisition, implications that I was somehow responsible for
my husband's behavior, incorrect and unwanted instruction, and obvious discomfort
with and inability to discuss emotions—hers or mine.

The damage caused by this meeting and the interactions that followed were devastating.
While I did not know yet exactly what was happening to me, I came to realize these
experiences exacerbated my post-traumatic stress disorder (PTSD) into complex PTSD
(C-PTSD). Why? Because Double Abuse uniformly exacerbates PTSD into C-PTSD.

What Do These Pivotal Terms Mean?

Within the work of The M3ND Project, **original abuse** is seen as the fundamental harm inflicted upon one or more persons by another person(s). There are multiple forms of original abuse: physical, sexual, verbal, emotional, psychological, spiritual, therapeutic, and economic. Such abuse is ubiquitous in societies and cultures worldwide. Equally important is that abuse can be *overt* (obvious to the victim) and/or *covert* (difficult to discern). Covert emotional abuse is found in all types of abuse, like sexual harassment, domestic violence, molestation, and bullying. ***Overt emotional abuse*** consists of behaviors such as raging, name-calling, and put-downs, while ***covert*** *emotional abuse* is far more subtle and difficult to detect, as in blame shifting, rewriting history, and gaslighting, to name a few (detailed information is available in the chapter on covert emotional abuse). Abuse, both overt and covert, can happen to anyone anywhere, regardless of gender, shape, size, race, age, or socioeconomic group. There are no exclusions.

Post-traumatic stress disorder (PTSD) is a condition of mental, emotional, and physiological stress occurring as a result of injury or severe psychological shock. PTSD is also known as an involuntary reaction that develops in some people who have experienced a shocking, scary, or dangerous event with a beginning, middle, and end. Thoughts, sensations, or situations can trigger a recurrence of the trauma, causing the person to feel what they originally experienced, even when not in danger anymore. Symptoms often include flashbacks, nightmares, irritability, outbursts of anger, fearful thoughts, and intense physical reactions, such as uncontrollable shaking.[2] Those individuals with PTSD may also experience "flash forwards," which is the gushing of past traumas into today, with high levels of anticipatory fear about looming future traumatic events.[3]

This portrayal warrants a qualifier: there are multiple ways PTSD can manifest. Not all people display the same symptoms in the same way. Some people isolate themselves, some become aggressive, and others experience intense fear, horror, paranoia, or fragmentation of thinking. While some people experiencing these symptoms are thoughtfully validated by health care professionals, they can also be subjected to rejection.

There have been multiple stories about abuse recently in the media since the #MeToo movement went viral. Often, we have heard news people reporting, "She was afraid if she spoke up or went to the police, she would lose her position on the team or her job." There is so much more at stake than losing a job or position. Victims instinctively know that they risk losing much more than that—the support of their loved ones, their spiritual and/or professional communities, and their lives as they know it. Author and psychotherapist Belleruth Naparstek examined over seventy studies of individuals who experienced traumatic events to determine why certain groups or individuals did *not* develop PTSD.[4] The meta-analysis showed that disturbances in social support *after* trauma are a stronger predictor for PTSD than a person's *pre-trauma* situation. She found that those who escaped suffering PTSD were the ones who were believed, supported, respected, and even exalted by their communities for their sacrifice and experience.[5]

Recovery from a single-event PTSD episode can take several months on average. Recovery starts when the individual moves into an acceptance and understanding of their traumatic event. Often *receiving acceptance and understanding first from others* is the catalyst that helps them move toward acceptance within themselves. Once that shift has occurred and is sustained, then the integration of new coping methods, developed and implemented over time, help to manage any re-triggered PTSD symptoms. The use of these new and effective skills ultimately helps to soothe and heal the traumatized brain.

Double Abuse

How can we stop what does not have a name? **Double Abuse** has to have a name because it is what allows all forms of original abuse to remain unchallenged. Double Abuse occurs when individuals or organizations respond to reported abuse through a lens of cultural bias, with criticism, minimization, taking a neutral stance, asking pointed questions, imposing advice, or pulling away—all forms of condemnation, rather than expressions of compassion.

When victims come forward for help, they are desperate for clarity to unravel their confusion and for intervention to stop recurring traumatic experiences. In these instances, the harm caused to victims inadvertently or intentionally by untrained responders cannot be overemphasized. The most impactful form of Double Abuse occurs when untrained responders (in positions of perceived or actual authority or misguided family and friends), suppress the voice of the victim by defining the situation through the lens of their own ideals, perspectives, or biases. Many times, this leads the responders to impose harsh expectations on how the victim should react, even giving them further consequences if they don't comply.

Well-meaning pastoral and other first-line professionals often refer a couple to couple's counseling first without having the necessary education to decipher whether covert or overt emotional abuse is present within the relationship. Couple's therapy is recognized as being strictly contraindicated by experts working professionally with abuse cases, but many pastors and therapists don't realize this, which compounds harm. Not every therapist is an expert in detecting abusive behaviors and knowing how to treat them, however, they should have the integrity and humility to consult with and/or refer to an expert when they do not. Unfortunately, the disconnect occurs when these first responders do not know what to look for because they have not been trained in spotting domestic violence and its many forms, and they do not recognize when such abuse is occurring.

We can see how the victim becomes tangled in layers of Double Abuse that exacerbate the victim's trauma. Double Abuse ensues when:

1. The victim reaches out for help but is met instead by responders (personal, lay, or professional) who do not know the definition or signs of domestic violence abuses
2. The victim is overtly or covertly rejected, ignored, or treated with apathy by the responder and is pushed further into oppression
3. When couple's therapy has been recommended even though it is contraindicated in cases of abuse
4. The referral may be to someone who is not trained in either recognizing or treating abuse.

Double Abuse then becomes systemically embedded and pervades the environment, and victims are met with these additional layers of harm, chaos, and oppression. The second and possibly third or fourth layer comes in multiple forms, protecting the abusers and laying burdens of responsibility at the victim's feet, where they do not belong. When the focus shifts onto the victim's behavior and they are told to ignore problems or to submit, forgive, or pray more, each of these forms of Double Abuse interferes with opportunities for victims' healing and pushes them toward incorrect interventions while increasing emotional and physiological harm and exacerbating their trauma. Any one of these secondary reactions to original abuse is an urgent signal of an ever-deepening problem inside a family, therapist's office, institution, or micro or macro culture.

Victims rarely come forward because they are lying, want to humiliate their partner, or gain monetary benefit. The vast majority of victims need validation from responders and for the abuser to face the consequences of their actions. Validating victims allows them to feel safe and ensure that the culture will not remain toxic for themselves or others. The main motivation for victims is simply to stop the abuse in a culture where they are heard and respected. The result of Double Abuse is usually the upgrading of the diagnosis of Post-Traumatic Stress Disorder (PTSD) into Complex Post-Traumatic Stress Disorder (C-PTSD).

Complex post-traumatic stress disorder (C-PTSD) has its own consequences beyond the symptoms and effects of PTSD, most particularly what Bessel van der Kolk characterized as profound despair and *helplessness* due to the loss of the sense of self.[6] More dramatically than any other conditions, both PTSD and C-PTSD represent conflated disturbances in the regulation of our neurobiological, endocrinological, and immunological systems. Trauma changes the body and simultaneously changes the brain.[7] As a result, the effective regulation of these important systemic functions becomes disturbed and distressed. What this means is that an individual suffering from PTSD and C-PTSD will be especially challenged in managing a wide variety of physical, emotional, and psychological responses to many aspects of daily life and specially to triggering elements with responders and interpersonal relationships.

While some doctors do diagnose C-PTSD, it is still considered a *proposed* diagnosis for the *Diagnostic and Statistical Manual of Mental Disorders* (DSM-5), the diagnostic handbook used by psychiatrists and psychologists.[8] *However, the International Classification of Diseases Eleventh Edition* (ICD-11), an internationally recognized publication of the World Health Organization, added C-PTSD as a new diagnostic term in 2018.[9] Only the United States lags behind. Since C-PTSD is not yet in the DSM-5, it is easy to understand how most professional therapists are unaware of the serious cautions that need to be in place when treating someone experiencing abuse or with PTSD.

As already stated, post-traumatic stress can be successfully mitigated when met with healthy support, respectful connection, and trauma treatment therapy within a reasonable period of time. But when relational cumulative trauma occurs, combined with Double Abuse, learned hopelessness and despair lead to C-PTSD, which can take a minimum of five years to heal, even in concert with multiple treatment modalities.

In my situation, I struggled with the need to seek help, fearful that my doing so would negatively expose my husband, who inflicted the covert emotional harm, and me. My interactions with the leaders, and all but one couple in my Bible study group to whom I turned, were uniquely destructive because this group was much more than just a Bible study group. I considered them my close friends. I saw them every week and broke bread with them on hundreds of occasions. We depended upon one another. I believed our attachment was mature and based on a shared love for each other and a deep commitment to our faith.

Our time-tested connection made their responses far more traumatic. *With Double Abuse the severity of the effect is dependent upon the victim's reasonable expectations not being met.* I came to them in a compromised condition seeking understanding and help for my husband and me. Instead, I discovered the hidden conditions they placed upon their acceptance of me. Patriarchy, especially that wives must submit to and respect their husbands, was an underlying theme that bound this group together. They were nearly united in their support for my husband and in their maltreatment of me. I was never invited to share a meal with them again, largely because I had disparaged my husband and taken steps to separate.

Soon thereafter, the male leader of the Bible study group phoned me and said, "This is going to be a difficult conversation, Annette." He proceeded to give me, but *not* my husband, the ultimatum to reconvene our current (though unsuccessful and harmful) couple's therapy within ninety days, or I—but again, *not* my husband—would be kicked out of the group and never invited back.

I responded by saying I would do *anything* if my husband would do just *one* thing: enlist the help of an accountability partner for transparency. My requirement fell on deaf ears. While my husband was now willing to seek solutions, the group interfered with what would have been the proper interventions, which were to separate, stop couple's therapy, replace it with separate collaborative therapy, and enlist an accountability partner. The group's refusals delayed the path to restoration because it emboldened my husband's faulty thinking and behaviors.

Religious communities, particularly where patriarchy dominates the culture, can hold the "institution" of marriage as more deserving than the wellbeing of the victimized spouse and children within the marriage. Other than in cases of adultery, the woman is expected to submit and hold the lion's share of the responsibility to keep her man happy and the marriage together. Double Abuse was being practiced under the guise of this group's religious dogma, which brandished at me the precepts of a scripturally distorted Christian microculture.

I find it difficult to convey how sick I had become when I initially came forward. The ongoing emotional abuse I was enduring at home and the maltreatment incurred during multiple therapeutic sessions with two different couple's therapists who had not been trained in abuse took their toll on my mind, body, and soul. These challenges were manifesting disease throughout my body.

My immune system was in a state of collapse, compromising my ability to fight infection. The doctors searched to identify viable diagnoses, including cancer, Lyme disease, and diabetes. I was diagnosed with latent autoimmune diabetes and Lyme disease. I had bouts of uncontrollable shaking, dangerous endocrine system fluctuations, and difficulties with organizing speech, balance, and cognition. Sudden drops in blood pressure landed me in the emergency room thirteen times. At times I was unable to care for myself, finding the normal activities of daily living overwhelming. The ways my C-PTSD was manifesting appeared to some as though I was emotionally unstable, while my husband's aloofness made him seem in control.

As you can see, these were frightening times for me. I had not yet discovered that I was experiencing symptoms of PTSD and C-PTSD. This was long before understanding original abuse and identifying covert emotional abuse and Double Abuse. Finally, I was significantly traumatized as I learned that, in an effort to drive me back into meeting their demands, the group had breached my confidentiality and reached out to others in our broader Christian community requesting that they not speak to me either. I leaned on more supportive friends and found my way to Dr. Henry Cloud and Dr. John Townsend's Life Coaching class where I gained a new perspective on what Christ teaches. There, John led me to an individual therapist who was an expert in trauma, abuse, and PTSD. Then, after painstaking discussions with my husband and his eventual agreement to disconnect from the Bible study group entirely, my husband and I were able to begin treatment with

Dr. David Hawkins of the Marriage Recovery Center, a Christian therapist who is a known expert in abuse. My husband began intensive therapy and group therapy, and he volunteered to join a batterer's prevention course even though physical abuse was not part of our story. Nonetheless, all provided essential turning points toward my validation and healing and my husband's acceptance of responsibility for his harmful emotional behaviors. After two years, including separation, these successful interventions saved our marriage.

What happened with my Bible study group still astounds me and always will. Three years later, even after my husband and I reconciled and came forward with our story in a local paper, they continued to publicly criticize me.[10]

I am proud to say I am a Christian. I am not proud of the ways in which we treat each other at times. Approaching the problem of abuse with a humble and open heart has always been my intent and is evident in my interactions with victims and audience members when I conduct The M3ND Project trainings and speaking engagements. I choose to divulge my story so we as Christians, and others of different faiths, can change what is happening to so many victims of abuse when they come forward. The first hurdle to overcome when embarking on a journey of repair is extinguishing Double Abuse.

Some Christians can be judgmental, and their pulling away, disconnecting, and shunning is an overt act meant to cast out others. This is contrary to a fundamental point of being Christ-like. In a seemingly ironic twist, through my research I found that it is mostly the unchurched individuals who advocated best against abuse, oppression, and trauma. How life changing would it be if churches were leading the way? It is the church's responsibility to deliver compassion to victims and stop allowing both overt and covert behaviors to be perpetrated without consequence to those inflicting the abuse. Double Abuse in the church would be extinguished if leaders became educated, talked openly about it from the pulpit, and properly intervened against such abuse. Victims would be set free, and many abusers would be set free as well through accountability and reparations.

My experiences with original abuse and Double Abuse led me to the founding of The M3ND Project, guided by this principle from Scripture:

It is shameful even to mention what the disobedient do in secret. But everything exposed by the light becomes visible—and everything that is illuminated becomes light. (Eph. 5:12–13, NIV)

At The M3ND Project, we seek to expose the hidden issues of original abuse and Double Abuse and bring them into the light. Listening with respect, strengthening connections, proclaiming truth, and doing no further harm are four core values we hold sacred.

The iceberg analogy

At The M3ND Project, we use The Iceberg Analogy to demonstrate the nature of abuse. The smallest part of the iceberg is above the water line, which we identify as the original abuse: any violence of a sexual, mental, emotional, physical, or financial nature, bullying, molestation, deprivation, or neglect. The greater part of the iceberg is under water. Original abuse is supported by this larger base where all aspects of Double Abuse reside. If we could tackle those things that reside below the waterline, then the top of the iceberg would melt into the water, not having the support to carry on.

THE ICEBERG ANALOGY.

Double Abuse® Allows All Forms Of Original Abuse To Remain In Place

Professional Sabotage

Sexual Harassment   Domestic Violence

Original Abuse ————   Child Abuse   Psychological Abuse   Bullying

Double Abuse® ————   Ultimatums   Placing Conditions
                                                                                      Limiting Scope of
                                            Pulling Away   Shunning   Conversations
                                                                              Blaming
                              Criticizing
                                            Asking Pointed   Silencing
                                            Questions   Ignoring
                              Setting Boundaries to   Giving Unrequested
                        Serve Personal Comfort Level   Advice
                                                                                      Judging
                                            Not Believing

THEM3ND PROJECT
educate. equip. restore.

Imagine a world where victims reach out with courage, overcoming their sense of helplessness as a first step. If we tackle the attitudes, blind spots, and pervasive systemic blindness toward abuse, then a victim's life will not be damaged but redeemed.

The M3ND Project's Antidote to Double Abuse

I created the Healing Model of Compassion (HMC, see below) to serve responders in their interactions with victims when those victims first reach out for help. For those who have been traumatized, compassion is a specific set of responses as defined in the HMC. We do not have to be experts, but in using this tool, we will not be doing further harm.

If families or institutions do not support the victim, layers of toxicity and ongoing trauma are added. When a safe space is offered for victims to unfold their story, find help, and be able to leave or separate, they will have the validation and assistance they need for doing so. While the symptoms of PTSD and C-PTSD may present in unattractive or challenging ways, the patience of a responder is a health-giving balm in the healing process. Practicing the Healing Model of Compassion ensures a responder will not inadvertently condemn those who come forward in their struggle to report their abuse.

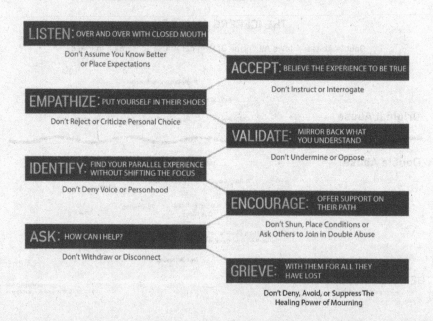

HEALING MODEL OF COMPASSION

LISTEN: OVER AND OVER WITH CLOSED MOUTH
Don't Assume You Know Better or Place Expectations

ACCEPT: BELIEVE THE EXPERIENCE TO BE TRUE
Don't Instruct or Interrogate

EMPATHIZE: PUT YOURSELF IN THEIR SHOES
Don't Reject or Criticize Personal Choice

VALIDATE: MIRROR BACK WHAT YOU UNDERSTAND
Don't Undermine or Oppose

IDENTIFY: FIND YOUR PARALLEL EXPERIENCE WITHOUT SHIFTING THE FOCUS
Don't Deny Voice or Personhood

ENCOURAGE: OFFER SUPPORT ON THEIR PATH
Don't Shun, Place Conditions or Ask Others to Join in Double Abuse

ASK: HOW CAN I HELP?
Don't Withdraw or Disconnect

GRIEVE: WITH THEM FOR ALL THEY HAVE LOST
Don't Deny, Avoid, or Suppress The Healing Power of Mourning

Here are the basic tenets for working effectively with this model:

- **Listen** from a posture that provides the victim a safe *space* and *time* to process their experiences. Do not assume you are more knowledgeable or that you've figured out why the abusive experience might be occurring. Do not place expectations on or redirect any aspect of the conversation.

- **Accept** the story to be true, at least until there is strong conflicting evidence. There is no harm in believing a victim as an initial mindset, but there is measurable harm that comes from disbelieving authentic stories.

- **Empathize** with the victim by putting yourself in the victim's shoes and adopting the mindset that the story is true. Do not criticize them or their decisions. Victims cannot heal in isolation; meaningful connections are an essential part of overcoming their situation and managing their trauma.

- **Validate** by mirroring what you understand, telling them they have every reason to feel harmed by emotionally or physically abusive behavior. Do not undermine their position or perspective. Your role is to provide them the human connection to feel heard and respected. Do not breach confidentiality.

- **Identify** by finding your parallel experience *without* changing the focus. You might say, "What you are describing reminds me of one experience I had in college. I'm sorry you're going through this." The idea is not to shift the focus onto yourself, but rather strengthen your connection by demonstrating that you are listening attentively.

- **Encourage** them by offering support. You might say, "You're going to get through this, and I'll be standing with you during the process." You may feel tempted to place demands and say something like, "If you don't leave, I can't listen any longer." Or you may say the opposite, "If you don't stay, I cannot support you." Leaving or staying is the victim's choice (not yours) that involves multiple complications.

- **Ask** what you can do to help? This one question is the only appropriate one to ask when a victim is trying to find clarity. Provide resources rather than pull away.

- **Grieve** *with* them for all they have lost or are going to lose. Don't deny, avoid, or suppress the healing power of mourning. Grieving with someone is a shared experience of deep connection. Victims are feeling immense pain as well as loss of connection from others. They have often been forced into isolation by their abuser, or they have pulled away on their own accord due to their unstable circumstances. Deeply connecting with a victim in one's care by grieving with them creates a new sense of being respected and valued.

Realize that the victim is in a mindset of anticipatory fear as they share their story. They are monitoring your facial expressions and body language, as they desperately scan to see if they will be accepted by a supportive first responder. They may just be coming to terms with the realization that they have been or are being emotionally, physically, or sexually abused, and their world is turning upside down. When a deep connection is offered, it can have a powerful impact on their steps towards healing.

I want to emphasize that using the HMC requires less effort or danger for the *listener* than inquisition or advice. The listener is *not* responsible for the victim's feelings or for fixing anything. The false notion that the responder is responsible impedes many people from engaging in meaningful and longstanding ways. Using the HMC empowers the responder and the victim and ensures that the listener will do no further harm. These actions minister to the heart and mind of the victim, which truly defines compassion.

I frequently find that when we reach the "Ask" portion of the HMC and say, "What can I do to help you?" the victim's answers are rarely imposing. They usually say something reasonable like, "Can you please just let me call you and talk with you periodically," or, "Will you come with me to my appointment with my attorney? I'm afraid to go by myself."

Bottom line: these are extremely manageable tasks for you.

A Close-up Look at Double Abuse in Action

One of the forms of Double Abuse mentioned earlier is that of *therapeutic abuse*. In the remainder of this chapter, we are going to focus our attention on this particular version of Double Abuse, both because it has been largely unexplored previously, and because it is one of the key understandings emerging from my personal experience and subsequent in-depth research.

The first step in knowing if you are in a relationship with an abusive person is clarity regarding specific abusive experiences and understanding what constitutes domestic violence, including emotional abuse. When covert emotional abuse (CEA) occurs, such abuse does not necessarily involve outwardly controlling behaviors, like physical violence or harsh criticisms or blaming. Instead, CEA is much more confusing. It might be framed as helpfulness, such as what my Bible study group used to justify their toxic behaviors. The key to deciphering these subtleties is determining whether the actions that are framed as helpful to the victim are actually exploiting the victim's vulnerabilities. One victim expressed her own confusion and doubts when she told me in an interview how her abusive husband insisted he loved her so much that what he was doing was *for* her. Since he presented to the world, as my husband did, as a successful and devoted husband, she felt "crazy" as she saw him differently behind closed doors.

Too often, victims do not believe they are experiencing abuse, because the abuse has become so habitual or so confusing or chaotic that they do not realize how seriously they are being harmed, even though they are experiencing the prolonged stress and traumatic effects from it. The inherent task of trying to unravel what is happening is a significant clue to someone that they may be in a relationship with an abuser. Once someone has determined that they are indeed in a relationship with an abuser, they need to explore whether their couple's therapy is making their situation worse.

Double Abuse in Couple's or Pastoral Counseling

As we have seen, trained therapists and pastors cannot be expected to know everything about every aspect of life and its challenges. They are not uniformly and thoroughly trained to diagnose and treat characteristics of abuse, trauma, or marital complications. In my research, I found that most states require licensed therapists only ten to fifteen hours of education concerning matters of abuse. I became convinced by this research that this is a seriously flawed practice that misinforms well-intended therapists into believing they are adequately prepared to diagnose and treat such cases. More so, it confounds clients into thinking a clinical license means someone is qualified to diagnose and treat emotional and physical abuse and trauma. I found victims to be largely unsuspecting regarding the imperative to carefully interview and seek out an expert therapist who will not re-traumatize them.

Understanding that active abuse cannot be healed in couple's therapy is of crucial importance for victims to understand. If there is abuse, then abuse is the *only* issue that should be addressed. Victims need to be aware that if they find themselves experiencing abuse (physical, emotional, psychological, verbal, sexual), and the *abuser* suggests couple's therapy as a way of working things out, this prompt is a common trap used by abusers to further crush a victim's spirit. And, victims, in their desperate need for help, wrongly seek couple's therapy as a potential solution.

If any of the following is happening in already established couple's therapy, the therapist does not have the expertise or is not equipped to diagnose or handle such cases:

- Victims are experiencing chaos or confusion in their couple's therapy
- The feelings of the abuser are the focus rather than first resolving their faulty thinking and worldview
- A therapist or pastoral counselor tells a victim to better meet the abusive partner's needs in order to stop the abuse
- The therapist implies that the victim is in *any way* responsible for the destructive behaviors of the abuser
- The therapist treats the relationship as fifty-fifty or even eighty-twenty (the abuser's fault), the abuser will solely focus on the victim's portion
- The therapist refuses to confront abuse by taking a moral stand thereby withholding validation from the victim along with the justice that is desperately needed

No amount of behavioral change on the victim's side will change the false ideas the abuser has of the victim's position. No one is meant to live a silent, confused, chaotic, or fearful life with his or her partner. There is no excuse for abuse. These are foundational problems that the abuser must face, having nothing to do with the victim's behavior.

An uninformed, incompletely trained therapist focuses only on the *feelings* of their clients rather than the reality of the situation. This approach not only re-traumatizes and damages victims further, but it reinforces the abuser's feelings, emboldens their behaviors, and supports them in avoiding remorse, accountability, reparation, and the possibility of restoration.

The only feelings that have a space in the therapeutic process are those of the victim's, until such time as the abuser's faulty thinking has been addressed and resolved. If the abuser's entrenched beliefs and behaviors are not addressed and resolved first, there will be no change in an abuser's behavior, and couple's therapy will be premature, traumatic, and harmful. Both the victim's and abuser's well-trained counselor or therapist will recognize and clearly state that the abuse is not about the victim, nor is it the victim's fault. That does not mean there may not be abuse that goes back and forth between victim and abuser. More commonly any abuse on the victim's part is a reaction to the abuser's abuse, not something the victim initiates.

Until the abuser has undergone a rigorous two-year batterers' prevention program, preferably in a faith-based environment or long-term abuse therapy, the abuser's feelings will be distorted and not grounded in rational thinking. They are about the abuser's belief systems and psychological dynamics, hierarchical thinking, and blaming others for their behavior. These skewed perceptions are problems of the abuser's worldview.

Many people wonder *how long it might take for an abuser to change.* Experts in the field emphasize that it takes significant, repeated efforts over an extended period of time, with cycles of successes and setbacks (that are strongly confronted) to change, and sadly, the majority of abusers do not.[11] Regardless, the ability of the abuser to change is *not* the barometer of whether a couple should remain together. Rather, the barometer needs to be whether the victim can manage the high stress, recurring trauma, duration, and repeating successes and failures of the process.

Over-Confronting and Under-Informing

Over confronting the victim occurs when the therapist inaccurately uses generalities about domestic violence or abuse. They may ask, "Why did you choose someone who's not emotionally available?" or "Why do you stay in this relationship?" or "Why do you tolerate abuse?" This unfairly blames the victim before they have the understanding necessary to process the accuracy of their situation. By illustrating the stonewalling behaviors of the abuser, the victim can unfold their own understanding, becoming more ready to learn that the problem within the relationship is abuse.

Equally important is not to *under inform* the victim. Some therapists say things like, "Your spouse has never cherished you." This is too vague, leaving the victim to wonder if their spouse might ever cherish them. Or they may think, *Am I unlovable?* Gently describing patterns and specific behaviors of the abuser is the necessary first step to validating the victim, providing the clarity they need to begin to heal.

Is it Ever Better to Allow Abuse Than to Confront It?

Has a family member, friend, or parishioner ever come to you personally to discuss some form of abuse? You may not know what to do. You may feel caught off guard, uniformed, and ill-prepared as to what steps to offer, which can motivate your avoidance in confronting the abuse. A willingness to confront specific abusive behaviors (if the victim has given you permission) and taking further action on someone's behalf takes knowledge, compassion, and courage.

Confronting an abuser and taking the vital steps to resolve it is often met with the *double-down effect*. This means it is very challenging to stand firm when the abuser desperately seeks to protect their *image* by recruiting others to join in the deception. Doubling down is a highly traumatic experience for the victim.

Family is a strong microculture, and for the victim, the idea of possibly destroying a family's connection and losing support is not easy to override. Such ruptures are costly, emotionally, relationally, and often financially. This usually means that relationships are going to be altered or broken, possibly forever. Not only victims but their therapists are fighting against family systems and cultures where changing such systems' beliefs, opinions, and behaviors pose great difficulty. Breakthroughs for abusers are not common.

Professionals who lack expert training might also permit abuse to continue rather than confront it in therapy because they either think that to confront is not what their clients are paying them for or that the abuser might flee, leaving the therapy forever, and with that, all hope for the relationship will be lost. Commonly abuse escalates over time, therefore it is imperative to understand the potential dangers that may even result in serious physical injury or death. The victim's wellbeing must always be the priority because trauma is measurable and harmful.

Remember how my Bible study placed the institution of marriage above the individuals inside the marriage, as many churches do. Because of the strong religious culture that discriminates against divorce, lay and some professional counselors work with families to stay intact, often with tragic results. There are times when the dissolution of marriage is the best, healthiest decision, especially when abuse and trauma are present. When a particular faith rejects the notion of divorce, the leaders of that faith need new education and training to address abuse with compassion, finding new pathways for resolution to mend families, within or outside of marriage.

My husband and I strove hard to save our marriage. For us it worked, and we have found the awareness, comfort, and fellowship of informed therapists and a new faith-based community. The more educated we become, and the more willing we are to work hard, the more likely our chances of success. But as emphasized earlier, this work to change takes time and sustained effort, and not all victims are capable of enduring the process, and very few abusers care enough to face confrontation for extended periods of time.

Is it easier *not* to confront abuse? It might feel that way in the moment, but if we do not, we are colluding with the abuser. Even the position of neutrality favors the abuser and traumatizes the victim. Evaluate actions. Depend upon the integrity of morals, legal guidelines, and ethics. "It is very tempting to take the side of the perpetrator. All the perpetrator asks is that the bystander do nothing. . . . The victim, on the contrary, asks the bystander to share the burden of pain."[12]

Minimizing the harmful actions of others, trying urgently to "clean things up," or failing to come to the aid of others when they come forward constitutes Double Abuse. Whether intended or not, any inaction or half effort to address abuse causes harm to the victim and those within and around the situation.

A Note About Emotionally Focused Couple and Family Therapy

There is a form of therapy that has become popularized in the last few years called emotionally focused couple and family therapy (EFT). According to Dr. Susan M. Johnson, primary developer of EFT, a positive therapeutic alliance with both partners is considered to be a prerequisite of successful treatment.[13] However, Johnson goes on to say that EFT is *not* designed to be used with couples where abuse is present or separating couples.[14] Unfortunately, there are therapists practicing this method of therapy who are either unaware of this caution or ignore it even with couples where abuse is present.

EFT requires that both parties be open and vulnerable about early traumas and responses that are emotionally triggering. For example, a husband and wife share each other's biggest fears so both can be sensitive never to trigger those fears. If you're dealing with an abuser in a relationship, the last thing a victim should do is share their vulnerabilities with that person, because the abuser lacks emotional awareness and maturity and will prey upon those vulnerabilities. They may exploit them publicly, and they'll do so privately. EFT becomes appropriate only after therapists successfully confront and help overcome the abuser's behaviors.

Unfortunately, among the substantial number of therapists I interviewed, many of them were using EFT with couples who should not have been in couple's therapy due to the presence of overt or covert abuse. They stated, "My single modality is EFT." Obviously, therapy is not a one-size-fits-all endeavor and to impose their "chosen modality" upon every client regardless of the needs of the client is not considered best practice. During my questioning of the counselors, I cautioned, "But these couples are not appropriate for emotionally focused therapy, and they're not even appropriate for couple's therapy." Uniformly, these therapists responded, "If I send the abuser away, who will take care of him? He won't be back."

This attitude demonstrates that the counselors are caring as much for the abuser as they are for the victim. But the victim is the one being harmed by the dangerous effects of trauma. The traumatized individual must be the priority because the cost of trauma is so life altering. The abuser might rail against the confrontation or fear the work ahead or feel hurt, but hurt for the abuser is what helps them grow. Facing consequences, accountability, and reparation are what the abuser needs, and the victim needs to experience the validation.

Several years earlier, in two other attempts to find help, my husband and I turned to marriage enrichment and intensive programs. They proved unreliable and painfully frustrating and traumatizing. On a larger scale they were built upon a similar foundation as EFT or couple's therapy for marriages where abuse is present: giving 50/50 percent responsibility and preferential weight to each partner's feelings, while not addressing the abuse that was occurring. In my later research when I went back to interview the leaders of these renowned multi-day programs, even though they presented themselves as "experts" they did not have training in domestic violence. They claimed that they had asked their attendees if they had been abused. If the attendees who experienced abuse said they had been in therapy, then the leaders allowed them to participate. If such abuse had not been addressed in therapy, the leaders recommended therapy to them. There was no vetting process for victims who did not yet understand that what they were experiencing constitutes abuse. And, without exception, these leaders were completely unaware of covert emotional abuse or Double Abuse.

When leaders become appropriately and thoroughly trained, they will realize that too often victims do not know they are being abused, and in their desperation readily agree to such programs in hopes of finding help. Or, at other times victims are "dragged" to these marital programs by abusers and victims dare not risk telling anyone the truth of what is happening, especially in group settings. The leaders' responsibility then is NOT to encourage the marriage programs but to refer the victims to individual therapy and the abusers to long-term abusers' treatment.

What is Essential for Effective Couple's Therapy

Judith Herman wrote in her renowned book, *Trauma and Recovery: The Aftermath of Violence—From Domestic Abuse to Political Terror,*

> The technical neutrality of the therapist is not the same as moral neutrality. Working
> with victimized people requires a committed moral stance. The therapist is called
> upon to bear witness to a crime. . . . This does not mean a simplistic notion that
> the victim can do no wrong; rather it involves an understanding of the fundamental
> injustice of the traumatic experience and the need for a resolution that restores
> some sense of justice.[15]

Abuse treatment experts understand that the primary therapeutic goals of equality, respect, and reciprocity in communication in couple's therapy cannot be realized if an abuser does not believe in, and pursue equality with and mutual respect for, their partner.

Once each member of the couple is fully and productively engaged in individual therapy, and the abuser has completed a comprehensive and lengthy program, and if/when all concerned agree to embark on couple's therapy, that therapy needs to be *collaborative therapy* rather than simply conjoint therapy. This means that the individual therapists work with their clients and each other in a collaborative manner, something not many therapists are willing to do. There are very good therapists and groups, as in The Marriage Recovery Center and others, who are experts in and capable of dealing with abuse within the context of individual and couple's therapy; it is essential to consult only those who are so capable. Most well-trained therapists realize that for the abuser there must be a breakdown before there can be a breakthrough.

If your couple's therapist, pastor, or lay counselor does not understand the dynamics of domestic violence, including emotional abuse and PTSD, an even inadvertent destructive therapeutic experience creates Double Abuse, which causes PTSD to escalate to C-PTSD. If you believe you have suffered in any of the ways mentioned throughout this book, I recommend that you follow up with an individual therapist who specializes in abuse, as well as PTSD and C-PTSD.

There will be times when we family members, friends, and first responders must step up and take action. If you are a person mandated to report claims of abuse, harassment, bullying, or other forms of abuse, ensure that your practices for taking action are ethically accurate, in place, and being practiced. If legal action is required, I encourage you to do your research. If you are not trained to manage these incidents, consult with professionals who specialize in handling abuse to devise an appropriate plan.

One of the fundamental goals I am striving for in The M3ND Project is the improvement of those best practices for all of us who may become responders, personal and professional, in order to meet ever-growing needs of both victim and abuser. Another goal is to encourage professionals to acquire the abuse and trauma treatment training that is so urgent. My—and The M3ND Project's—primary mission is to educate, equip, and restore all those impacted by original and Double Abuse and put an end to it.

How Abuse Impacts our Health

EDITH JOHNSON

Physical and emotional abuse not only impacts a victim's health through direct injuries but also has long-term negative impacts on many areas of health. Victims of abuse can experience various problems, like trouble healing from wounds, gut health issues, autoimmune diseases, as well as numerous mental health issues. Abuse stimulates and even reshapes the brain causing lasting effects, particularly when the abuse occurs in childhood. Research studies of babies and children demonstrate that from the beginning of our lives, love, kindness, and gentle touch are necessary for healthy development. Abuse, in both childhood and adulthood, causes negative changes in the body, the brain, and the emotions that lead to illnesses of all kinds. Sadly, these health issues are too often misdiagnosed, blaming the victim and perpetrating further abuse rather than helping the victim heal. Knowing and understanding the impact that abuse has on a person's health is the first step in offering godly, helpful counsel.

Relationships Are Made for Love. Abuse Destroys.

Intimate relationships require nurturing to grow and succeed. Top marriage researchers, John Gottman and Robert Levenson, have been studying couples' interactions during conflict for more than forty years. They have found that during conflict couples need five or more positive interactions for every negative interaction in order to have a stable, happy relationship.[1] Contempt, criticism and stonewalling, all common behaviors used by abusers, have proven to be very destructive in relationships. This research validates the Bible's repeated instructions to "encourage one another," "build one another up," "love one another," and "serve one another." We were made for positive, supportive relationships. Physical and emotional abuse have just the opposite impact—they tear down and destroy.

One form of abuse in relationships is betrayal. An intimate partner having an affair is a form of betrayal, but so is "lying, absenteeism and coldness, withdrawal of sexual interest, disrespect, and breaking promises."[2] Women and men who experience betrayal have intense reactions that affect their hearts, their breathing, and their emotions. Moreover, when the victim reacts to one of these forms of betrayal, he or she is often diagnosed as codependent rather than being recognized as having Post Traumatic Stress Disorder (PTSD). However, the victim's brain is trying to make sense out of their experience and has become hypervigilant, which is a normal adaptive response to trauma and should not be discounted.

The way we are designed to emotionally attach and remain connected creates a lot of confusion for a person when an adult relationship turns emotionally abusive. What appears to be attentiveness and caring can turn into harmful, controlling behavior. "We are hard-wired to preserve our attachment relationships (our connection with our primary attachment figure who, after childhood, is often a romantic partner) above all else. After a person has attempted fight, flight, and freeze in the face of a physical or verbal attack, they will often surrender as a final defense mechanism."[3] An onlooker watching a woman stay with her abuser will assume that the relationship must not be that bad. Instead, compliance may be submission to the abuser's will in order to stay attached.

Often the controlling partner manipulates the victim, causing her to feel incompetent and to think she needs the help of the abuser. The victim may be isolated financially or physically from family and friends. As a result, no one knows how bad it is. Researcher Evan Stark has written about this in a book entitled *Coercive Control: How Men Entrap Women in Personal Life*. Research shows that this type of control and emotional abuse is just as injurious to women as physical abuse. The victim becomes anxious and may go on to develop many physical and emotional symptoms.

Medical Repercussions of Abuse

When stress levels get too high, it is as if a circuit breaker flips, and the body no longer has the energy to manage life. Individuals in hostile relationships will heal forty percent more slowly when they are wounded than those in happier marriages. The risk of "heart disease, cancer, arthritis, type 2 diabetes, and depression"[4] increases significantly in unhappy marriages. Depression and stress contribute to a greater risk for infection, prolonged infectious episodes, and delayed wound healing; all processes that can fuel sustained serious inflammatory and autoimmune responses.[5] In addition, "Teitelbaum reports that people who have been through abuse, including being abused as children, are twice as likely to develop fibromyalgia as others."[6] Gut issues which are common in stressful situations such as an abusive relationship may include irritable bowel syndrome or leaky gut, both of which cause significant physical distress and lead to long-term health issues.

If the abuse progresses to battering and the victim ends up in the emergency room (ER), the physical injuries can be quite serious. If the abuser is the one who takes a woman to the ER, and she is dependent on him in any way, he may represent her as needy. Then the doctor may not pick up on the abusive nature of the relationship or may not take it seriously. A woman in this situation cannot speak up and tell the doctor what really happened. That would likely lead to more abuse when they get home. Women are often blamed for their circumstances, and through "clinical insensitivity and inappropriate care, abused women are reported to be hypochondriacs, crocks, hysterics, women with vague complaints and 'total body pain.'"[7]

The most common injuries that women sustain in domestic abuse situations are blunt force trauma to the head, face, and neck. "Although Traumatic Brain Injuries [TBI] and strangulation injuries are common, they are frequently undiagnosed."[8] TBIs can have short and long-term negative consequences on functioning. This can include eye damage leading to dizziness, inflammation of the brain, memory issues, and much more. In addition, any physical attack will likely activate the part of the brain called the amygdala which is where our fight, flight, and freeze responses originate.

Children Need Love and Peace for Healthy Development

Parents and adults who are struggling to treat each other well should take seriously the negative impact they will have on their children if they do not get help or escape from their abuser. The brains of infants and young children are dependent on their caregivers. When a parent or caregiver is responsive to a child's needs, the child calms and learns how to regulate his or her behavior, emotions, and physiology. "With time and with successful experiences in co-regulation, children increasingly take over these functions themselves. Abuse and neglect represent the absence of adequate input (as in the case of neglect) or the presence of threatening input (as in the case of abuse), either of which can compromise development."[9]

While parents are usually the ones to offer comfort and closeness which leads to adequate development, on occasion others may be able to provide this as well. In 1995, a set of twins were born twelve weeks early. One twin was growing and gaining weight while the other was failing and not expected to live. Nurse Gayle Kasparian violated hospital protocol and put the stronger twin in the same incubator as her ailing sister. The photo of what happened when they were put together by a gutsy nurse has changed the world of neonatal nursing: "The stronger baby wrapped her arm around her sister, and her touch allowed the struggling baby's heart to stabilize and her temperature to return to normal."[10]

This life-giving hug shows the power of appropriate loving touch. Warm, loving hugs help reduce stress, boost immune function, increase serotonin, balance the nervous system, and protect against heart disease. Being held lovingly reduces levels of cortisol, the hormone released when a person is stressed, and increases levels of oxytocin, the hormone associated with empathy, trust, and relationship building. However, once there has been violence in a relationship whether as a child or an adult, the victim can almost never relax in the presence of the abuser again, so those benefits will not be experienced.

Closeness and bonding are a part of God's design for us. We enter the world as babies for a reason, and the Bible says that we are fearfully and wonderfully made (Ps. 139:14). God knit each one of us together in our mother's womb. He entrusted us as little babies to our parents knowing that we can only thrive with lots of love, nurture, attention, and a safe environment—not just physically safe but also emotionally and spiritually safe. Children in a safe, peaceful environment with attentive parents develop a secure attachment which allows them to develop healthy relationships later.

Abuse Impacts the Brain Negatively

None of us were designed to experience domestic violence, sexual abuse, war, or a whole host of other traumatic experiences. Even witnessing someone else being abused, as in domestic violence, is extremely disturbing. Our brain is wired to respond to danger by activating the amygdala, a very small part of the brain which is especially attuned to threat and fear. When a bear is chasing us, or in other dangerous situations, this part of the brain takes over and reacts with either a fight, flight, or freeze response depending on how serious the threat is. However, when the amygdala stores the emotional memory of this event and its reaction and replays it repeatedly, it is retraumatizing. When a memory is properly stored the person can relax because he or she is safe again.

Furthermore, when the amygdala is overactive in a traumatizing situation, the prefrontal cortex, the thinking part of the brain, shuts down. Additionally, the anterior cingulate cortex, the part of the brain which regulates emotions, tends to go offline, overwhelming the person. Once a person is safe again, if the stressful situation is completely over and was not devastating, a person's amygdala will calm down, and their prefrontal cortex and anterior cingulate cortex will take over again allowing a person to think clearly and manage their emotions well.[11]

However, when there is ongoing abuse or extreme trauma, the brain may not recover well. The amygdala remains on high alert causing hypervigilance, which makes it difficult to calm down or to sleep. This internal alarm can stay activated for months or years. In addition, there may be a loss of ability to think clearly or concentrate and difficulty controlling emotional responses to even non-threatening circumstances. Many children diagnosed with attention deficit/hyperactivity disorder (ADHD), "oppositional defiant disorder," or "disruptive mood dysregulation disorder" are actually trying to block out the memories of their own or another family member's abuse.[12] It is very difficult to focus on schoolwork when you know you will get beaten or molested again that evening. Similarly, if you witness your mother being attacked regularly, you have no interest in history or math, because survival and safety are the only things that matter. Additionally, you are bound by a spoken or unspoken rule that you cannot talk about what is going on at home.

Children are torn between wanting to tell someone so the abuse will stop and fearing punishment for telling or loss of a parent if they do tell. Many children who are abused are told that they deserved this, they asked for it, or that they should like it. Almost every molester either bribes the child to be silent or threatens the child. Shame is also a strong silencing factor. Years later, the person will still believe that they were somehow at fault and caused the abuse. Even more difficult is the guilt they may feel for not having told when a sibling was being abused despite having been too young at the time. A cognitive approach to healing is rarely effective because the lies are embedded in intense emotional memories that need to be healed simultaneously for the person to recover.

PTSD Is Often Misdiagnosed

Recurrent trauma, or even a single severe trauma, can lead to post-traumatic stress disorder (PTSD) with its accompanying nightmares, flashbacks, and intense reactions to triggers such as a sound, a sight, or a smell. A teacher raising his or her voice might completely derail learning for the day because the brain links it to the abuse at home. The brain goes offline, and the child goes into fight, flight, or freeze mode. This can lead to aggressive behavior or total shut down from the child. Either way, learning cannot take place. "The impact of ACEs (adverse childhood experiences) on children can manifest in difficulties focusing, self-regulating, trusting others, and can lead to negative cognitive effects. One study found that a child with four or more ACEs was thirty-two times more likely to be labeled with a learning or behavioral problem than a child with no ACEs"[13]

The definition of PTSD in the *Diagnostic and Statistical Manual of Mental Disorders* (DSM5) is quite straightforward: "A person is exposed to a horrendous event 'that involved actual or threatened death or serious injury, or a threat to the physical integrity of self or others,' causing 'intense fear, helplessness, or horror,' which results in a variety of manifestations: intrusive re-experiencing of the event, persistent and crippling avoidance (of people, places, thoughts, or feelings associated with the trauma, sometimes with amnesia for important parts of it), and increased arousal (insomnia, hypervigilance, or irritability)."[14]

Most children who have been repeatedly traumatized by caregiver abuse or neglect suffer in significant ways. These children "demonstrate chronic and severe problems with emotion regulation, impulse control, attention and cognition, dissociation, interpersonal relationships, and self and relational schemas."[15] These children cannot identify what they are feeling or calm themselves down when they are upset. They may throw a tantrum or alternately withdraw and go silent, even at times blanking out and losing touch with the here and now.[16] This scares teachers and others and often results in over medication.

Children who have experienced a number of ACEs suffer numerous negative developmental, behavioral and mental health outcomes. These include learning difficulties, problems relating to peers, depression, anxiety, and other disorders mentioned above. "As adults, these children continue to show increased risk for psychiatric disorders, substance use, serious medical illnesses, and lower economic productivity."[17]

The brains of children and adults who experience the world as a dangerous place release an overabundance of stress hormones sending them into fight, flight, or freeze mode.

> "With their brains overloaded with stress hormones and unable to function
> appropriately, they can't focus on learning. They fall behind in school or fail
> to develop healthy relationships with peers or create problems with teachers
> and principals because they are unable to trust adults. Some individuals do
> all three."[18]

Young people struggling with despair, guilt, and frustration many turn to food, alcohol, tobacco, methamphetamines, inappropriate sex, high-risk sports, and/or work and excessive achievement for comfort. They don't regard these coping methods as problems but rather as methods to escape from depression, anxiety, anger, fear, and shame.[19] Adults in abusive situations develop addictions for the same reasons: "They (are) twice as likely to be smokers, twelve times more likely to have attempted suicide, seven times more likely to be alcoholic, and ten times more likely to have injected street drugs."[20]

Sadly, many of these children are punished, isolated, labeled as slow, or otherwise mislabeled and judged. This leads to an attempt to use behavioral modification to address a damaged brain that needs love, acceptance, and understanding to heal. Children do not understand why they are acting out and often accept the adult's narrative that they are bad kids or stupid. This further traumatizes and stigmatizes an already injured child. Negative beliefs and low self-esteem lead to all kinds of self-harm. Left untreated, many of these children grow up to be abusers or victims of further abuse themselves. The church can become a place of healing for children and adults when they begin to understand that these behaviors have reasons far beyond simple defiance. We too often judge and misunderstand a child, a teen, or an adult's acting out when they need compassion and support.

Adverse Childhood Experiences Are Common

Household dysfunction:	
Substance abuse	27%
Parental sep/divorce	23%
Mental illness	17%
Battered mother	13%
Criminal behavior	6%
Abuse:	
Psychological	11%
Physical	28%
Sexual	21%
Neglect:	
Emotional	15%
Physical	10%

Used with permission of Dr. Vincent Felitti. The chart presents data from the CDC-Kaiser Permanente Adverse Childhood Experiences (ACE) Study. The data is from a 17,337 adult sample from a clearly middle-class population that was 80% white, 10% black, and 10% Asian. 74% had been to college and all had high-end medical insurance. The 10 categories were selected because they were the 10 most common in the major Obesity Program that triggered the ACE Study to see if they were at all common in a general population.

Recently, studies have been conducted on the impact on adults of negative events in childhood (ACEs), such as witnessing domestic violence, experiencing neglect or a parent's death or divorce, or experiencing sexual or physical abuse. These experiences are very common; so common that two-thirds of a study of 17,421 people had experienced at least one ACE. "The patients . . . surveyed were not troubled or disadvantaged; the average patient was fifty-seven, and three-quarters were college educated. There were 'successful' . . . with good educations, . . . middle class, with health benefits and stable jobs."[21]

Dr. Vincent J. Felitti, chief of a preventative care initiative at Kaiser Permanente in San Diego, observed a connection between obesity and traumatic incidents in childhood, particularly sexual abuse. Although patients started to lose weight, many dropped out of the program and regained the weight they had lost. Eating not only addressed a person's anxiety, fear, and depression, but being overweight also provided some protection from unwanted physical attention.[22] In 1990 Felitti determined that, "'certain of our intractable public health problems had root causes hidden 'by shame, by secrecy, and by social taboos against exploring certain areas of life experience.'"[23]

"There was a direct link between childhood trauma and adult onset of chronic disease, as well as mental illness, doing time in prison, and work issues, such as absenteeism."[24] Suffering in childhood has all kinds of negative impacts. The life expectancy of a person with six or more ACEs is twenty years fewer than those with no ACEs because ACEs affect us on a cellular level, causing our cells to age prematurely.[25]

"Time," says Felitti, "does not heal all wounds. One does not 'just get over' something—not even fifty years later." Instead, he says, "Time conceals. And human beings convert traumatic emotional experiences in childhood into organic disease later in life."[26] The higher the number of ACEs, the more likely a person was to be diagnosed with cancer, to be hospitalized for an autoimmune disease, to become diabetic, to have heart disease, to suffer from migraines, chronic bowel disorders, anxiety, or depression.[27]

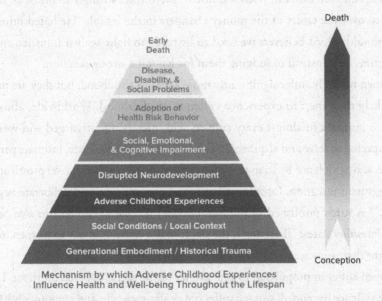

Mechanism by which Adverse Childhood Experiences
Influence Health and Well-being Throughout the Lifespan

The ACE Pyramid represents the conceptual framework for the CDC-Kaiser Permanente Adverse Childhood Experiences (ACE) Study, accessed August 1, 2021, https://www.cdc.gov/violenceprevention/aces/about.html.

Sadly, women experience far more adversity as children than men do, leading to more medical problems as adults. Women more often suffer from "fibromyalgia, chronic fatigue syndrome, obesity, irritable bowel syndrome, and chronic pain."[28] Felitti believes that medicine has yet to recognize the impact that a woman's gender has on her health; pain in childhood leads to illness in adult women.[29]

Women who were victimized as children are more likely to end up in abusive relationships, although that is not always the case. Some women who grew up in healthy, happy homes end up in unhealthy relationships as well, often because abusers can be very charming at first. How these women are viewed when they try to get help or talk about their partner's treatment often causes them more pain. Rather than understanding how the brain functions and the impact of trauma on a person, women have been considered overdramatic and attention-seeking. Psychosomatic symptoms were diagnosed as malingering, rather than being recognized as an overactive amygdala. Sadly, for many years women with strong emotional reactions have been considered hysterical. When helping professionals don't acknowledge the symptoms of a very real brain disorder and instead perceive the victim as overreacting, victims are further traumatized. Additionally, the victim's strong reaction to injustice can be very legitimate and even biblical. Jesus was not afraid to react strongly to injustice when he turned over the tables of the money changers in the temple. He hated injustice and so should we. As believers we need to be ready to fight against injustice and to help victims heal instead of judging them for having a strong reaction.

Women not only suffer significantly more abuse in childhood, but they are much more likely than men to experience violence in adulthood. Worldwide, abuse of women is rampant in almost every culture, with men being privileged and women being expected to serve and acquiesce.[30] This leads to "dating violence, intimate partner violence, sexual violence by strangers, rape during armed conflict, forced prostitution, female genital mutilation, forced marriage, female infanticide, and deliberate neglect of girls."[31] A study published in the *International Journal of Humanities and Social Science Invention* states, "Battering is the single major cause of injury to women, more significant than auto accidents, rapes, or muggings."[32]

Women suffer in proportion to the severity of the abuse inflicted on them. Long after the violence has ended, women suffer physically, mentally, and emotionally.[33] One of the most obvious impacts of violence are the physical symptoms: broken bones, bruises, lacerations, burns, or head injuries. Sadly, women are "most likely to be killed by someone close to them—male intimate partners commit 30–70 percent of all murders of women in settings as diverse as Israel, South Africa, and the USA."[34] This includes honor killings, dowry killings, or even infanticide against baby girls.

Female genital mutilation (FGM) is an inhumane practice which does permanent harm to girls and women. FGM leads to increased pain, increased rates of infection for women and girls, as well as "the risk of obstetric complications and perinatal death."[35] Furthermore, sexual violence against women results in many different gynecological problems, including "vaginal infection, pain during intercourse, chronic pelvic pain, and urinary tract infections. . . . Gynecological trauma may include tearing of the vagina; fistula (a tear between the vagina and bladder or rectum or both); hemorrhaging, infection, or ulceration; . . . or complications during childbirth."[36] There is also an increased risk of HIV infection among those who have experienced sexual violence for a variety of reasons. Among them is the reduced use of condoms with forced intercourse, increased risky sexual behaviors after childhood abuse, and fear of violence if testing shows HIV infection.[37]

The risks extend beyond the abuse of women and their own health to that of their children. "Evidence links physical and sexual violence during pregnancy to many complications, including: low maternal weight gain, miscarriage, and stillbirth, and low-birth-weight babies."[38] Around the world, violence against intimate partners leads to the death of many pregnant women.[39] Men who struggle with control issues can feel threatened by the addition of a new little one who will demand their partner's time and attention. This jeopardizes both the life of the mother and that of the infant.

Overall, the evidence indicates that pregnancy, infancy, and childhood are sensitive periods during which exposure to social adversity can induce behavioral, psychological, and epigenetic changes in children that may persist into adulthood.[40] Studies showed that incidents of prenatal stress caused by intimate partner violence cause a mother to release stress hormones which lead to much higher levels of these hormones in the unborn baby. A recent study on the impact of this stress on newborn children shows a link between the abuse of pregnant women and "trauma symptoms in their children within the first year of life. Symptoms include nightmares, startling easily, being bothered by loud noises and bright lights, avoiding physical contact, and having trouble experiencing enjoyment."[41]

Living under the threat of or experiencing physical, sexual, or emotional abuse creates intense stress reactions. The release of adrenaline and cortisol helps a person survive a dangerous threat to one's well-being. Adrenaline "mobilizes energy stores and alters blood flow," while cortisol "mobilizes energy stores, enhances certain types of memory, and activates immune responses."[42] This is very adaptive in a crisis and helps us survive. However, when these hormones are constantly flowing through our body as a result of chronic toxic stress, "longer-term effects can include suppression of immune function, other types of memory, and contributions to metabolic syndrome, bone mineral loss, and muscle atrophy."[43]

The amount of cortisol released has a direct impact on whether a person's memory of an event is enhanced and vivid, or whether it is "fuzzy, fragmented, or apparently non-existent." "Too much cortisol, and you just have bits and pieces instead of a whole memory."[44] This is very confusing for a person who may have strong physical or emotional trauma reactions but no memory of an actual trauma. "The emotions and physical sensations that were imprinted during the trauma are experienced not as memories but as disruptive physical reactions in the present."[45] The symptoms these victims then display are often diagnosed as mental illnesses and medicated rather than figuring out the root causes of the trauma reactions and helping people heal. Moreover, "hallucinations" can be (1) a way to cope with unspeakable trauma, (2) a way to escape abusive situations without acknowledging to oneself, or others, the desire to escape, or (3) fragmented memories of events that the brain could not store. "We now know that more than half the people who seek psychiatric care have been assaulted, abandoned, neglected, or even raped as children, or have witnessed violence in their families."[46]

A further complication is that severe chronic stress can overtax the system to the point that the body can no longer produce much cortisol. "This means that ongoing trauma or stress can make it hard to remember stuff because you don't have enough cortisol, and a single stressful or traumatic event can be hard to remember because you have too much."[47] Both extremes, too little or too much cortisol will alter memory so that the trauma may not be remembered. This makes it far more difficult to understand a victim's responses.

The effects of trauma, domestic violence, and sexual abuse on a person's mental and physical health are unending. Research continues to uncover more and more impacts on our bodies and minds. Dr. Rachel Yehuda is doing research on the impact of trauma on transforming a person biologically.[48] This research has shown that children of Holocaust survivors are similar to children of war veterans and children of women who were pregnant when 9/11 occurred. If the parents develop PTSD, the children will have low cortisol levels which predisposes these children to stress related psychiatric disorders, including PTSD, chronic pain syndrome, and chronic fatigue syndrome.[49] "Yehuda was one of the first researchers to show how descendants of trauma survivors carry the physical and emotional symptoms of traumas they have not directly experienced."[50] Additionally, "when cortisol levels are compromised, so is our ability to regulate emotions and manage stress."[51] Learning and identifying with what a person's parents or grandparents experienced helps a person heal. Without this the dysregulation of emotions causes a myriad of mental health issues.

Another researcher, Dr. Bruce Lipton found that, "The mother's emotions, such as fear, anger, love, hope among others, can biochemically alter the genetic expression of her offspring."[52] The children of mothers who live in fear of being abused will be more reactive later in life with increased fight or flight responses.[53] "In an August 2015 study published in the *Biological Psychiatry*, Yehuda and her team at New York's Mount Sinai Hospital demonstrated that gene changes could be transmitted from parents to their children."[54] It is increasingly clear that a mother's safety and well-being before and during pregnancy is of utmost importance to her unborn child.

We used to think that children would not remember or that they would get over it; however, we now know that that is not the case. "Childhood abuse isn't something you 'get over.' It is an evil that we must acknowledge and confront if we aim to do anything about the unchecked cycle of violence in this country."[55] Not only is violence that children witness or experience changing their lives, but also the violence that their parents witnessed or experienced before they were born impacts them in significant ways. We live in a highly traumatized world.

The research has weighed in: domestic violence, sexual abuse, emotional abuse, and spiritual abuse, along with the unspeakable horrors of war, have devastating effects on children and adults that change people and how they respond to life. The cost is great medically, mentally, relationally, and in every other way.

The good news is that there is hope and healing available. At the same time science is exposing the awful impacts of abuse, it is also showing us paths of healing. Science is confirming what Scripture has told us for centuries. We need to experience comfort, understanding, and peace in order for our brains to calm down and our bodies to relax after trauma. Paul told us to "weep with those who weep" (Rom. 12:15, RSV). We as churches need to become better at this, especially when the loss is related to abuse. We need to become people and places of safety and healing where people can be honest about their pain and where they can find understanding and peace. Healing takes time and hard work on the part of the person who has been wounded as well as on the part of the people walking with this person through their pain. It also requires some level of expertise. It should not be assumed that we have all the answers for a person who has experienced abuse. We need to engage professionals, both in helping us learn more about abuse, as well as in helping survivors heal. God has made provision for us in his Son, Jesus, "For to us a child is born, to us a son is given, and the government will be on his shoulders. And he will be called Wonderful Counselor, Mighty God, Everlasting Father, Prince of Peace" (Isa. 9:6, NIV). Now it is our privilege and responsibility to become more like him so that we can be agents of his grace and peace.

Ideas Have Consequences

DR. MIMI HADDAD

Plato said *ideas* rule the world. All action begins with an idea. Paul said, "Take every thought captive to Christ" (2 Cor. 10:5). Why? Because ideas have consequences.

The most prominent indicator of whether a girl will be sold to a brothel, killed as a fetus, abused in her marriage or family, or denied a place of decision-making in her church, community, or marriage is not based on her gender but the value ascribed to the female gender. In study after study, research suggests that when a culture values females as much as males, we are more likely to see equal numbers of girls surviving to adulthood. Gender justice begins with an idea—that males and females are of equal value.

Thus, for every devaluation based on femaleness, there is a consequence in the form of marginalization, abuse, and injustice. To say it another way, when communities value females by sharing authority and resources, not only is abuse reduced, but economic stability also increases within families and communities. Non-governmental organizations (NGOs) call this *the girl effect*.[1] Christians might call this phenomenon *the ezer effect* because *ezer* is the Hebrew word God used to describe the strong help females provide (Gen. 2:18). *Ezer* is found twenty-one times in the Old Testament, and, of these, fourteen describe God's help. According to R. David Freedman, the Hebrew word used to describe woman's help (*ezer*) comes from two Hebrew roots that mean "to rescue, to save" and "to be strong."[2] In Psalm 121:1–2, *ezer* is used for God's rescue of Israel: "I lift up my eyes to the mountains—where does my help come from? My help comes from the Lord, the Maker of heaven and earth" (NIV). What stronger help is there apart from God's rescue?

Scripture teaches that females were created to provide a strong rescue—a reality that NGOs are now recognizing because support for women's leadership leads to significant social benefits. Denying girls and women equal value places them at risk for abuse. As so many have observed, the well-being of whole communities is linked to the value we ascribe to females. In this chapter, we will explore how ontological devaluation of females—that is, seeing them as inferior with respect to their being—is inseparable from their marginalization and abuse. We shall then consider how the early evangelicals first observed this fact and offered a biblical challenge to females' devaluation. Next, we shall explore the parallels between slavery and the emancipation of women as they inform our interpretation of Scripture. Finally, we will consider how Scripture supports the equality of females. We begin with several personal examples.

Ontological Ideas Have Daily Consequences

Brenda and Scott are Christian campus pastors at a secular university. Building relationships with college students, they also lead Bible groups around every possible context. They laugh, cry, pray, and encourage students and help carry many burdens. Brenda is single and Scott is married. Their campus work is funded mostly by a large Baptist church that invites Scott to preach (giving him an edge on fundraising). But, because of her gender, Brenda is never invited to speak from the church's platform. Brenda is not bitter, but one day she took me aside and said, "Mimi, giving Scott regular opportunities to preach and denying me the same tells me one thing: there is something wrong with being a female. It tells me that being female is less than being male."

Consider Laticia, whom I met in my workshop at a nationwide missions conference. Laticia was a lawyer working on a PhD. She wanted a private moment with me to tell me that she was thinking of leaving the church. When I asked her why, she said it was because she wanted to get married. When I asked for more information, she said that Christians from her community believe that males hold authority over women in church and marriage—not because they are more holy, more intelligent, better able to discern God's leading, or because they have leadership and logic skills, but simply because they are male. It is injustice, she said, to give a sector of humanity unilateral authority while denying the same benefit to another group based not on character but on gender. She concluded that she would not be party to injustice and, therefore, could not marry and remain in the church.

A pastor friend of mine was seated on a plane next to a person who could not stomach religion because there was not one that treated women as equal to men. Brenda, Laticia, and the man seated next to my friend are asking significant questions about gender and justice from an ontological perspective.

What do we mean by ontology? The term comes from two Greek words *ontos* ("being") and *logia* ("study"). Ontology is the study of being, nature, or essence which is fixed and unchangeable like gender or race. One's ontological status is routinely assessed through comparisons. For example, it has often been assumed that men are more godlike than women because men are presumed to be more rational and morally able. Therefore, it follows that men should hold positions of authority over women because of men's innate, unchangeable, ontological superiority. Similarly, it was believed that royalty were ontologically superior to commoners, and that whites were ontologically superior to people of color.

The devaluation of people groups at an ontological level is deeply entrenched throughout history. Observe the ontological assumptions the Greeks made of women. Aristotle (384–322 BC) said, "The relationship between the male and the female is by nature such that the male is higher, the female lower, that the male rules and the female is ruled."[3] Plato (427–347 BC) concluded that "[woman's] native disposition is inferior to man's."[4] These ideas have consequences.

The daily lives of females reflect their ontological status. In ancient culture, patriarchy was noted in the primacy of males, the vast number of girl babies exposed and left to die after birth, the lack of women's participation in philosophy and politics, the absence of women in social gatherings with males, and men's many sexual partners (including slaves, female prostitutes, and boys/men) in addition to their wives. Marriage was to ensure a man's legitimate heirs.[5]

Gender and Ontology in the Early Church

We notice a difference between Christians in the early church who rescued girl babies, and the Romans who abandoned them. Christian women participated in *agapē* meals.

They served beside men as teachers, evangelists, missionaries, apostles, prophets, and coworkers with Paul. By doing so, they engaged with men in social and theological spheres. Women were also martyred beside men for advancing the gospel with equal influence. Christian marriages were monogamous, and Paul asks both husbands and wives to submit to and obey one another (1 Cor. 7:3–5; Eph. 5:21). Marriage is viewed as a one-flesh relationship for the purposes of love, intimacy, and reflection of the mutual love and sacrifice within the Trinity.

Notice Paul's transformation from his life as a Jewish male who prayed daily, "Thank you [God] for not making me a Gentile, a woman, and a slave,"[6] a prayer that implicates women's ontological devaluation that prevented them from studying Torah or participating equally beside males in worship. Scholars suggest that Paul wrote Galatians 3:28—"There is no longer Jew or Greek, there is no longer slave or free, there is no longer male and female; for all of you are one in Christ Jesus"—to reveal how the gospel redresses prejudice based on gender, ethnicity, and class.[7] Men and women, slaves and free, Greek and Jew constitute one body—the church, Christ's New Covenant community which, though diverse in gender, ethnicity, and class, functions without favoritism based on these attributes.[8] Thus, males in the early church shared leadership with females, as Scripture and archaeological evidence suggest.[9] Unfortunately, the ontological and functional equality of male and female believers in the early church was short-lived.

Perils of Devaluation

A devaluation of individuals based on a fixed and unchangeable condition is noted throughout human history. For example, Nazi Germany mounted an extensive campaign to devalue Jews at the level of race. Before they were able to convince Germans to round up Jews and send them to death camps, the Nazis first had to insist upon their innate and unchangeable inferiority. Triumphantly, Nazis noted their great success in "reeducating" Germans:

> . . . there are only a few people left in Germany who are not clear about the fact that the Jew is not, as previously thought, distinct from "Christians," "Protestants," or "Catholics" only in that he is of another religion, and is therefore a German like all of the rest of us, but rather that he belongs to a different race than we do. The Jew belongs to a different race; that is what is decisive.[10]

By suggesting that Jews comprise a different race, the Nazis were able to construct a distinct and inferior ontological category for Jews. The genocide of the Jews was made plausible by first positing that the Aryan Germans were the superior race and by showing that the Jews had no share in their blood line.

In a similar manner, American slavery was based on a perceived inferiority of African Americans because of race—which is fixed and unchangeable. The French scholar Compte Adrien de Gasparin said that slavery was centered on "a native and indestructible inferiority" of those of African descent.[11] This so-called innate inferiority was rooted not in one's moral choices, but in one's ancestry, and was, therefore, an unchangeable condition. It was African ethnicity, noted in skin color, that placed Africans under the permanent domination of those said to be their superiors—whites. The reason the Civil War failed to redress ethnic prejudice is that the so-called inferiority was associated not with slavery, but with ethnicity—an unchangeable attribute. Slavery was the consequence of an idea: that Africans were inferior. Slavery was not the root cause; an ethnic devaluation was. One can amend the United States Constitution and free the slaves, but new forms of ethnic abuse will emerge because the root problem—ethnic prejudice—has not been addressed.

Like slavery, the subjugation of women is made plausible by insisting that males are innately superior. There can be no question that Christians have advanced, uncritically, the inferiority of females throughout history. Here are a few examples:

- Irenaeus (AD 130–202): "Both *nature* and the law place the woman in a subordinate condition to the man."[12]
- Augustine (AD 354–430): "Nor can it be doubted, that it is more consonant with the order of *nature* that men should bear rule over women, than women over men."[13]
- Chrysostom (AD 347–407): "The woman taught once, and ruined all. On this account . . . let her not teach . . . for *the sex is weak and fickle.*"[14]
- John Calvin (1509–1564), in his commentary on 1 Timothy, wrote that women are *"not to assume authority over the man . . .* it is not permitted by their *condition."*[15]
- John Knox (1514–1572) said, "*Nature*, I say, does paint [women] forth to be weak, frail, impatient, feeble, and foolish; and experience has declared them to be inconstant, variable, cruel. . . . Since flesh is subordinate to spirit, a woman's place is beneath man's."[16]

Even today, one popular pastor of a megachurch writes:

> [W]hen it comes to leading in the church, women are unfit because they are more
> gullible and easier to deceive than men. . . . [W]omen who fail to trust [Paul's]
> instruction . . . are much like their mother Eve. . . . Before you *get all emotional*
> *like a woman* in hearing this, please consider the content of the women's magazines
> at your local grocery store that encourage liberated women in our day to watch
> porno with their boyfriends, master oral sex for men who have no intention of
> marrying them . . . and ask yourself if it doesn't look like the Serpent is still trolling
> the garden and that *the daughters of Eve aren't gullible* in pronouncing progress,
> liberation, and equality.[17]

Women Lead the Modern Missionary Movement

Despite such disparaging assumptions made by Christians, females as a whole have not
performed according to the devaluations made of them. In fact, throughout church history,
we observe women providing enormous moral, spiritual, and intellectual leadership
within the church even without official church authority. This was never more the case
than during the modern missionary movement, when women outnumbered men on
mission fields around the world two to one. Their leadership combined evangelism
with humanitarian service, and their work gave rise to new centers of spiritual vitality
throughout Asia, Africa, and the Americas—so much so that their leadership shifted
the density of Christian faith from the West to broadly scatted locations in the global
South and the East.[18] Without the vote, without a legal voice, and without the world
wide web, these women established highly productive mission organizations, and they
occupied all levels of service and leadership. Their leadership in organizations such as the
Women's Christian Temperance Union, the Society for the Abolition of the Slave Trade,
the American Antislavery Society, and the Salvation Army gave enormous momentum
to suffrage, abolition, and temperance, demonstrating that their humanitarian focus was
inseparable from their commitment to evangelism. Moreover, as the early evangelicals
worked to free females from sexual slavery, they also discovered that the abuse of females
was always accompanied by a deprecation of their being.

Working in India among brothels established by the British government to attract
and retain soldiers and officers, Katharine Bushnell (1856–1946), a medical doctor,

infiltrated British garrisons to learn firsthand the abuses female prostitutes suffered. According to her findings, these abuses were justified not only to satisfy the sexual needs of the British military, but also because females were viewed as innately inferior. Bushnell eventually realized that the global abuse of women was inseparable from a devaluation of females as a whole. In response, Bushnell wrote *God's Word to Women*, based on one hundred scriptural teachings concerning gender, a whole-Bible approach to show that Scripture values males and females equally.[19] Her painstaking research on Greek and Hebrew words, archaeology, and ancient history is a death blow to what philosophers call "ascriptivism," a system that ascribes value, dignity, and worth to groups based on attributes such as gender, ethnicity, or class. Bushnell's arguments were biblical and systematic, adding momentum to the first wave of feminism—a deeply biblical movement that advanced suffrage, abolition, and the leadership of women in church work. Bushnell was joined by other early evangelicals such as Sojourner Truth, Catherine Booth, Fredrik Franson, Frances Willard, Amanda Smith, A. J. Gordon, Josephine Butler, and others who together published more than forty systematic biblical treatises supporting the ontological and functional equality of women and slaves.[20]

Bushnell engaged the whole of Scripture, particularly the early chapters of Genesis, concluding that, according to Scripture, Adam and Eve were both created in the image of God;[21] both were called to be fruitful and to exercise a shared governance over Eden[22] that did not place Adam in authority over Eve. Eve was not the source of sin,[23] and God does not curse women because of Eve.[24] Rather, it was Satan, not God, who inspired the domination of men over women.[25] God bestows leadership on those who do what is right in God's sight regardless of their gender, birth order, nationality, or class.[26]

For Bushnell, Scripture locates women's status not in the fall, but in Christ's completed work on Calvary. Therefore, a consistent interpretation of the Bible as it relates to women's value[27] should be determined in exactly the same manner as men's value, based on the atonement of Jesus Christ. "[We] cannot, for women, put the 'new wine' of the Gospel into the old wine-skins of 'condemnation.'"[28] Bushnell condemned the prejudice noted throughout church history which routinely aligned women's status with Eve's sin rather than through their full redemption and inheritance in Christ.

Katharine Bushnell recognized that female subjugation and abuse was often linked to flawed methods of biblical interpretation—failing to differentiate what is descriptive in Scripture from that which is prescriptive. While patriarchy is part of the cultures depicted in the Bible, patriarchy is at odds with the moral teachings of Scripture. After years of working beside women to dismantle sex slavery around the world, Bushnell recognized that the abuse of women was inseparable from a devaluation of females promoted by religious and philosophical teachings justifying and codifying male dominance and female subservience. Bushnell argued that the abuse of women will persist as long as "the subordination of woman to man was taught within the body of Christians."[29] Bushnell wrote:

> [W]e must have the whole-hearted backing of the Christian church in our [work], and that we would not have it until men came to understand that a woman is of as much value as a man; and they will not believe this until they see it plainly taught in the Bible.

> Just so long as men imagine that a system of caste is taught in the Word of God, and that they belong to the upper caste while women are of the lower caste; and just so long as they believe that mere flesh—fate—determines the caste to which one belongs; and just so long as they believe that. . . . Genesis 3:16 [teaches] "thy desire shall be for thy husband, and he shall rule over you" . . . the destruction of young women into a prostitute class [will] continue.

> But place Christian women where God intends them to stand, on a plane of full equality with men in the church and home, where their faculties, their will, their consciences are controlled only by the God who made man and woman equal by creation . . . then the world will become a much purer [place] than it is today. . . .[30]

Bushnell was compelled to challenge the devaluation of women that drove the sex industry. Her theological work was the first systematic, biblical approach to women's ontological equality and the first to oppose the distorted view that females are more gullible and inferior to men, and, thus, in need of male authority.

The Egalitarian View Gains Strength

Thanks to Bushnell and others, by the end of the 1800s, two views on gender ontology were circulated. First, the patriarchal view that insisted women were unequal in being and therefore unequal in authority. The second view was egalitarian which perceived women as equal in being and equal in authority. However, by the mid-1980s a third view emerged. Referred to as "complementarian," it depicted women as equal in being, but unequal in function or authority. We can summarize each position as follows:

1. The patriarchal view: unequal in being; unequal in authority or function.
2. The egalitarian view: equal in being; equal in authority or function.
3. The complementarian view: equal in being; unequal in authority or function.

Each view had its social consequences. As the egalitarian position gained acceptance, women's suffrage was instituted and immediate human flourishing ensued. For example, in the United States, maternal and child mortality decreased dramatically after women gained the vote. Prior to suffrage, more women died giving birth than did all men in United States wars combined to that date. Further, child mortality dropped by 72 percent.[31]

Not only do we observe less abuse and greater health for women and children as American culture became more egalitarian, but we also find that, when authority is shared, marriage relationships are happier. Couples who share decision-making are less likely to experience abuse, according to research by the Prepare and Enrich Premarital Inventory—one of the most widely-used population samples in the world with more than 4 million datapoints. Equally important, their research indicates that an authority relationship of men to women is a significant predictor of wife abuse, but not a predictor of husband abuse.[32] Couples with the highest levels of abuse are those where one partner is dominant, most often the male, and the other avoidant or submissive. Research by Prepare and Enrich also shows a statistical association between violence and unequal power in decision making.[33]

Similarly, studies by NGOs suggest that when communities are more egalitarian, there is less gender abuse. Amartya Sen, a Nobel Prize-winning economist, documented a correlation between a culture's devaluation of females and steep drops in their numbers.[34] By contrast, in those communities where women and therefore gender equality is valued, the ratio of females to males is more balanced.[35]

South Korea has turned the tide on male preference. In the 1990s, the nation had a gender ratio almost as skewed as China's. Now, it is heading toward normality, "because the culture changed. Female education, antidiscrimination suits, and equal rights rulings made son preference seem old-fashioned and unnecessary."[36]

Clearly, gains have been made as culture has become more egalitarian, yet there is still much work to be done. For example, women have not yet attained equal leadership politically or professionally. Though outnumbering men in medical school, law school, and many graduate programs, women lag behind men in income and in holding top positions in corporations, political parties, and organizations, because, in part, society has not dealt completely with the root problem—an idea—that women are not as able as men. The idea that God does not give women positions of leadership is also taught as a biblical principle by missionaries and churches worldwide. There remains much work to do, and yet many significant strategies can be learned from reform movements throughout history, particularly abolition. Significantly, reform movements are often led by prophetic individuals who challenge indifference, biblical ignorance, and moral failings. Such reformers are often people who have been deeply renewed themselves. Finding like-minded colleagues across denominational and geographic boundaries, reformers appeal to reason through academic discourse. Eventually, they popularize more academic ideas through the arts, literature, and song, making visceral the injustices under critique. Ultimately, reform movements bring needed change theologically and socially.[37]

Theological Foundations of Slavery and Gender Reform[38]

New principles of biblical interpretation

Consider the similarities between the abolitionists and egalitarian reformist movements. Both challenged a shallow reading of Scripture by taking into account the historical and cultural context of the critical biblical passages. Both also elevated the moral teachings of Scripture rather than of the patriarchy and slavery of biblical culture. Through the struggle to upend slavery and women's subordination, principles of biblical interpretation emerged, including the following:[39]

1. *A plain reading of the Bible must include the historical and cultural context.* The proslavery camp, like those opposed to women's leadership, relied upon what they called a "plain reading" of Scripture. To avoid abusing Scripture for personal gain (after all, slaves and women provided an unpaid service industry), passages must be read within their historical and cultural contexts. A "plain reading" is only plain within its own cultural and historical context.

2. *The full testimony of Scripture must be considered.* The obscure portions of Scripture must be interpreted by what is obvious. In considering the passages on Abraham,

for example, the point is not that he had servants, possibly slaves, but that he trusted God's promise. Similarly, the point of 1 Timothy 2:11–15 is not that Paul subjugates all women to silence and male authority, but that those who teach should be educated and should not domineer over others. A confusing passage, like 1 Timothy 2, should not be ignored, but instead be informed by other, more clear parts of the word of God.

3. *A portion of Scripture should be viewed for its primary emphasis, not for its attendant or cultural features.* Slavery and patriarchy are part of Bible culture. These are attendant or cultural features which do not constitute the moral teachings of Scripture.

4. *Be scrupulous in assessing selfish motives when reading the Bible* (Matt 20:25–28).

Through these and other interpretive strategies, reformers equipped the church with better methods of understanding the value, dignity, and equality of those who once had been viewed as ontologically inferior. We can see how these ideas empowered the work of individuals like the freed slave, Amanda Berry Smith (1837-1915).

One of the most successful missionaries of her day, Amanda Berry Smith, while speaking at a revival in England in 1882, located her true identity in her relationship to God. She said: "You may not know it, but I am a princess in disguise. I am a child of the King."[40] Smith realized that, "if she was God's child, she was also an heir of God!"[41] Embracing her full inheritance in Christ, Smith declared herself an heir with Christ. Regardless of her gender, ethnicity, or class, Berry Smith fearlessly fanned into flames God's gifts within her. What was the result? One man told her that he had learned more about Christian leadership from observing her lead than from any other life example. Smith's self-confidence was infectious, even as she pushed past a number of critics and gatekeepers. She recognized that her truest identity was not in her gender, but in her union with Christ.

Leaders such as Amanda Berry Smith allowed the fullest teachings of Scripture to inform more obscure passages like 1 Timothy 2:11–15. Rather than reading all of Scripture through the lens of 1 Timothy 2:11–15, the early evangelicals began to read 1 Timothy 2:11–15 through the whole of Scripture, particularly Paul's work beside women leaders. In doing so, they noticed that Paul built the church working beside women such as Phoebe, Junia, Lydia, Chloe, and Priscilla. The experiences of combating slavery and female subjugation enabled the early evangelicals to push past shallow interpretations to perceive, embrace, and celebrate those liberating biblical passages where the moral principles of Scripture prevail over slavery and male-rule—both part of the milieu of Scripture. And, slaves and women were among the first to notice liberating moments in Scripture.

Jesus

Katharine Bushnell observed that Jesus never devalued women. Welcoming women as fully human and equal to men, Jesus was strangely and authentically comfortable in their presence. He approached them as he did men, in public, regardless of cultural taboos. Consistently challenging the devaluation of women's bodies, Christ healed a hemorrhaging woman in public. Allowing her to touch him in public, he declared that she had been healed of her disease. She was not unclean, but ill. Women were the first to notice the liberating message in Christ's words and deeds.

Jesus spoke with women unselfconsciously, in broad daylight, despite the disapproval of his disciples (John 4:4–42). Unlike the rabbis of his day, Jesus allowed women to sit at his feet and study his teachings (Luke 10:38–42), preparing them for service as disciples, apostles, evangelists, and teachers. In all ways, the equality of women was self-evident, implicit, and, most importantly, consistently part of Christ's teachings and practice. These passages were given new meaning by early evangelicals like Katharine Bushnell.

When a woman called out to Jesus, saying, "Blessed is the mother who gave you birth and nursed you," Jesus responded, "Blessed rather are those who hear the word of God and obey it" (Luke 11:27–28). For Jesus, a woman's value resides not in her cultural roles, but in her response to God's revelation in her life. This becomes the standard for every member of Christ's New Covenant—male and female. Women are now daughters of Abraham (Luke 13:16), a phrase first used by Jesus to welcome God's daughters as heirs and full members of Christ's body, the church. The life and teachings of Jesus fractured the patriarchy of his culture.

Pentecost

Consider Pentecost—the birthday of the church (Acts 2:1–18)—mediated not through an elite group of Jewish males, but through God's Spirit poured out on many tribes and nations, on both men and women. Pentecost was the fulfillment of Joel's prophecy: "In the last days, God says, I will pour out my Spirit on all people. Your sons and daughters will prophesy, your young men will see visions, your old men will dream dreams. Even on my servants, both men and women, I will pour out my Spirit in those days, and they will prophesy" (Acts 2:17–18). There is no gender, ethnic, or age preference noted in the birth of the church or in the gifts expressed at Pentecost.

Baptism

In the New Covenant, baptism rather than circumcision became the outer expression of our union with Christ, and baptism was open to male and female, Jew and Greek, slave and free. The significance of Christian baptism is cited in Galatians 3:28, a verse etched into early baptismal fonts celebrating the inclusivity of Christian faith. To be united with Christ in his death and resurrection constitutes a rebirth that redefines our value with respect to God and all other Christians.[42] Because Christ established satisfaction and reconciliation between sinners and God, we receive newness of life and power from the Holy Spirit to work for mutuality among the members of Christ's body, the church. To state it another way, our doctrine of salvation shapes our doctrine of the church.[43]

The notion that Jews and Greeks, slaves and free, male and female are all one in Christ (Gal. 3:28) was an affront to a culture where identity, value, and influence was established through ethnicity, class and gender. Remember, more than half of the population in Paul's day were slaves and women. To his culture, Paul suggests that to be clothed in Christ means all believers are heirs with Christ. What we inherit through our earthly parents cannot compare to our heritage through Christ. Therefore, our newness of life in Christ recreates the status of females, slaves, and ethnic minorities, an idea with daily consequences.

Paul continually places the ethos of the New Covenant above the gender and cultural norms of his day. For example, Paul asks Philemon to welcome Onesimus as a Christian brother (Philem. 16). With these words, Paul allows kingdom values to take precedence over cultural expectations for slaves, pointing to the fact that the cross changes everything (1 Cor. 2:6, 7:31). It is believed that Onesimus became bishop of Ephesus.[44]

Ephesians 5

In the same way, husbands and wives are called to submit to one another in marriage (1 Cor. 7:3–4), just as all Christians submit to one another (Eph. 5:21). Interestingly,

Paul asks those with cultural authority—husbands—to love their wives as they love themselves, even to the point of death. Certainly, this request would have been radical to first-century husbands. As men and husbands held ultimate authority over their wives, Paul asks husbands to sacrifice themselves for their wives, just as Christ sacrificed himself for the church. This is a complete reframing of gender and authority in marriage. Christian authority in marriage reflects authority in ministry—it is the call to serve without self-regard and cultural privilege: to lay down one's life for another.

Paul realized that God was building a new creation—the church—with each member born of the Spirit and joined equally to Jesus as head. The new wine of Jesus would require a new wineskin where slaves and women can serve equally in accomplishing the purposes for which God had called and gifted them. That is why Paul did not hesitate to celebrate the woman Junia as an apostle. Nor was he reluctant to require respect for Phoebe as a deacon and *prostatēs*—that is, a leader in the church of Cenchreae. Nor do Paul and the other apostles shy away from celebrating the leadership of women teachers such as Priscilla and house church leaders such as Lydia, Chloe, Nympha, and Apphia.

Spiritual gifts

Notice that the spiritual gifts are not given along ethnic, class, or gender lines because the spiritual gifts are first and foremost an equipping for service. All believers are called to serve. In referring to the spiritual gifts, Paul reminds Christians in Rome not to think more highly of themselves than they ought, but with sober judgment to count others as better than themselves, remembering that, though each person receives spiritual gifts, the gifts are for serving, and each of us also depends on the gifts we receive from other Christians. For as Paul said, "each member belongs to all the others" (Rom. 12:5b). Likewise, Paul tells the Christians at Corinth that they are mutually dependent upon one another for, "The eye cannot say to the hand, 'I don't need you!' And the head cannot say to the feet, 'I don't need you!'" (1 Cor. 12:21). The eye needs the hands, just as the head needs the feet. The parts of the body are not divided from one another but function best when they have equal concern for, and mutual submission toward, one another.

Therefore, service is not determined by gender or class but arises from God's gifting and is established by one's character, moral choices, and intimacy with God. Here,

Scripture deals a death blow to any notion of ontological superiority based on gender, ethnicity, or class. Here are just two examples:

Notice that, in 1 Timothy 2:12, Paul limits women at Ephesus from teaching, not because of gender, but because of their behavior. While this passage is frequently used to limit women's authority as a whole, notice that the intention of Scripture is quite different. What is often missed by those unfamiliar with Greek is that Paul selects an unusual Greek word when speaking of authority in verse 12. Rather than using the most common Greek terms for healthy or proper authority or oversight (*exousia*), Paul selects the term *authentein*—a word that would have caught the attention of first-century readers!

Authentein implied a domineering, misappropriated, or usurped authority. *Authentein* can also mean to behave in violent ways. It can even imply murder! *Authentein* appears only once in Scripture, in 1 Timothy 2:12. It was used by Paul as well as extrabiblical authors to connote authority that was destructive. For this reason, various translations of Scripture rendered the special sense of this word as follows:

- Vulgate (fourth to fifth century AD) as, "I permit not a woman to teach, neither to *domineer* over a man."
- The Geneva Bible (1560 edition) as, "I permit not a woman to teach, neither to *usurp authority* over the man."
- King James Version (1611) as, "I suffer not a woman to teach, nor *usurp authority* over a man."
- The New English Bible (1961) as, "I do not permit a woman to be a teacher, nor must woman *domineer over* man."[45]

This unusual Greek verb makes it clear that what Paul is objecting to in 1 Timothy 2:11–12 is an ungodly, domineering usurpation of authority.

Leadership concerns character. Thus, in determining who may or may not serve as an elder, overseer, deacon, pastor, or church board member, it is not gender, ethnicity, education, wealth, age, experience, or a person's capacity to influence others that Scripture celebrates. Rather, it is one's moral choices tied clearly to one's intimacy with Christ. The following table describes the character qualities required in elders, overseers, deacons, and widows—who also served as leaders. These qualities are, interestingly, very similar to the fruit of the Spirit (Gal. 5:22–23).

Elders/Overseers (1 Tim. 3:2–3)	Temperate, sensible, respectable, hospitable, an apt teacher, not a drunkard, not violent but gentle, not quarrelsome, and not a lover of money
Deacons (1 Tim. 3:8)	Serious, not double-tongued, not indulging in much wine, not greedy for money
Widows (1 Tim. 3:11)	Women likewise must be serious, not slanderers, but temperate, faithful in all things
Fruit of the Spirit (Gal. 5:22–26)	Love, joy, peace, patience, kindness, generosity, faithfulness, gentleness, and self-control

Gifts of the Spirit

Biblical leadership is established not through gender, but through giftedness, character, and one's capacity to exhibit the fruit of the Spirit. In contrast, those who display the fruit of the flesh (e.g., fornication, impurity, licentiousness, idolatry, sorcery, enmities, strife, jealousy, anger, quarrels, dissensions, factions, envy, drunkenness, carousing, etc. [Gal. 5:19–21]) have disqualified themselves from leadership regardless of their gender, class, or ethnicity.

To follow the teachings of Scripture, our choice of leaders, deacons, pastors, elders, and teachers should be from individuals who best exhibit the fruits of the Spirit, regardless of gender, ethnicity, or class.

Conclusion

Through our rebirth in Christ, all people, including slaves and women, inherit a new identity—not of shame, marginalization, or abuse, but of dignity, inclusion, and shared authority and service because they too are born of the Spirit. Ethnicity, gender, or class no longer limit one's potential or service in Christ. As those who had once been subjugated began to read and interpret Scripture, they brought a wealth of insight to the world, expanding our gratitude for Christ through whom all people receive their truest empowerment and identity, regardless of the circumstances of birth.

Sexual Integrity in Healthy, Egalitarian Relationships

REBECCA KOTZ

While the church often focuses on sexual sin and exploitation, understanding healthy sexuality in egalitarian relationships is crucial.

Sexual consent is a framework frequently used in the anti-sexual violence movement. At the same time, there are many valid critiques of the *limits* of consent in determining ethical sexual behavior.

Catharine MacKinnon, a feminist lawyer and activist, critiqued the concept of consent in a sexist culture. She said, "when force is a normalized part of sex, when no is taken to mean yes, when fear and despair produce acquiescence and acquiescence is taken to mean consent, consent is not a meaningful concept."[1]

The concept of sexual consent is not worthless, but MacKinnon challenges us to dive much deeper and recognize our choices do not occur in a vacuum. Environment, oppression, power, relationship, and context matter and greatly influence people's choices. Truly free consent can only be a concept applied in a healthy relationship of equals. A person cannot consent when in a relationship with an abusive person. In an egalitarian world where all are free, sexual consent would be simple. In a patriarchal society where sex is used as a tool of oppression and subordination, consent is far more complicated.

Sexual consent as a concept remains shallow if it is only defined as surface-level agreement or a simple "yes" or "no." At the same time, a relationship grounded in a true consent ethic has great potential for mutual fulfillment, erotic pleasure, safety, trust, and respect. This chapter explores how sexual ethics, integrity, and consent help relationships flourish and how to respond to common issues in a healthy sexual relationship.

In the United States, the age of consent varies by state but is usually age 16 or 18. Besides age, a person cannot consent if they are asleep, passed out, mentally incapacitated, unconscious, unable to communicate, highly intoxicated, or when there is a significant power differential between the two individuals. For example, a child cannot consent to sex with an adult, a client (regardless of age) cannot consent to sex when under the care of a mental health professional, clergy member, or employer. In each of these cases, the victim's agreement is irrelevant because the power inequality negates consent.

Beyond power differentials due to gender or status, economics also significantly impact consent. If money is power, those who have less—especially those who are in poverty or financially struggling—have major constraints on their choices. Poverty is gendered. Men's and women's wages are unequal (especially for women of color and women who have children), "women's work" is undervalued and pays low wages or no wage, and men are promoted more and dominate leadership positions. Sexism is institutionalized and embedded within the economy. Men's control of money and resources is yet another sphere that limits women's power and keeps them dependent on men economically. The fear of financial struggle and homelessness prevents many women from leaving abusers. Submission, sexual or otherwise, to men can sometimes quite literally be for survival purposes. But having no other options but to agree to sex is never true consent. A "yes" is meaningless when you can't say no.

Although each state has different criminal statutes regarding sexual assault crimes, most statutes define sexual assault as "sexual activity without consent or involving coercion or force," Historically, there has been an ideological conflict between victim advocates and the criminal/legal system on how sexual violence is defined. Sexual assault crime laws, written by men, for men, and to protect men (primarily white, wealthy, and powerful men), continue to uphold patriarchal bias. To be a chargeable offense, an act of sexual assault often must involve overt coercion or force. However, men routinely violate and sexually traumatize women in ways that do not meet the level in which a perpetrator can be charged criminally.

Current laws fail to accurately capture experiences of sexual violation that do not involve such high levels of force/coercion (which is most of the time). Women's inferior social status, sexual objectification, and rational fear of male violence incite a submissive response to men.[2] As a result, sometimes very little overt coercion is necessary for a woman to comply with a man's unwanted sexual demands. All women and girls are socialized this way, but women who have been abused in the past, who are currently afraid of their partner, who are members of other subordinated groups due to race, socioeconomic class, sexual orientation, ability, or other vulnerabilities due to oppression, are taken advantage of and further exploited by abusers. However, no level of privilege protects an individual woman from sexual violence. Force is always an option. Men who rape will rarely face any consequence. Most women don't report sexual assault, and even when they do, only 2 percent of *reported* rapists will be incarcerated.[3] The numbers are even lower for perpetrators who are partners or ex-partners, when victims are people of color, and when perpetrators are white men.

Consent for Christian Couples

Speaking about sexual abuse is particularly taboo in the church because speaking about *sex* is still taboo in the church. People can't truly understand sexual abuse without knowing what healthy, ethical, consensual, God-honoring sex is. In addition, sexual violation can be a subjective determination by the victim, because each person has unique boundaries, backgrounds, comfort levels, likes, and dislikes. The differentiation between sex and sexual abuse can't be adequately unraveled without in-depth and explicit discussion of both. This overall discomfort is partly why both topics are often avoided—to everyone's detriment.

The message directed at Christians is usually abstinence until marriage, and Christian couples who have little sexual experience are sometimes ill-equipped for healthy sex when they choose to have sex. What people *need* to hear about sex is seldom discussed. Congregants need to understand sexual boundaries, mutuality in pleasure, sexual communication and assertiveness, and how to respond in practical scenarios such as what to do when one partner wants sex and the other doesn't.

Abusers benefit from, and take advantage of, sexual naiveté. **This overall lack of sexuality education does not protect people, it actually creates more vulnerable**

children and adults. The abuser then takes on this role and becomes the "educator" that normalizes abusive sex—he is unchecked and unaccountable when a healthy teacher does not educate.

Abusers in the church often use spiritual means to justify their abuse. An abuser may play the victim and whine about being "deprived" or how "Satan will tempt him" if his spouse doesn't comply with what he feels entitled to. Though biblical sexuality condemns violence, selfishness, lust, sexual immorality, and using power to dominate, certain verses may be conveniently manipulated for an abuser's self-serving purposes.

Abusers may distort scriptures on spousal submission in marriage (such as the Ephesians 5 "Household Codes"). They ignore mutuality and isolate verses to feel biblically righteous in their sexism by focusing on one-sided submission, convincing their female partner that submission is only required of *her*. **The belief in *one-sided* submission is the cornerstone of both patriarchal/complementarian theology *and* the belief system of theologically minded abusers.** In a dating or spousal relationship where there is abuse, one person has significantly more power and control than their partner while the other person obeys and submits. In contrast, egalitarian relationships are those in which both partners share power equally, have flexible roles, and lead and serve together, as God designed. Egalitarian theology genuinely practiced is a protective factor against abuse. Complementarian theology in practice is a risk factor for abuse because the theology itself provides the ideological framework for power inequality.

Complementarian men are often sent a message (usually indirectly) that marriage is *for* sex, therefore his wife's sexual submission is part of the "deal" and he can feel justified in expecting sex. Patriarchalists and complementarians may also convince victims that "respect" means she must meet *all* his expectations—including his sexual demands.

Tim Krueger describes his personal experience of the "respect principle" that can be easily manipulated:

> Because a patriarchal culture assumes the best of a man's intentions, a man can "love" a woman like he'd love a child, and the world will celebrate him for it. Through the twisted logic of patriarchy, disrespect, pride, and even abuse could be construed as love. When we say "women need love" in a patriarchal world, we allow room to believe this: "women need to be treated as men see fit." . . . Looking back, I now recognize that I had latched onto the love-respect principle because it allowed me to

define literally anything I disliked, especially if it embarrassed me, as disrespectful. And I, as a man, needed respect more than anything else. It was her job to ensure that happened. I had no equivalent obligation toward her, because what she needed most was love, not respect. If I publicly embarrassed her or dismissed her ideas or put her down, I could simply have said it was tough love.[4]

Andrea Dworkin shares a similar sentiment on how men sometimes redefine love to include abuse:

We have a double standard, which is to say, a man can show how much he cares by being violent—see, he's jealous, he cares—a woman shows how much she cares by how much she's willing to be hurt; by how much she will take; how much she will endure.[5]

Principles of Practical Consent

To counter sexual abuse and dangerous sexual ideology, it is imperative that we understand the antidote to it: healthy, ethical, consensual sexuality. Let's explore what consent truly entails, and, more importantly, how to practically apply it to our sex lives. Let's look first at the principles of consent. Sexual consent says, *"at this particular moment, I desire/want to engage in this particular act."* F.R.I.E.S. (Free, Reversible, Informed, Enthusiastic, and Specific) is an acronym in the sexual health field that summarizes the principals of consent outlined below:[6]

- *Freely given*: Sexual expression is ethical when authentic, mutual desire is expressed between two equal partners who are also legally able to give consent. This means they are of age, awake, able, and not intoxicated. For a person to truly consent, there must be a mutual trust, honor, courtesy, and esteem for oneself and the other. Both partners' "yes" or agreement to sex must be as respected as their "no." Both partners must feel safe to assert themselves, disagree, or deny their partner. Consent can never be free in the context of abuse, fear, threats, intimidation, intoxication, lack of options, survival, or any level of coercion. No pressure. No obligation.
- *Reversible*: Consent is a continual process, not a one-time event. A person can stop or change their mind at any time, and the other partner must respect their boundaries and not push them to continue an act (at any stage—even if right

before an orgasm). There is no "point of no return"—we are always in control of our actions. Prior relationship or sexual experience with a person is irrelevant because consent can only be given in the present moment—not in a future or past agreement.

- *Informed*: A person can only give true consent when they have "all the facts" about what they are consenting *to*. This requires communication between partners about their boundaries, what they are comfortable with, what/if they will use contraception, relationship status/fidelity commitments, and disclosure of STIs.

- *Enthusiastic*: A person should only do sex acts they *desire* and *want* to give or receive! Partners should check in and make sure the other partner is enjoying what is happening at all times. If they express ambivalence, discomfort, low enthusiasm, the partner should ask if the other partner would like to do something else or stop immediately.

- *Specific*: Consent to one thing does not mean consent to *any*thing. A person can consent to one/some sex acts, but not others. A partner may want to kiss, but not have sex. A partner may be comfortable with manual genital stimulation or oral sex, but not want intercourse. A partner may consent to sex with a condom, but never without. A person's sexual desires and preferences may change throughout their lifetime, day-to-day, and even during an act.

Sexual consent is the mandatory *minimum*, only a start to ethical sex. Someone can agree to sex, and it can still be unhealthy or abusive. Partners must evaluate the power dynamics in their relationships. Power inequality limits a person's ability to consent freely. What may look like agreement or choice in the eyes of a more powerful person could actually be coerced compliance on the part of the less powerful.

Although power inequality is intrinsic in relationships between couples of different sexes, races, classes, and abilities, couples can work toward equality within their interpersonal relationship, even if societally they are still unequal. In these cases, it is the responsibility of the person in the dominant group to yield themselves, and be sensitive and humble. The privileged person must build trust and, mutual respect, being keenly aware of these power dynamics. They must make an intentional choice and commit to never taking advantage of their power position. Authentically egalitarian relationships lay the groundwork for the safest sexual relationships.

Now let's get more practical. How do the principles of consent play out in a sexual encounter? What does consent look like and sound like in a couple's sex life?

A Sexual Invitation: Asking and Responding

A consent question is something like, "Would you like to have sex?" or "Can I take your clothes off?" Because true consent is enthusiastic, your partner should be authentically excited and be clear that they want to do this!

When you both want to have sex . . .

Some verbal questions/statements to gauge consent and pleasure *during* sex could include a question like, "Want to try a different position?" "How does this feel?" "Can you go slower?" "Could you move this way?" "I'm not really into that right now, can you try this?" "It looks like you're not comfortable/not into this/in pain, want to do something else or stop?"

Affirmative responses are essential to indicate that you like what your partner is doing. Most people can pick up non-verbal cues from their partner, especially the longer they have been a couple. Still, verbal enthusiasm and encouragement are vital to communication. *That feels good! Keep going! Right there! Yes!*

Some non-verbal responses that indicate a partner is *no longer* consenting or wanting to have sex may look like hesitation, freezing, grimacing, silence, seeming "zoned out," pushing a partner away, seeming unresponsive or tense, avoiding eye contact, shaking their head, or general lack of enthusiasm.

It's important to note that sexual abuse in SDPE (spouse, date, partner, or ex) relationships is not a result of miscommunication on the part of the victim. Abusers either ignore or disregard verbal and non-verbal communication.

When your partner turns you down . . .

An unenthusiastic response should be taken seriously. This might be, "Maybe," "I don't know," "Not right now," "I'm not sure," "I think we should wait," "Later, I would love to but can't right now," "I'm not feeling well," "I'm tired," "Fine, I guess," or "Ugh . . . okay." These are *not* words of consent. These are what I would describe as a "soft no."

A "soft no" is not encouragement to convince, pressure, persuade, or guilt a partner into sex. People (especially women) are often socialized to respond with a soft no so as not to offend their partner.

Neither partner ever owes their other partner sex. If one partner wants to have sex and the other doesn't, it is never okay to guilt, pressure, obligate, badger, manipulate, whine, complain, or force someone into having sex. Both partners deserve to have their boundaries respected at all times.

If a partner is consistently turning down sex, it's time to have an honest, vulnerable conversation. Is the partner stressed? Overwhelmed? Frustrated? Depressed or having mental health issues? On medication that lowers their sex drive? Does s/he not enjoy sex or experiences pain during sex? Is one partner not putting in enough effort to turn the other partner on? Is one partner sexually selfish? Is a partner abusive? Does a partner need more lubrication? Is the partner uncomfortable with their body or have they been criticized? Does a partner not feel safe and relaxed in this situation? Does a partner feel degraded, hurt, betrayed, or afraid? Does the partner feel too much pressure to orgasm or "perform" a certain way? Does a partner have past sexual trauma that is being triggered? Is a partner cheating with people or porn? Are there addiction issues?

Many times, when couples don't address sexual issues or risk engaging in vulnerable conversations that get to the root of the problem, they may resort to simplistic and untrue sex stereotypes. There are often much deeper reasons to explore beyond "they just have a lower/higher sex drive."

A couple's sex life is often a good indicator to gauge the health of the relationship overall. However, some couples have fantastic sex lives in the midst of an unhealthy relationship and vice versa.

Countering Patriarchal Sexuality

We, as the church, can fight for a real sexual revolution! Society has twisted something *so very good* into a pornified act of violence and degradation. But it does not have to be this way.

Honor is one of the words commonly associated with love and sex in the Bible. In Romans 12:10, Paul encourages those in all relationships to "outdo one another in showing honor." A high respect for, or a reverent posture toward all people is important.

Honoring sex, your partner, their body, and their choice to share all of the above in vulnerability is the first step in countering a sexually toxic culture. Patriarchal attitudes *dis*honor and lack high respect for the other because the other is not seen as truly equal. Instead, the woman is seen as an object to fulfill men's desires.

Treating a date or spouse, their body, and sex with reverence doesn't mean your sex life has to be somber, serious, and boring. Sex that honors yourself, your partner, and God *should* be just as fun, creative, playful, exciting as any other kind—but this type of liberated sexuality cannot thrive in a relationship where both partners are not equally respected and do not feel safe enough to be truly vulnerable and known.

In a patriarchal society, the sexual landscape is male defined. Sex is seen as something men do *to* women. Men are the subjects; women are the objects. But what if it was never intended to be this way? What if sex were truly as good as God intended it to be? Tina Schermer Sellers calls us to renew our understanding of sex as an experience that is "collaborative, non-goal-oriented, pleasure-focused, experience-rich, and whole-body oriented."[7]

When making ethical sexual choices, go back to the basics: 1 Corinthians 13:4–7. Replace "love" with "healthy sex" in the most fundamental, well-known passage to describe love:

> [Healthy sex] is patient, [healthy sex] is kind. It does not envy, it does not boast, it is
> not proud. It does not dishonor others, it is not self-seeking, it is not easily angered,
> it keeps no record of wrongs. [Healthy sex] does not delight in evil but rejoices
> with the truth. It always protects, always trusts, always hopes, always perseveres.
> (1 Corinthians 13:4–7, NIV; "love" replaced with "healthy sex")

Does a couple's sex life reflect a spirit of patience and kindness? Do they each honor their partner in their sex life? Do they each give and receive fully or are they more self-seeking and focused only on their own pleasure? Do they each protect their partner's vulnerability or do they exploit/take advantage? Do they each work to create an atmosphere of trust?

Or how about the fruits of the spirit? Are they each operating out of a spirit of self-control? Faithfulness? Gentleness? Kindness? Joy?

It is easy to assume your partner would affirm and respond "yes" to the above questions, but instead of assuming, ask your partner. If they don't respond in the way you expect, disagree, or bring up an issue, avoid getting defensive. They may not bring it up again if they feel you can't handle feedback. Thank them for telling you candidly and ask how you can improve and be a healthier partner.

The church can play a role in equipping people to have courageous conversations about sex. Because the media and porn have become the primary sex educator of the public, we have a responsibility to counter these messages. Most depictions we see of sex in the media are inaccurate at best.

What makes "good TV" does not make good sex. Most sex scenes show unrealistic portrayals of bodies and of quick sex where both partners are immediately "ready to go." After a few kisses and a few thrusts, both partners have mind-blowing orgasms at the same time. They never have to communicate. They don't ever have to reach for a condom or lubricant, or worry about pregnancy or STIs. The first sexual experience with a partner is portrayed as smooth, romantic, magical, and earth-shattering. Somehow, each partner knows what to do and exactly how the person wants to be touched.

Navigating what is real versus a myth or stereotype is not always easy, especially since people are often uncomfortable talking about their experiences. It's difficult to have good sex when you can't talk about it. Sexual assertiveness is key to a healthy, satisfying sex life. Sexual assertiveness means you can communicate directly with your partner about sex—giving and receiving, taking direction, and your desires, likes, dislikes, boundaries, and feelings

Language is powerful and shapes sexual perceptions. Androcentric sexuality is encoded in our language. When people use the term "sex," they almost always mean penetrative, penis-in-vagina sex. Intercourse is considered the "main event," while sex acts that are sometimes most pleasurable for women are trivialized as "foreplay." This also reinforces the belief that sex ends when the man has an orgasm. Because only 25 percent of women orgasm from intercourse, women may internalize that *pleasing the man* is the main event, and her desires are secondary. In addition, women may feel pressure (whether internally or from their partner), to have intercourse, even if it is uncomfortable, painful, or simply not pleasurable.

Because most people receive highly inadequate sexuality education, many people assume intercourse is the *only* way to have sex, instead of just one option among many ways to enjoy a sexual relationship with their spouse. Because there is so much silence surrounding women's sexuality, many Christians will probably never hear the word "clitoris" ever said out loud. Some people do not even know what a clitoris is, do not know where to locate it on a woman's body, and do not know that God created it for no other purpose but women's sexual pleasure! If intercourse is the main event and procreation the only reason for sex, why is the most sexually stimulating area on a woman's body externally on the vulva, rather than inside the vagina? Clitoral stimulation, manually or orally, is usually necessary for women to orgasm. This is almost never talked about, especially in church. If the church cares about women's sexuality, it must be!

If we desire to practice egalitarian sexuality and resist the patriarchal, hierarchical sexuality of the world, we must re-evaluate our language, messaging, gender stereotypes, and sexual norms. The recognition that patriarchy socializes men's and women's sexuality differently means women and men must resist patriarchal sexuality in different ways as well.

Again, the person with more social or individual power within the relationship has more responsibility to create a safe atmosphere.

How men can counter patriarchal sexual socialization

Men can counter patriarchal sexual socialization by refusing to use porn and consume sexist media. A man can treat his partner as a real equal in every area of their lives together. He can genuinely share domestic, emotional, and mental labor with his partner. He can prioritize serving *her* sexually—and serving her first. He can ask her about her sexual experiences, how those experiences have affected her, and recognize that most women have varying levels of sexual violation and trauma. He can empathize with the fact that this will likely affect her sexually. He will learn her body and her desires, and work to be in tune with her verbal and body language. He will humble himself and take sexual instruction from her seriously and not as a threat to his ego. He can ask what she wants rather than assume what she wants. He will be diligent about making sure she feels safe, respected, honored, and adored inside and outside the bedroom. He will never badger, guilt, obligate, or pressure her into having sex or doing sex acts she doesn't want. He can focus not solely on sex but affection, affirmation, and sensual touch that doesn't always lead to sex. He can sexually pleasure her without expecting anything sexual in return. He will not do sex acts that hurt her or ignore her discomfort. He will not put so much pressure on himself recognizing that sex is an expression, not a performance. He will do the work to educate himself on rape culture, sexism, men's violence and abuse, and egalitarian relationships and sexuality—rather than burdening his partner with the expectation that she will educate him.

How women can counter patriarchal sexual socialization

Women can counter patriarchal sexual socialization by being an active, assertive, mutual participant in sex. A sexually free woman is unafraid to initiate sex or be sexually assertive when she feels desire. She will intimately know her body and be vocal and comfortable sharing with her partner her boundaries, desires, and turn-ons without shame. She will stop worrying about how her body looks and accept herself as God created her to be—more than a body. She will be present and in-the-moment during sex, not worrying about the next thing on her to-do list. She will believe she is worthy of great sex, and not feel selfish or unworthy for indulging in this God-given gift. She will prioritize her own pleasure as much as her partner's. She will agree to sex only when she wants sex and only the type of sex acts she is comfortable with. She will not feel she must endure sexual pain or discomfort. She will prioritize her healing if she has experiences of past sexual trauma.

How couples can counter patriarchal sexual socialization

Both partners should avoid pornography and sexist/sexually violent media—these can truly be toxic to a couple's sex life. Couples can also consult a mental health professional or sex therapist if they have further issues—especially if one or both partners are survivors of prior sexual trauma. However, beware: some therapists are not well-trained on issues of sexual violence, and some therapists may even "prescribe" pornography and condone sexually violent behavior.

How pastors can use their platform and position to counter patriarchal sexuality

Talk about egalitarian relationships and sexuality from the pulpit. Screen couples for abusive attitudes such as entitlement, control, sexism, narcissism, image/reputation-obsessed, power-over/hierarchal mentality, gender roles, glorification of violence, etc.

Educate youth AND adults on sexual coercion vs. consent, how to talk about sex with a partner/spouse, differences between healthy sex and pornography, and asserting boundaries before and after marriage. Invite experts from local sexual and domestic violence advocacy centers to speak to adults and youth or consult with them when writing a sermon. Consult egalitarians and feminists in your community. Poll your church to see what topics on sex, relationships, and abuse they would like to learn or talk more about. Share the information in this chapter and book in pre-marital and marriage counseling, classes, and conferences. Share the Duluth Model's Power & Control Wheel and Equality Wheel.[8] Always consult victims/survivors, experts, and professionals when any topic or issue is not your expertise. Refer victims and perpetrators to professionals. Hire as many female pastors as male pastors. Pastors should not sexualize or objectify their spouses or anyone in the congregation. Avoid messaging that makes women responsible for men's actions. Read egalitarian theological perspectives before preaching a sermon on sex or gender. Consult CBE International's website for books, blogs, articles, etc. Publicly support CBE and egalitarian theology, relationships, and sexuality in your church. Host groups on egalitarian books or authors, etc.

Conclusion

Rather than continuing the damaging legacy of silence, shame, and blame surrounding sexual violence, we as the body of Christ are called to make a different choice that lifts and empowers. We are called out of our comfort zone to take on the challenging, exciting, difficult, and courageous work of reclaiming our sex lives and taking back what the forces of evil have tried to destroy. We will bring forth a vision of counter-cultural sexuality without power-plays, manipulation, degradation, and objectification. We will reimagine the sexual revolution as God intended—a humanizing sexual ethic of mutuality, equality, connection, safety, playfulness, freedom, and respect for every part of ourselves and others—so that our sexuality can be as *good* as God promises!

Teaching and Preaching about Domestic Violence

JOHNRICE NEWTON, RN, M.DIV.

It was during the Samuel DeWitt Proctor Conference for African American pastors and seminarians that I first heard Judges 19 preached, the passage regarding the Levite and the concubine. As the preacher read, the audience was captivated and repelled by the horrific events that occurred in the passage, in the Sacred Text, the Bible! As the female pastor skillfully exegeted the passage and brought to life the abuse of the young concubine by males in a patriarchal society, I was convicted to be intentional about examining the scriptures that have been preached, largely by males, that cast some female biblical characters in a negative light. It caused me to think back to my church upbringing. Had I ever heard a sermon preached speaking out against domestic violence among women? I had not.

Discussing domestic violence, including sexual abuse, in a church setting can be uncomfortable because it exposes the dark side of human nature. But Scripture is not silent about abuse. The same Scripture that encourages and uplifts also acknowledges that abuses, especially toward women, do indeed occur. Pastors, ministers, and clergy have a unique responsibility and opportunity to respond to, and care for, those suffering from domestic abuse in their midst. One way is by guiding your congregation to examine what

Scripture has to say about domestic abuse and God's response to it. By speaking out, pastors can help establish that abuse will not be tolerated in the home, church, or community.

It requires commitment and dedication to present this difficult topic with transparency and compassion for those in the congregation who may be victims, survivors, advocates, or perpetrators. It is important to:

1. Offer Scripture as the voice of hope, restoration, resistance, and safety to victims/survivors of domestic abuse.
2. Make the church a "Safe Place" where abuse victims can come for help and support, a place where they can speak openly about their experiences confidentially without fear of judgment, persecution, or gossip.
3. Show the church's commitment to bring healing by breaking the silence around domestic abuse. The voices of victims and survivors can shed new light on scripture and deepen our understanding of God's response to abuse in the Bible.

There are multiple ways leaders can provide information about domestic abuse. It can be presented from the pulpit as a sermon or a youth group talk. Another way to discuss abuse is in small groups, such as Bible studies, educational series open to the public, parenting classes, teen relationship lessons, premarital counseling, or marriage enrichment sessions.

The topics that should be covered include:

1. What is domestic abuse?
2. Who is a victim?
3. Who is a perpetrator?
4. Who and where is God in the midst of struggle?
5. Finding hope in crisis.
6. Exposing evil and embracing God's grace.
7. Healing as a marathon, not a sprint.

Depending on the setting, it is important to keep several things in mind when speaking to a congregation on domestic violence:

- Realize that your sermon may be the first one many in the congregation have ever heard that speaks against domestic abuse or even speaks positively about women in the Bible, especially those biblical figures who have normally been presented as immoral and evil.

- Be aware that it is likely there are victim/survivors in your congregation.
- Be aware that perpetrators may also be in these groups, perhaps accompanying their victims, or having a history of abusing.
- When we preach from the pulpit regarding domestic violence, "we find ourselves preaching about the powerful ambiguities of violence, who is violated, and why, while still proclaiming genuine hope amid the gaps between our human selves and the divine."[1]
- Realize that because much of the Bible is presented from a male point of view and was written in a patriarchal environment, it is beneficial to "re-read" the passages that often demonize and berate women, and search for a fresh way to present these women as being worthy of God's love.
- To appropriately preach texts that present female victims of abuse, you first must place the passage into the context of the patriarchal system of the biblical society. Understanding the patriarchal structure of male dominance and its impact on human society forms a foundation for understanding the element of violence as a tool to maintain power, and how God transforms all human cultures. When we have a clear picture of the culture's attitude toward women and men, we can make a more informed judgment about the nature of the violence in the text.

Re-Reading the Text Through the Lens of the Victim

Often the cries of domestic violence victims fall on deaf ears, making these cries "silent noise." After abuse happens, there is pain, there is crying out, and there is suffering, but because the abuse has not been named for what it is, all this crying out is "silent noise." When the church is silent regarding domestic abuse, ". . . it is not really silent. It sends a clear 'hands off' message to victims, perpetrators, and bystanders. At the very least, this silence communicates to perpetrators that the church will not hold them accountable for their evil actions. To bystanders it says that it is okay to remain on the sidelines of a brutal and sometimes deadly game."[2] Scripture challenges us to speak about this very issue. However, it can take some excavating to figure out how and where. We need to think faithfully about how to find truth long buried in some very painful texts.

As a case study, consider Psalm 6, a lament in prayer. This psalm exposes and recognizes the forces of evil and violence. These words could be the words of many victims who cry out in the night, longing to know when and how God will hear their cries and rescue them from the hands of their abusers.

> Have mercy on me, Lord for I am faint; heal me, Lord for my bones are in agony.
>
> My soul is in deep anguish. How long, Lord, how long?
>
> Turn Lord and deliver me; save me because of your unfailing love.
>
> Among the dead no one proclaims your name. Who praises you from the grave?
>
> I am worn out from my groaning.
>
> All night long I flood my bed with weeping and drench my couch with tears.
>
> My eyes grow weak with sorrow; they fail because of all my foes.
>
> Away from me, all who do evil, for the Lord has heard my weeping.
>
> The Lord has heard my cry for mercy; the Lord accepts my prayer.
>
> All my enemies will be overwhelmed with shame and anguish;
>
> They will turn back and suddenly be put to shame." (Psa. 6:2–10, NIV)

Psalm 6 provides an easy example of reading through the lens of the victim. One can imagine the psalmist wronged by others, in pain and desperate, because he or she is writing from the perspective of the victim. Many texts dealing with abuse, especially the abuse of women, are not written in this way. However, it is still possible to *read* them from the perspective of the victim. Because Scripture provides a vast richness of truth through which the Holy Spirit can speak to us in our own circumstances, there are always many things to be learned from any particular text. A faithful reading requires close attention and deep analysis of the issues at play. When Paul tells Timothy to rightly divide the word of truth (2 Tim 2:15), we might easily think of a surgical operation on a text: there is much to find in any passage, more than may first meet the eye. The Holy Spirit guides us to find wisdom for today. We can call this exploration of a text's many facets "ways of reading." One way of reading is from the perspective of a figure in the narrative. Reading through the lens of the victim in a story can be a very helpful way of preaching compassionately for victims and survivors in a congregation.

In the next section I will present insights for sermon writing and victim-perspective readings of three biblical stories that have potential to hurt or heal hurting women: The Levite's concubine (Judges 19), Hagar (Gen. 16 and 21), and Tamar (2 Sam. 13). Even though they are difficult and perhaps triggering to read, the Holy Spirit is still speaking through these texts, and has something to say to survivors, victims, perpetrators, and their communities.

Giving Voice to Silent Noise: The Levite's Concubine, Judges 19:1-30

This passage could easily be unfamiliar to you or your congregation, but here it sits in the middle of a book filled with patriarchy and violence. This story centers on the evil that results from disregard for the human dignity of women, and ultimately the terrible consequences of men acting according to "whatever seem[s] right in their own eyes" (Judges 21:25 NLT). The story of the Levite's concubine may sound like a modern-day soap opera or a cartel movie, which only shows that human behavior hasn't changed much over time.

The first thing to note is that we do not hear from the concubine (a secondary or lower status wife). She says not a word in thirty verses. She is human, so we know she has feelings and thoughts, but like the "silent noise" of the abuse victim, they go unrecorded. Rather than patriarchal bias in the text, we could read this as a literary choice—a point being made about the woman's desperate position. A preacher can give voice to her "silent noise" in the midst of the voices and actions of the abusers.

In this story a young Jewish girl (pre-teen or early teen) from Bethlehem has been married off by her impoverished father for financial gain. The father considered the Levite a good catch as a son-in-law, because being from the priestly clan, he came from good stock. He had money (two donkeys, a servant, and a home), he was probably well spoken and well dressed, and he paid a generous bride price. The obedient daughter was sent away with the stranger/husband to be his secondary wife, a term that implies lower status in the household than the "real" wives. After she settled into her new role as secondary wife to the Levite, he revealed his true colors: he was an abuser.

Here is where the biblical story picks up. She becomes angry with her husband and makes a bold choice to leave the relationship. She runs home to her father and is there three or four months. The Levite devises a plan to retrieve his wife from her father—after all, he paid good money for her. Perhaps she made him look bad in front of his friends, insulted him, or wounded his ego by leaving him. He will teach her a lesson not to defy his authority. He goes to win her back by "speaking tenderly to her" (Judges 19:3a). Perhaps he threatens the father with a demand for the bride price to be repaid. In any case, the two men enjoy days of friendly socializing and the girl is finally sent back with her husband. Though the Levite supposedly goes to make up with his wife, it seems he spends his time sweet-talking her only defender instead. He sets out once again with his wife. This time, the twenty-mile journey from Bethlehem to Ephraim would be tragic.

Halfway to their destination the Levite decides to stop in Gibeah, a Benjamite territory, to rest and refuel. It is late evening in a rough neighborhood, and danger is present. An old man and his daughter, originally from Ephraim, take them in and feed the Levite, his servant, and the donkey—but no mention is made of hospitality to the young girl. Late in the night loud knocks on the door wake the household. Men from the community are demanding that the Levite be sent out to have sex with them. Neither the Levite nor his servant want to accommodate them. Can't you see them, nervously arguing in pecking order, looking down at the young, teenage, secondary wife, a sold-out daughter who had publicly defied her husband—the least of these—as the best candidate to be thrown to the mob? Maybe she spoke up: "No way! Why Me? Husband, why don't you protect me?" But the text does not record this "silent noise."

We can imagine the girl screamed and cried, beating on the door, pleading to be let in, and begging for mercy as the mob of men overpowered her and took her screaming into the dark night. The men tear her clothes, leaving her frightened and shamed as they take turns raping her, repeatedly, all . . . night . . . long. After hours of abuse, she loses her voice from screaming and crying out, eventually passing out. Perhaps they mistook her silence for submission. When the mob of men have satisfied themselves and dawn is approaching, they leave her there, exposed and forgotten. Neither her husband, nor her host, nor the servant have come looking for her. Surely, they have heard her screams! As dawn breaks, she is alone, torn, bloody, beaten, bruised, and near death. But with her last bit of resilience she crawls to the old man's house, not for help, but to remind them of the tragedy they had subjected her to. Here a subtle shift in the text signals that the narrator recognizes that the Levite's abuse has ended his marriage to this woman: where he was previously called her husband, now he is called her master. Perhaps she thinks, *If I can make it back to the threshold of the house before I die, they will have to deal with my dead body. They will have to let my father know what he sent me to. They will have to recognize that I am, that I was. I will be a part of history.*

After a good night's rest, ready to set out for home, the Levite likely thinks the mob has done his dirty work for him, humiliating and disposing of the girl. After all, he thinks, he is not responsible for what happened to her, it was the mob's fault. Whatever happened to her, she deserved it for embarrassing him by leaving. It is not clear if the girl died at the threshold of the house, or still had some life left in her body, but to the Levite's surprise, he almost trips over her limp body as he leaves the house. With no regard for her wellbeing, not taking her to the doctor, not tending to her wounds, he coldly and calmly says to her, "Get up, let's go" (vs 28). He expresses no grief for the loss of his wife, no lamenting, no words of sorrow for the dead or dying. Just, "Get up, let's go." When she does not respond, he picks her up like a sack of feed and tosses her bloody, broken body across his donkey to head home. Now she is damaged goods, no longer of any use to him. In her condition she would not be able to bear children, cook, clean, or be a wife to him. He has to come up with a plan to publicly get rid of her while proclaiming himself the victim. After all, he lost money on this deal. Her purchase has only caused him inconvenience and trouble—good riddance!

When the Levite gets home, he parades his concubine through town with cries of sorrow that the Benjamites have violated and killed his poor wife and should be punished for their crime. He remembers his priestly training in the art of preparing sacrificial animals and meticulously cuts her body into 12 pieces. He sends a body part to each of the 12 tribes of Israel with his idea of what has happened to this girl. Her story is not told. Of course, this horrible incident incites outrage against the tribe of Benjamin. Their words are recorded: "Such a thing has never been seen or done, not since the day the Israelites came up out of Egypt. Just imagine! We must do something! So, speak up!" (Judges 19:30). This verse instructs us to speak to the "silent noise." We must tell this young girl's side of the story and expose the lies about violence against women. We are called to SAY SOMETHING!

What can we learn from this story?

1. We should give women experiencing harm a *voice* by providing a safe place to be heard. Educate the congregation on what domestic abuse is, and how to report abuse. Preach from the pulpit that it is not okay for women to be abused, raped, beaten, and marginalized.

2. We should hold the perpetrators of domestic violence accountable for their actions. It is easy for perpetrators to follow in the Levite's footsteps and make themselves out to be the victim, especially in public. When the pulpit is intentionally silent about domestic violence in churches, we absolve the perpetrators of their wrongdoing and teach that there are no consequences for their violence.

3. God's love supersedes the unimaginable violence, greed, and injustice in this passage. The question of why a good God allows bad things to happen to good people arises and we cannot make sense or justify the harm and suffering we see in this passage and the world. We are not God, and we cannot begin to understand the mind of God. We have to trust God's work in the midst of undeserved suffering that God's message and purpose goes forth in ways that we cannot imagine or comprehend. When the abused tell their side of the story, healing can begin.

4. Judges was written to show us that God's people need a king. Though the book begins in a good place, with God's prophet Deborah in spiritual and political authority, by the end of Israel's centuries-long spiral into chaos women are barely considered human. Our eternal king, Jesus, calls us to turn from the sin of sexism.

5. Women victims of abuse can now give this young woman in Judges 19 a name. Her name is their name. Her name is the name of any woman who has been subjected to abuse, assault, rape, neglect, slavery, or murder. This young girl crawled to and clung to the threshold so that others like her can be restored, renewed, and heard.

Reflection:

1. A voice is a powerful tool when justice, safety, sanity, and dignity are at stake. When we witness these things in our own church or community, how can we speak up to make a positive change?

2. How have you used your voice to speak on behalf of others whom society has rendered voiceless?

3. When and how have you questioned God about a tragic event in your life that you felt you did not deserve? What was God's answer? Has God ever redeemed or healed your suffering?

4. How do you look at abuse victims? Do you think it is a faraway problem or not an issue in your community? How can you listen to survivors and be an agent of healing?

All Things Domestic Violence: The Story of Hagar, Genesis 16:1–16; 9–21

The saga of Abram, Sarai, and Hagar tells the story of the beginning of two nations. Sarai, the privileged first wife, was free, wealthy, beautiful, righteous, and barren. Hagar, the slave given to her mistress' husband as a concubine, is a young girl (possibly about 11–12 yrs. old), bound, poor, foreign, and fertile. Both women, in fact, were victims of sexual exploitation. When Abram presented the beautiful Sarai as his sister out of fear for his own life (Gen. 12:10–20), she was taken into Pharaoh's palace. Hagar's bodily autonomy was stolen from her so that Sarai could have a child. One situation of abuse does not supersede or justify the other.

Hagar exemplifies all the ways a woman can suffer abuse, then and now. In this passage she becomes a symbol of oppression, rejection, and exploitation. She was a marginalized African woman, a surrogate mother, a runaway youth, an expelled wife, a homeless woman, and welfare mother.[3] Her victimization starts in the heart of Sarai, who was aged and barren. God had promised her and Abram a child, but she could not see past her age to trust in God's plan. She crafted her own plan to bear children through her servant Hagar. God had promised Abram that his offspring would be more numerous than the stars. But his wife Sarai was old and childless.

Whether Sarai wanted to please her husband, herself, or God, she took matters into her own hands. She presented Hagar to Abram to bear an heir on her behalf. Hagar was given and taken. She became pregnant.

The text paints a picture of Hagar and Sarai's relationship in light of the giving and sharing of Hagar's body without consent. After Hagar became pregnant, these two women from two different worlds and ways of being found themselves at odds with each other (Gen. 16:4–6). Hagar hated Sarai and Sarai was abusive toward Hagar. There are a number of underlying reasons for the contempt between these two women. It seems likely that Sarai was jealous of Hagar's youth, fertility, and ability to bear children with Sarai's husband. Hagar could see Sarai and Abram as a powerful couple disregarding her humanity for their own needs. She was abused by another woman, and perhaps felt betrayed, believing that Sarai should have been her ally. She probably felt Abram's emotional detachment. Because of Sarai's abuse, the pregnant Hagar ran away to an unknown wilderness rather than face the hostility at home. Abram was ambivalent, offering no solution to Hagar's dilemma.

This was the first exodus of Hagar from Abram and Sarai's home. Whether due to naiveté or desperation, Hagar fled with no support or protection. She just needed to be free from the abuse. God met Hagar in the wilderness with a message:

> "Hagar, slave of Sarai, where have you come from and where are you going?" "I'm
> running away from my mistress Sarai," she answered. Then the angel of the Lord told
> her, "Go back to your mistress and submit to her." The angel added, "I will increase
> your descendants so much that they will be too numerous to count." (Gen. 16:7–10)

The angel of the LORD informs Hagar that she is pregnant with Ishmael, and he will be a "wild donkey of a man."

This text presents a challenge. The message to Hagar to return to her abusive household can be misconstrued as a message to victims of abuse to do the same. Is God being irrational, asking too much of Hagar, that she reenter the fire? This was an exceptional "God moment," when Hagar instinctively realized she must survive for the sake of her unborn son. It also gave her a sense of worth, because GOD SAW HER! God saw her sorrow, her anger, her silence, her abuser, the abuse, her son, and her destiny. Oh, to realize that God sees our true selves and our true essence! God did not see her as Abram and Sarai did, a means to an end, but saw her as the mother of a great nation. When God sees you, you do not appear as the world sees you—limited and diminished. Instead, God sees you as loved, valued, and blessed!

There is a wrestling with this message from the Angel of the Lord to Hagar telling her to return to the place of her abuse. Hagar saw harm behind her and harm before her when being questioned by the angel, ". . . where have you come from and where are you going?" (Gen. 16:7). Hagar was willing to risk death in the wilderness—both for herself and her unborn child—to avoid returning to her abuser. This is an unusual divine moment when the Lord's messenger allows this victim of abuse to see what the outcome of her survival would look like, while asking her to return to the fire. God the liberator is not seen in these words. This call for Hagar to return to an abusive setting is not a call for the abuse victims to return to abuse, God forbid! But a reassurance that survival, protection, and restoration are possible when God intervenes. God assured Hagar that whatever was to come, she and her child would survive and prosper. Most abuse victims can only see the horror of the moment they face, with no assurances of safety and survival in the future. We pause at this proclamation by the Angel of God and claim this as a call for church and community to be the intervention for those women who feel there are no other alternatives to survival but to return to their abuser in order to secure shelter, food, and clothing. With the intervention of God's called people in the lives of the abused, returning to abuse is not an option, but a source of safety and provision.

Because of God's revelation, Hagar made the decision to return to her "assignment" in order that her son would be a legitimate heir of Abram, securing for him access to wealth, power, status, and honor. She returned to the household of Abram and Sarai with a new mission: endure at all costs, because her child's future was on the line. Without Abram legitimizing Ishmael through recognition and circumcision, God's promise to her for Ishmael's future would not be fulfilled.

In returning, Hagar endured the reality that she did not own the rights to her womb; Sarai claimed Hagar's child because he was birthed on Sarai's behalf. In this society, surrogate births took place on a birthing stool. The primary wife, who would be the child's mother, sat with the birth mother on her lap. When the baby was born, he or she would fall into the lap of the primary wife. When Hagar's son Ishmael was born, he was Abram's and Sarai's son, not Abram's and Hagar's son. Ishmael's falling into the lap of Sarai gave him legitimacy and inheritance, which was not only Sarai's goal, but Hagar's goal as well. Whatever the cost, her son would be his father's heir.

Sarai's jealousy did not dissipate after Hagar gave birth. In fact, the presence of Hagar and her son Ishmael seemed to infuriate her even more. With Sarai well into her late 70s when Ishmael was born, Sarai's prospects for motherhood seemed bleak. When Abram was 99, once again the unfailing God appeared to him with the promise of a son with Sarai. Their son Isaac would be the father of many nations. This was such a miraculous occasion that God changed their names from Abram and Sarai to Abraham and Sarah, for they would no longer long for a child, but would finally have a son in their old age, the establishment of God's covenant for all generations.

When Sarah gave birth to Isaac in her old age, she joined the ranks of motherhood. She would no longer be mocked or looked down upon for being barren. As Sarah's son grew older, she noticed Ishmael mocking Isaac and reported to Abraham that it was time for Hagar and Ishmael to leave their household. Again, Abraham took the low road and sided with Sarah, sending Hagar and Ishmael out into the wilderness with only bread and water. At the time of Hagar's second exodus, she was a mother, a woman with new experiences and some measure of status. This time she did not need to return to her abuser, she had to forge a new reality for her and her son. A child with a promise.

The power of motherhood is a force like none other. It will make you bear the unbearable, fight the unconquered, and tolerate the unfathomable. In the wilderness Hagar was facing death when the tangible supports of life ran out. She could not bear to see her child's face as he cried, staring death in the face. Hagar felt helpless and almost suicidal. Once again God, the intangible, came to her rescue and provided water, shelter, and food. She was reassured again that God would make her a great nation. With God's provision, she conquered the desert and returned to Egypt a woman with a promise. She had been sold against her will, as a girl without voice or power over her own body, but she returns with Abraham's legitimate heir. As his mother, Hagar is now connected to a male protector who would cover her, provide for her, and give her a place of honor.

What can we learn from this story?

1. Sometimes a victim can be abused by multiple people in a family. Domestic abuse extends beyond physical and sexual violence to coercion and domination. Family systems can produce toxic patterns that attack vulnerable members from many angles. Sometimes a perpetrator is a victim him/herself.
2. God intervened at every crossroads of Hagar's life and brought safety, reassurance, and restoration. This is the message of hope that the abused and victimized need to hear.
3. God's plans for our lives are almost never what we envision. God's intervention is always exactly what we need.
4. Hagar's life at the beginning of the text was out of her control as long as she was under human authority. When she realized that God saw her, had her, and heard

her, human affliction was minimized in light of the promise of God. No affliction endured could abort the favor of God.

Reflection:

1. How has God spared you in the deserts of your life?
2. What has God promised that has come to pass, or are you still in a place of waiting?
3. Trace the broken pieces of Hagar. What areas of abuse do you note that she endured?
4. How was Sarai/Sarah victimized by a patriarchal system?

The Young and the Restless: Tamar, 2 Samuel 13:1-22

King David was warned by the prophet Nathan, "The sword shall not depart from your house because you have despised me and have 'taken' the wife of Uriah the Hittite to be your wife" (2 Sam. 12:10). David had lusted after Uriah's wife Bathsheba and plotted to have Uriah killed in battle in order to take her as his wife. We see this same spirit of lust in his son Amnon. The son carried the arrogance and entitlement he had seen in his father into his own life.

What else is there to desire if you have money, fame, and power? King David had all these things and more. He had many wives and children. 2 Samuel 13:1–22 shows that even amid all this grandeur, appearances may deceive. The tale takes place in the royal house of King David and involves three of his children: Absalom, Amnon, and Tamar. David was known as a slayer of giants and a military genius, but had problems in his camp with troubled children. His children Absalom and Tamar shared the same mother, while Amnon was half-brother to them both. The siblings were young, handsome, beautiful, and restless. The palace of King David should have been a safe place for Princess Tamar to grow and thrive because virgin princesses were protected by the palace eunuchs to make sure their virginity was preserved. Oftentimes, the princesses were pledged to marry at birth to ensure peaceful access to goods and services.

Amnon developed a sexual attraction to his sister and believed he was in love. Tamar was a young girl and Amnon was a young teen. Because she was a virgin and well-guarded, he couldn't get to her. He became obsessed with her, so much so that he made himself sick. His first cousin Jonadab saw his misery and devised a plan for Amnon to reach Tamar. The plan was for Amnon to pretend to be ill, and when his father came to check on him, to ask if Tamar could fix and serve him some food. Does this story sound familiar? We see some of David's trickery in his son Amnon, recalling David's plot to have Uriah killed so he could marry Bathsheba. The apple does not fall far from the tree.

Amnon's plan worked. When David heard his handsome, strong son was ill, he came personally to see about him. When Amnon asked his father if Tamar could prepare and serve him food, David gladly agreed and ordered Tamar to prepare the food. Anything for his son. Amnon did not share with his father the desire he had in his heart for his sister for fear of being denied her. The proper and least hazardous way for Amnon to have Tamar legally was to ask his father to bend a few rules and let him marry her. Instead, he resorted to trickery. When Tamar had prepared the food and brought it to her brother, Amnon cleared the room of all servants, removing Tamar's protection and intentionally making her vulnerable. Because he was a prince, he had the power to clear a room, and he used it. She in her innocence and sisterly love was willing to serve her ill brother, but Amnon took advantage of her naiveté and willingness by grabbing her and asking her to have sex with him. Amnon should have been her protector from outside dangers, but instead he became the threat within.

Despite Tamar's pleas for mercy, her brother raped her. "No, my brother!" she said to him. "Don't force me! Such a thing should not be done in Israel! Don't do this wicked thing. What about me? Where could I get rid of my disgrace? And what about you? You would be like one of the wicked fools in Israel. Please speak to the King; he will not keep me from being married to you." But he refused to listen to her, and since he was stronger than she, he raped her" (2 Sam. 13: 12–14, NIV). Tamar was forced, like many women before and after her, to bargain with her attacker. Of course, it did not work.

Tamar's plea is filled with questions, truths, and solutions that went unanswered. She made it clear that his attention was unwelcome. She called him her brother, but Amnon disconnected himself from that relationship and saw her as a vulnerable, available female. She brought up the legal implications for them both—she would be disgraced, and he would be labeled a fool. She even gave him the option of marriage to preserve their dignity. Amnon's desire was undignified and evil. He wanted to use her body for a fleeting experience of power and pleasure,

When Amnon overpowered Tamar physically, he altered the course of her life, stealing her future. Not only would she not be a physical virgin any longer, but she would be ineligible to marry, to be a mother, even to be used as a bargaining chip for her father. His choice for evil made her an outcast in the palace and none of that mattered to him, only what he wanted. When she still tried to salvage her honor by proposing marriage, he sent her away. His "love" had only been lust—lust for sexual pleasure and lust for power, and rape was his weapon. Is it any wonder, then, that afterwards he was revolted by the sight of her? His loathing seemed to be even greater than his lust. Even though the physical act was finished, the rape itself was not over. Tamar's life was permanently ruined by Amnon's sin.

Just as Amnon had cleared the room in order to rape Tamar, he ordered the servants into the room to remove her from his presence and bolt the door behind her. In her pain she saw the loss of her virginity and the violation of her body as an offense to be grieved. She took the very ashes from the fire she had made to cook her brother's food and covered her head as a sign of grief. She tore her clothes and wailed throughout the palace hallways covered in ashes, letting all know a crime had been committed against her. She demanded to be heard.

Tamar's full brother Absalom plotted revenge for what had happened to his sister, planning his brother's assassination and eventually attempting a coup against his father. What is missing in the aftermath of this rape is the King's reaction. David did nothing to console his distraught daughter. He did not even treat her rape as a crime. David had the ultimate power to punish, exile, love, and make rules in his household but he did not exercise this power to restore his daughter to a respected status. He could have commanded Amnon to marry Tamar to preserve her status. He could have exacted harsh justice for Amnon's wickedness. But when Amnon staunchly refused to marry Tamar, David did nothing. He didn't even bother to punish his son for his crime. He protected the abuser instead of the victim.

David's silence and indifference toward his daughter in the wake of her rape sent a message to all his subjects—that neither Tamar nor any other woman was valuable or respected in her own right. It is also notable that probably none of the women of status in the palace came to Tamar's aid, perhaps to prevent their own status from being tainted by associating with her. She would eventually become silent and disappear, the crime committed against her dismissed. As a response to the silence of his father regarding the crime against his sister, Absalom took matters into his own hands; thus the sword remained in the house of David, as was foretold by Nathan the prophet.

What can we learn from this story?

1. The message of hope and redemption for Tamar in this passage seems to be missing, but consider that this story of betrayal by a brother toward his sister made it into the canon, and we are witnesses. Such stories disrupt the idea that "all is well" in the Word of God and force us to reckon with the sins of our "heroes." This reminds us that no one is above temptation and even our leaders can fall.

2. This story not only shows the ineffectiveness of "protective" patriarchy, but the injustice that women truly can be punished just for being women. We as pastors/ministers/leaders must began to reread and retell the biblical stories of those lives that have been violated unjustly, especially women, so that we will not continue to perpetuate those injustices. Tamar stands out boldly in this text to remind us that she will not be silenced and that she had a voice. The crimes committed against her will not go unnoticed, because we will tell the whole story.

Reflection:

1. Consider society's view of women in Tamar's day. How is it similar or different from your experience? Are there places in the world today where Tamar's story could be repeated? What cultural values would make it possible for Amnon and David to behave as they did?

2. In the world of power and prestige that David and Tamar inhabited, how could David have used his influence to change things for women like his daughter?

3. What similarities do you see in the stories of David's lust for Bathsheba and Amnon's lust for Tamar? What are the differences?

4. When women are violated, how can we be present as advocates and allies?

5. What are some characteristics that David and Amnon share?

6. Imagine alternate endings to Tamar's story. How could respect and redemption be her outcome?

Breaking Down Barriers for Women in Church Leadership

DR. JEANNE PORTER KING, PH.D.

In my early days of ministry, I was blessed to be mentored by a male pastor who encouraged, supported, and served as a sponsor of women in ministry leadership. This pastor recognized my preaching gift, as well as my leadership training. He carved out a role for me to serve with our church's leadership development team and included me in our church's preaching rotation. Many of my conversations with my pastor and mentor stand out for me, but one in particular comes to mind as it relates to developing women for leadership.

I was holding a spirited dialogue with him and another pastor and enjoying our intellectual exchange, discussing some of the most challenging issues of the day. In the middle of our conversation, my pastor said, "Jeanne, one day I want you to sit down with me and tell me what it has been like for you as a woman leader. I imagine you have some stories to tell."

I was quietly awed for no man had ever asked me that question before. Yet it is an important question. For no pastor can adequately develop women leaders without understanding the stories of women who lead in and out of the church. Any pastor (male or female) who is committed to nurturing an egalitarian church culture must be open and willing to listen to the experiences of women. Our stories give insight into the struggles women have faced while breaking into leadership as well as in leading. These stories also shed light on the barriers that have existed and still exist in far too many places. In this chapter I will share some stories that reveal barriers to women's leadership and offer some strategies for removing those barriers. Even in churches led by egalitarian pastors, there are barriers, intentional or not, that must be identified and removed in order for women to gain full inclusion into church leadership.

First let's start with some definitions. According to Mary Crawford, author of *Transformations: Women, Gender, and Psychology*, sexism is defined as "prejudice on the basis of sex or gender,"[1] and entails beliefs and practices that stem from and support the negative and unequal treatment of women. Sexism can operate both consciously and unconsciously, explicitly or implicitly.

Overt examples of sexism include sexual harassment, domestic violence, and discriminatory hiring practices.[2] These overt forms of sexism still exist, and a great deal of this volume has been dedicated to addressing these explicit barriers that women in our churches face.

However, there also exists subtle forms of sexism that have negative effects on women, including negative mental health outcomes.[3]

In my consulting work with churches and other organizations, I have found there are four levels of barriers that prevent women from accessing and advancing into leadership, particularly senior levels of leadership in church and denominational ministry. These four barriers include: personal, interpersonal, institutional, and societal/cultural. These four levels of barriers to women's leadership in the church include both overt and subtle types of sexism.

The Personal Level

Personal barriers to women's leadership exist in the thinking patterns and biases of church leaders and members toward women leaders. These barriers abound in traditional thinking and can pop up anywhere any time in unexpected ways!

I had just published my first book on women's leadership in the Bible. I was invited to do an interview about the book on a television program hosted by one of the local radio personalities in Chicago.

After asking a series of general questions about the book and me as the author, the interviewer began to wind down his interview by lobbing a question to me which seemed meant to put me on the defensive. His tone was somewhat defiant. He asked, "Should women be pastors?" I remained calm, thinking my book did not expressly address women pastors, and he's trying to set me up. So, I replied, "Women are pastors." He tried again, asking the same question. I gave the same response, using the same steadfast resolve, "Women are pastors. It's not a matter of should; they are pastors."

It turns out this interviewer, unbeknownst to me, was part of the segment of the church who does not believe in women serving as pastors and allowed his biases to show during his interview with me. This interviewer's bias became quite apparent, but often in many of our more egalitarian churches today, biases against women leaders can be subtler and not as overt.

Yes, even in our most egalitarian churches, there are members or family members who visit with members, or leaders who transfer in from other churches, who hold an implicit bias against women in ministry leadership, especially women preachers and pastors. Many people in this day and age will not admit it.

This phenomenon is called by many names, including implicit bias, implicit association, unconscious bias, or hidden bias. Social psychologists Mahzarin Banji and Anthony Greenwald describe these hidden biases as "bits of knowledge about social groups. These bits of knowledge are stored in our brains because we encounter them so frequently in our cultural environments. Once lodged in our minds, hidden biases can influence our behavior toward members of particular social groups, but we remain oblivious to their influence."[4]

These implicit associations or hidden biases often connect leadership with maleness and support roles with femaleness. In this thinking, men are the natural leaders and women are the nurturers. For some people who have been socialized against women in church or ministry leadership, their cognitive biases associating men with leadership and women with support roles influence their responses and reactions to women who lead in church. A man preferring male pastors, preachers, or denominational leaders would be an example of personal-level bias. When those men are decision makers or opinion leaders in the church or denomination, and they act out of their biases, they create barriers for women who aspire to ministry leadership roles. Furthermore, according to Jioni Lewis in discussing gender bias in the workplace, "it is also possible for women to internalize these sexist beliefs and thereby prefer male supervisors or assume female supervisors are less competent."[5] I would suggest that it is also quite the case that some women do indeed internalize sexist beliefs and prefer male pastors, preachers, and denominational leaders.

As egalitarian leaders, we must provide a means for helping members who react based on hidden biases to slow down and become more thoughtful about the reality of women in ministry leadership. For instance, providing role models and examples of women who preach, serve communion, teach Bible studies, evangelize, and lead ministry departments will begin to offer an alternative view for those who resist accepting women in such roles.

Finally, including women in Bible study series helps to expose the congregation to the varied roles women play in Scripture. Sometimes these women only get brought out in women's ministry studies or at women's conferences. Yet, women were the first proclaimers of the gospel, and some people today try to limit our inclusion in ministry, using against us the very Bible in which women's voices are authoritative. As New Testament scholar Kline Snodgrass reminds us:

> We need to take seriously that women are the source of specific biblical texts. Miriam's prophecy, Deborah's song, Hannah's song, the words of the wise woman of Tekoa, and Mary's Magnificat are all beloved and *authoritative* passages, to say nothing about the words of other women like Anna who are mentioned in passing. Dare we suggest the voice of women may be heard in Scripture but not in the church?[6]

Including women of the Bible along with men of the Bible when illustrating biblical topics normalizes the reality that women leaders *are* and *have always been* a part of the redemptive story of God.

The Interpersonal Level

At the interpersonal level, implicit biases get enacted through interactions and encounters. These include the microaggressions that get displayed toward women leaders in everyday encounters. According to Elizabeth Hopper,

A microaggression is a subtle behavior—verbal or non-verbal, conscious or unconscious—directed at a member of a marginalized group that has a derogatory, harmful effect. Chester Pierce, a psychiatrist at Harvard University, first introduced the term microaggression in the 1970s.[7]

A microaggression is the seemingly small assault on a person's humanity based on their identity. Further, "gender microaggressions are the nonverbal and verbal ways in which sexist beliefs are communicated to women on an interpersonal level."[8] Using the taxonomy of gender microaggressions identified by Jioni Lewis, here are examples of how these gender microaggressions show up in our churches:[9]

1. *Sexual objectification* is the act of reducing women to sexual objects through word or deed. This occurs when men use the church as a place to prowl and pick up women. I have had numerous single women describe being "hit on" in church. As egalitarian pastors, we must maintain the safety of our spaces and confront people who violate our Christian relational ethics.

2. *Second-class citizenship* is when leaders infer that God only uses women when men are not in their rightful places. This belief places women in a second-class citizenship position and diminishes their true equality with men in God's sight.

3. *Use of sexist language* includes the use of male terms when referring to both men and women, such as using "men" or "mankind" instead of "humankind" or "humanity."

4. *Assumptions of inferiority* happen when teaching Bible lessons that infer women were created for and exist as subordinate to men.

5. *Restrictive gender roles* hold women to traditional roles in our church using a limited view of Scripture to support that view.

6. *Denial of the reality of sexism* suggests sexism does not exist in the church.

7. *Denial of individual sexism* occurs when church leaders deny their sexism. For instance, church boards and search committees may claim they could find no qualified women to candidate for a senior pastor role when key people on the search committee do not believe in women pastors.

8. *Invisibility* overlooks women's contribution in the church or ignores their voices in meetings.

9. *Sexist humor or jokes* used in sermon illustrations or everyday talk that demean or objectify women or that reinforce traditional gender roles.

Pastors and church leaders would do well to inventory their church practices for evidence of any of the above gender microaggressions and work to change practices that reinforce them.

The Institutional or Organizational Level

The above personal—and interpersonal—level barriers create a culture in a church or ministry that can be uncomfortable for women in leadership. The institutional-level barrier goes beyond discomfort to actually excluding women from leadership or from advancement. These types of barriers include the gendered practices, policies, and systems of the local church, denomination, or parachurch organization.

Denominational barriers

Despite more and more denominations ordaining women and giving top ecclesiastical leadership roles to women, many denominations still exclude women from full and equal leadership. Women can't serve in the highest ranks of these denominations because their polity excludes women from being elders or ordained clergy. Instead some will license women into special tracks for ministry (e.g., Christian education, missions, evangelism).

The leaders in one egalitarian local church I worked with were part of a strongly complementarian denomination. Women's ministry for the denomination was segregated to ministry to other women and children. Yet this denomination's polity left room for the local church to operate somewhat autonomously. In this church, there existed two cultures: adherents to the ministerial licensing traditions of the denomination in which women were licensed but men could be ordained, and members who had never been a part of the denomination and embraced far more egalitarian beliefs.

This church implemented a ministry training program open to men and women from the congregation responding to the call to ministry service in the local church. Women were included in the training program on the same level as men and anyone completing that certificate program received the same local license. Men and women were free to then continue with the denomination's gender-segregated parallel ministry tracks, but anyone serving in the local church was not segregated based on their gender. In this way, the leaders of this church instituted egalitarian practices while still within a complementarian denomination. Change starts small, but it does start locally.

Language barriers

The language church leaders use in the pulpit, in classrooms, in meetings, and in their writings reinforces a culture of inclusion or exclusion. As mentioned above, persistently using gender-biased language is a type of microaggression that hurts women, whether intended or not. Use gender-inclusive words such as *humanity* or *humankind* instead of *man* or *mankind*. Resist exclusively using the male pronoun to refer to God. Orthodox Christian theology reveres God as Father, yet Scripture provides insight into many feminine qualities of God. According to John 4:24, we are clearly told that "God is spirit," and therefore is not gendered as humans have constructed gender. In addition, there are numerous places where God is revealed through the use of feminine imagery (see Deut. 32:11; Ps. 22:9–10; 71:6; Isa. 49:15; 66:9; Hos. 13:8; Luke 15:8–10). The Bible even describes how Jesus lamented, desiring to gather the people of Jerusalem like a mother hen longs to gather her chicks under her wings (Luke 13:34). One way to honor the complexity of the nature of God is to unlock God from a gendered box. Instead of only using "he," periodically use God instead of the pronoun; instead of himself, use "Godself." It may sound awkward at first, but it will help you make the shift toward more inclusive language for God.

In addition, there are other ways to shift the privileging of male language that get people to think about our gender norms in language. For instance, a few years ago, I spoke on women's leadership development at a conference. During the question-and-answer time a young woman was rattled by something I had written in the opening chapter of one of my books. I had transposed the order of the names of the first humans. I referred to Eve and Adam. I wanted readers to think about their co-leadership and challenge the thinking around gender. This truly made her think!

Leaders, you can find creative ways to address language barriers in your church. Do a survey of your sermons and your training sessions and determine the ways in which you privilege men's experiences and language over women's. And then by all means make your language more equal.

Finally, let's face it, across Christendom we have hermeneutical differences that have led to the very definitional differences around women's roles in leadership. But if you claim to be an egalitarian pastor you must find resources and tools that help you be authentic to an egalitarian hermeneutic.

Intersectional barriers

Intersectionality is an academic concept that has entered popular culture and justice movements. First coined by critical race theorist and law professor, Kimberlé Crenshaw, intersectionality revealed the "conceptual limitations of the single-issue analyses"[10] in which gender or race, for instance, is the single issue. Intersectionality speaks to the ways intersecting power structures oppress and/or create unequal power dynamics for people. As a black woman, I have been aware of how both sexism and racism have created challenges for me in my ministry in church and in the marketplace. In my broader corporate work, in my early days as a rising corporate professional, I lost count of the times that some well-meaning coworker noted that I was a "twofer" for my company. This microaggression revealed their notion of affirmative action and their assumption that I was hired just because I am black and a woman, and my company could check off two affirmative action boxes by hiring me. It didn't matter that I had an advanced engineering degree from a stellar engineering program and a certificate in organizational development from an Ivy League program.

Yet in the black churches and parachurch organizations I was a part of I experienced being silenced, being put in my place as a "daughter of the church" who was to submit to the elder male leaders of our organization. These are just a few examples. But both, in my opinion, stem from a patriarchal culture that has erected barriers to the full inclusion of women and, specifically relevant to me, women of color.

I also have found that many advances of women into leadership have often focused on white women—intentionally or not. This focus stems from a privileging of whiteness and European ideas and ideals to the exclusion of African, Asian, Latina, and Native voices. Conferences and ministry events aimed at advancing women in ministry provide a platform for white women and very few women of color. Topics aimed at advocating for women in ministry and leadership often do not address the intersectional nature of issues facing women of color. White women leaders must become far more open to hearing the different experiences of women of color. As leaders of egalitarian ministries, we must be more intentional in diversifying our representation of women leaders to include the presence, experiences, and wisdom of women of color.

The Societal/Cultural Level

The barriers at this level include the memes and popular cultural images and narratives that reinforce women's exclusion from leadership or reinforce women in support or ancillary roles. We often use a phrase in church circles that we are to be "in the world but not of the world." The fact remains that the culture of the world influences the church just because we are in this world. Over the past few years we've become more sensitized to misogynistic culture that dominates women and leads to domestic violence, sex trafficking, sexual harassment, and sexual violation.

We are bombarded with images of women in print and video that situate women in a subordinate or subservient position. This explosion of sexual imagery in media has been attested to in studies and documentaries.[11] This proliferation of sexual exploitation in media is harmful to women and girls. "When women and girls are repeatedly objectified and their bodies hypersexualized, the media contributes to harmful gender stereotypes that often trivialize violence against girls."[12]

According to a review of sexual images of women and girls in media by UNICEF:

> A report by the American Psychological Association (APA) on the sexualization of girls in the media found that girls are depicted in a sexual manner more often than boys; dressed in revealing clothing, and with bodily postures or facial expressions that imply sexual readiness. In a study of print media, researchers at Wesleyan University found that on average, across 58 different magazines, 51.8 percent of advertisements that featured women portrayed them as sex objects. However, when women appeared in advertisements in men's magazines, they were objectified 76 percent of the time.[13]

These images are not only harmful to the wellbeing of women and girls, it also reinforces the concept of women as subject acted upon and not agent, as powerless not powerful.

Gendered leadership stereotypes also abound in our cultures. Almost two decades ago, a leading women's advocacy group documented the stereotypes that exist in the minds of CEOs around women and leadership. "Women 'Take Care' and Men 'Take Charge'" was the headline of Catalyst's research report on gendered stereotypes in the workplace.[14] Today, this double bind of leadership exists in all professions. If a woman is caring, she may be labeled as "office mother" and deemed not strategic enough for leadership; if she is a take-charge leader, she is labeled as not a good fit for the organizational culture or worse.

In church culture gendered stereotypes are evidenced by the positions in which women are afforded to serve. Make sure your church does not relegate women only to the nursery, children's church, or women's ministry. These are laudable and necessary ministries, but if they are the only places women are permitted to serve, you have in place a gender-segregated system.

We must continue to defy these stereotypes and expose our congregations to a range of images and roles for women. Studies confirm that women who are exposed to images depicting counter-stereotypical roles report stronger nontraditional gender role beliefs than women exposed to images depicting stereotypical roles.[15]

Consider the following questions as you reflect on the practices at your church or ministry. Does the congregation see women serving along with men? In your ministerial rotation, are women included in the preaching rotation? Are women and men equally scheduled to read Scripture and pray or serve communion? Are women included on your pastoral or congregational care team to be able to sensitively address issues for women (and some men) who would prefer to talk with a woman pastor? Do your church's print and digital images include women of a range of ethnicities in leadership roles or speaking roles?

Do your sermon topics include issues of gender justice and the ways gender justice intersects with racial justice? Do your sermons highlight the leadership of women in the Bible? These topics help to counteract the stereotypical images that serve as barriers to women of various races and ethnicities entering and advancing in leadership.

As pastors or church leaders committed to the full inclusion of women into leadership at every level, it behooves each of us to do an inventory of the barriers that exist in our church or institution and develop strategies for dismantling those barriers and opening access to women at every level of leadership.

Envision the Future Without Barriers

A few years ago after a seminary symposium, I got to spend some time with the leader of the symposium. We discussed my research, writing, and speaking objectives for providing tools that help prepare women for leadership in the church and beyond. He challenged me to envision what leadership could look like if we fully lived into the vision of the kingdom of God or the realm of God.

I envision the realm of God to be the place in which God, first and foremost, is sovereign and chooses whom God wills to do God's work based on God's grace. In this realm, God's choosing of each of us is not limited by our gender, race or ethnicity, social class, or personality. I envision a realm in which God's choosing of us to serve is not limited to certain offices prescribed by human hierarchy but is based instead on our gifting by God's Holy Spirit.

I envision the realm of God to be a place where God calls the very women and men that were created in the image of God into the service of God. I envision the realm of God to exist where men and women who have open hearts respond to the call and will of God graciously to serve together—each recognizing how we need each other to complete the mission of God. I envision the realm of God to be a place where God has gifted women and men and intended for every person to use those gifts in service to others and to God's glory.

What about you? What is your vision for your church? What is your vision for the women and men of your church to live out the realm of God here and now? Envisioning God's realm helps every church leader accept that the work of ministry and its leadership "is God's work, and God has enlisted women and men in a process that is led by Him. This insight helps to free the leader to trust and follow the leading of the Lord"[16] and not be limited or led by biases imposed by human systems.

Women's Ways
of Leading in the Church

DR. JEANNE PORTER KING

Over twenty years ago, I published *Leading Ladies: Transformative Biblical Images for Women's Leadership* to lift up four leadership archetypes that spoke to women's distinct ways of leading. I provided images and language about leadership that resonated with women. The book was hugely popular as women in churches, denominational offices, convents, and seminaries resonated with leadership images that were honed from women of scripture with examples of contemporary women leaders living out that leadership style. In two decades we've come a long way toward embracing women's leadership, but we still have a long way to go to ensure women's full inclusion in leadership of religious organizations. To that end, I have expanded those four images to six styles of leading that speak to the leadership capacity and potential of women today, especially for places that still limit women.

In this chapter, we will look to Scripture for biblical imagery that can help current church leaders recognize the leadership gifts in women around them. I will describe these six Bible-based leadership types and provide some examples of women who lead using each style and suggest attributes you as a senior leader may look for in recognizing these leadership gifts. These six images or types provide language that allows women to see their brand of leadership in the ancient Scriptures, while at the same time legitimizing women's leadership for today.

Puah and Shiphrah, the Midwife Leaders

In the book of Exodus, we are introduced to two midwives, Puah and Shiphrah, whom the king of Egypt commanded to kill all Hebrew baby boys as part of their midwifery duties. The two women were more than likely leaders of a network of other midwives that the king held responsible for the duties of all the midwives assigned to help Hebrew women give birth.

According to Drorah O'Donnell Setel, these midwives were two of "numerous women who play significant, although unelaborated, roles in the events described in" Exodus.[1] Setel suggests that these women's "stories may be remnants of a larger cycle that recorded women's as well as men's involvement in leadership of the people."[2] For the midwives, Setel explicitly argues, "The texts we do have imply that to the extent women provided guidance they acted in rebellion (1:17)."[3] Indeed these leaders of other midwives developed their own strategies for following God and resisting Pharaoh's scheme to murder Hebrew boys. Yet, in as much as the very nature of midwifery is relational, what we see with the midwives is an image of female leadership that is at once strategic and relational. What might the midwife type of leader look like today?

The leader as midwife tends to:

- See and bring out the potential in others
- Help to birth the dreams of others
- Encourage others to do their best and be their best
- Help others realize their potential
- Develop strategies that help develop people and systems

How to spot a midwife

Wanda[4] was a midwife leader. New to her church, she gravitated toward leadership and within her first year of membership, she enrolled in a leadership development program at the church. As a fairly new church member, she was sensitive to the need to provide mentoring for new members in order to help them connect to discipleship processes and become acclimated to the church. She asked about the feasibility of the church developing a mentoring program for new members. When asked, she agreed to lead a team to develop a proposal for how such a mentoring program could work. She eventually agreed to help facilitate the birth of the church's new mentoring ministry.

Leaders who are midwives help to birth the dreams and aspirations in other people, in groups and on teams, and within organizations. In contemporary leadership discourse the more popular terms are that of coach and/or mentor. Both of these are facilitating roles aimed at helping people reach their goals or navigate the culture of their organization.

There are women in your congregation who may be ready for leadership who see the potential in others and encourage them. Some of these women see the potential in your church and are capable of birthing new ministries that are needed. These women could be developed for discipleship, small group leadership, and more senior leadership. Leaders who help to birth others pay particular attention to leveraging their existing relationships while at the same time pushing others they work or serve past their own preconceived notions, limitations, or concerns. Midwife leaders have a passion for developing others. Listen for that passion and you can help them unlock their leadership purpose.

Priscilla and Aquila, the Partnering Leaders

Collaboration is at the heart of leaders who partner with others, and the New Testament provides an insightful snapshot of a unique couple named Priscilla and Aquila who partnered together to minister. In my second book, *Leading Lessons: Insights on Leadership from Women of the Bible*, I argued that "This husband-and-wife team of the first century exemplifies collaboration as a leadership strategy."[5] Collaboration entails identifying mutual goals for working together with mutual respect that enables each leader to optimize their contribution toward the outcome. Priscilla models this partnering leadership style.

First as we examine her in Scripture, we note that in each of the six times Priscilla and Aquila are mentioned, they are always mentioned as a pair, suggesting they were equal partners in ministry. As we are introduced to them in Acts 18:1–3, we learn they were expelled from Rome and settled in Corinth working as tentmakers. "Priscilla and Aquila would have needed multiple skills in various crafts to be successful in their business."[6] These skills could have included design, purchasing raw materials, negotiating, marketing, etc. Can you see how working together in the tentmaking shop could have also honed their skills for working in ministry? Leaders who partner can effectively accomplish most tasks when each has the opportunity to offer their specific gifts and skills. The effective leader understands the value of collaborating.

Further, the apostle Paul connected with them, as he also was in the tentmaking trade. He eventually traveled to Ephesus and invited them to accompany him. Paul left them in Ephesus presumably to lead the ministry there. Paul greets them in his letter to the Romans, calling them fellow laborers and notes the church "meets in their house" (Rom. 16:3–4; see also 1 Cor. 16:19 CEB). Priscilla was a valuable part of the leadership collaborative that Paul placed in Ephesus. So much so that Luke notes that this team mentored Apollos, an eloquent man, well-versed in Scripture, but he needed to be shown the way of God more accurately (Acts 18:24–26). As you see, Priscilla was a full partner in this pastoral teaching ministry and bears witness to an important church leadership role.

The leader who partners tends to:

- Seek out groups or teams to be a part of or to assist
- Work well toward mutual or collaborative goals
- Offer her skills and gifts in service to the whole, but does not expect to be a lone-ranger leader
- Jointly develop processes for working together
- Demonstrate the commitment for mutual interests

How to spot a partner

Thelma worked as a project manager for a large company. Though she volunteered in children's ministry, no one in her church knew of the leadership gifts she possessed. The leader of the women's ministry began to watch her. Thelma possessed a willingness to help with a number of ministry projects. She always said, "I just like helping." The women's ministry leader invited her to join the women's ministry leadership team, and within months Thelma was asked to serve as the logistics lead. Thelma's style of collaborative leadership grew clearer as she became a go-to person to partner with various ministry leaders on special projects. Creative and never desiring to take the spotlight, Thelma was often sought out to help with leadership tasks. Noting this pattern, the executive pastor of the church approached Thelma about serving in a newly created role that would allow her to lead special projects and partner with ministry leaders throughout the church.

The style of the partnering leader establishes mutuality very early on, so look for women who bring these collaborative gifts to their ministries. These partnering leaders demonstrate collegial respect for others in the ministry. They resist tendencies to work independently and include others in problem-solving and decision-making. They do their homework upfront to identify the potential benefits of working together; and they create a dialogue for others to buy into and commit to working toward the stated aims. They tend to be flexible enough to allow changes and modifications to emerge as they collaborate with others.

There are women in your congregation who serve on task forces, as project managers, and team leads at work. There are women in your congregation who faithfully attend small group ministry activities, perhaps never expecting to serve on a leadership team. Seek them out and engage them in ministry projects that can eventually lead to leadership roles. Pay attention to women in the congregation who gravitate toward small group ministry and take an interest in helping to include others.

Deborah, the Catalyzing Leader

Leaders who catalyze serve as sparks for the movement of other leaders. They are visionary and strategic. The Hebrew Bible tells us of a woman who was both a prophet and judge who ultimately catalyzed a movement of warriors to reclaim their community. That leader is Deborah. Catalyzing leaders are inspirational and transformative.

Indeed, Judges 4:4 describes Deborah as the "wife of Lappidoth," a phrase which scholar Danna Nolan Fewell argues could also be interpreted as "'woman of fire,' a designation that says more about Deborah's character than any familial relationship implies."[7] The passion of women of fire who are able to ignite the flames of others is really at the heart of the catalyzing leader.

Judges 4 and 5 gives us a glimpse into the current state of the Israelites in which the Canaanites had become occupiers, terrorizing the community. Deborah's song in chapter 5 gives even more insight into the harrowing conditions—the "highways were deserted, travelers walked along the byways." Village life in Israel ceased. (5:7, NKJV).

Yet Scripture tells us that "Deborah arose" (5:7). In fact, Scripture says Deborah "arose, arose a mother in Israel." What a powerful testament to the imagery of mother as leader. Too often in patriarchal cultures mother is limited to nurturer, and father is elevated as the dominant leadership motif. But not so with Deborah—she ignites vivid imagery of and for women leaders.

Deborah arose to catalyze Barak the military general who in turn galvanized his troops. In so doing, Deborah inspired leaders to rise and lead (5:2) and to ultimately bring their envisioned peace back to their community.

The leader as catalyst tends to:

- Envision God's preferred future for their community or organization or for their part of the organization
- Inspire entire groups and organizations to envision a better future
- Rally the troops around a vision
- Galvanize volunteers to serve
- Shape reality for others and help make meaning

How to spot a catalizer

Jenna served as a volunteer consultant to a large church for nearly ten years before being asked to join the pastoral staff. The pastor recognized that spark in Jenna and hired her onto the pastoral team to launch a new department that focused on the development of staff and volunteer leaders. Jenna had the education, experience, and passion for leadership development and now was being given the opportunity to launch a new department based on her unique gifting and the distinct needs of the church at that time.

Catalyzing leaders share their passion for new visions and projects, and they ignite passion in others. They create energy and enthusiasm for proposed changes without appearing to give a hard sell. They take the time to understand others' values and aspirations and seek to help them move toward the collective vision.

There are women in every one of our congregations who inspire us to be our best. They are women of faith who spark faith in others. They don't ignore the realities of the day, but they envision or align with the vision for the church and congregation and help move people forward toward their goals. They have a motivational gift. Listen to them paint the picture of a hopeful future. Get them involved in leading your church forward.

Lydia, the Influencing Leader

An influencer is one who gains the commitment of others by persuasion and the strategic use of power. Influencers do not overpower with their words or actions. Instead they effect change in people, teams, and organizations for the good of all. Influencers are persuasive.

Acts of the Apostles tells the story of a woman in Philippi who was part of a prayer meeting held on the outskirts of town down by the riverside. To this gathering the apostle Paul came, and his missionary crew "sat down and spoke to the women who met there" (16:13, NKJV). The text focuses our attention on a "certain woman named Lydia" (16:14). Lydia was a "seller of purple from the city of Thyatira, who worshiped God." According to Gail R. O'Day, as a woman who sold purple cloth, a luxury item for the wealthy, Lydia's "business therefore put her in contact with the elite of Philippi. The offer of her home as a missionary center and the information that she was the head of her household (16:5) suggest that Lydia was wealthy herself."[8] Lydia was a powerful woman who knew how to sell her goods. The Lord "opened her heart to heed the things spoken by Paul" (16:14). Lydia believed the message, and she and her household were baptized into the Christian family.

After her conversion, Lydia persuaded Paul and company to come to her house and stay. Lydia made a generous offer and the sense of the encounter lets us know she influenced Paul to set up his headquarters in her home. As a successful businesswoman whose clientele were people who used the purple fabric she sold, Lydia's house was large enough for the apostolic missionaries.

What is significant is that this businesswoman employed her skills of influence for the good of the ministry. Lydia used her power strategically in service to the ministry, out of which came at least two additional dramatic conversions—the slave girl being trafficked by sorcerers and the jailer who guarded Paul and Silas (Acts 16:16–34). Lydia's house became home to the church in Philippi, to which Paul maintained a close affinity (see Paul's letter to the Philippians).

The leaders as influencer tends to:

- Persuade others to move toward the greater good
- Use strategic power in order to accomplish their goals
- Convey their conviction about the rationale of a proposed action
- Gain commitment of others by selling them on a plan of action
- Communicate the costs and benefits of a proposed plan

How to spot an influencer

Leaders who influence set the appropriate tone that enables others to hear their pitch. They garner their facts and data to enhance their credibility and convey their trustworthiness and competence. When presenting a case for change, these leaders or potential leaders deal with resistance objectively using facts and data, not getting caught up in personal attacks. They work diligently to persuade others to commit and agree to the necessary next steps to move forward with the agreed upon plan.

Betty had a heart for sharing the gospel. It was her belief that every Christian should be engaged in evangelism. Betty belonged to a medium-sized church with a strong internal set of ministry programs but with little outreach. Betty capitalized upon what she saw as a gap and pitched to the senior pastor the need for a more formal outreach ministry. She was persuasive. As part of her development for this outreach ministry, Betty completed the church's ministerial training program and was invited to serve on a leadership team for a year in order to inculcate her into the ministry processes of the church and give her experience working on a leadership team.

Look around your congregation. Who are the women who influence others toward ministry or relational goals? Who are the women who may not seek a title but are clearly opinion leaders and influencers? Given opportunity and training and using models that fit them, these women could be developed into modern day Lydias.

Abigail, the Negotiating Leader

Leaders who lead through negotiation are adept at engaging others in mutual exchange. They see needs that others have and are willing to enter into give-and-take processes that ultimately end in solutions that are win-win.

Abigail was such a leader. First Samuel 25:3 describes her using a Hebrew word that gives the sense that she was "insightful," "intelligent" (NAB, NIV, GNT), even "clever" (NRSV) or "sensible" (NLT). Abigail was married to Nabal, a wealthy man whose very name meant fool and was described as "harsh and evil" (NKJV), or "crude and mean in all his dealings" (NLT). No doubt being married to such a man challenged Abigail.

During sheep-shearing season, Nabal received a visit from ten men of David, who had been anointed to be the future king of Israel, but was currently on the run in the wilderness from the current king, Saul. David's men came in peace, greeted Nabal respectfully, and requested food and supplies that were no doubt in abundance during the sheep-shearing feast. David's men informed Nabal of their own generosity in protecting Nabal's shepherds while they were in Carmel, so surely Nabal would see fit to be a blessing to David and his men now. The brutish Nabal scoffed at the request and insulted David, charging "David was a mere servant running way from his master. How dare David ask anything of me?" David's men reported all of Nabal's words to David, which in turn stoked David's anger and determination for vengeance. The making of one heated conflict was at hand.

In the meantime, one of Nabal's men came to Abigail, most likely knowing she would be of sounder mind. He explained all that David's men had indeed done for them. He implored Abigail to see what she could do to fix this impending mess brought on because no one could tell her husband anything. Sure enough, wise is the leader who can mediate, negotiate, or arbitrate a conflict. Verses 18–19 reports that without informing Nabal, Abigail took food and supplies, loaded up the donkeys, and instructed the servants to go ahead of her toward David. Knowing that David was coming to avenge his name, Abigail wisely sent gifts ahead of her.

As Abigail encountered David and his men, she reasoned with David that her coming was the Lord's way of keeping him from "shedding blood and taking matters into your own hand" (25:26, NET). In exchange for the gifts she had brought in response to his original request, Abigail assured David that God was going to bless him to be king one day, whether Nabal recognized it or not. She reasoned that as king David did not need the blood of Nabal on his hands.

As an astute negotiator, Abigail further implored David to remember her when the Lord brought him success (1 Sam. 25:31). Abigail got what she wanted—the preservation and protection of her and her household—while giving David what he wanted—respect.

The leader as negotiator tends to:

- Compromise tasks or tactics (not values) in order to get a needed change
- Facilitate a process of give and take to achieve desired outcomes
- Make personal sacrifices to resolve conflict
- Work hard to locate resources for the other person in order to help accomplish mutual goals

How to spot a negotiator

Leaders who negotiate are adept at setting the tone for eventually gaining consensus on a proposed solution. They do this by staying focused on the goal and creating space for dialogue between all parties involved. Because they are willing to give a little to get a little (or a lot), these leaders are good at recognizing and acknowledging what others bring to the table and how each person plays a role in getting to an eventual solution. These leaders stay focused on issues and the desire to achieve win-win, trusting that through a well-orchestrated dialogue, the solution will emerge for both them and the other people with whom they work.

Tonya is a negotiating leader. Yet she did not serve in leadership for the first ten years she attended her church. That season ended when the church's marketing director relocated, and Tonya's name was submitted as a candidate to head up the church's marketing team. The person who nominated her recognized her leadership gift, creativity, and keen eye for detail. The pastoral team invited her to serve in this capacity, and after a few short months in the role, she astounded the leadership team with her savvy for working with vendors and ministry leaders alike.

Miriam, the Choreographic Leader

Choreographers are connectors. They connect disparate groups of people, bring them together, and guide them into a unified dance.

As with Puah and Shiphrah, Setel includes Miriam's story as one of the stories in a larger cycle that recorded women's leadership. Setel suggests that Miriam's leadership was within a separate female sphere.[9] However, the prophet Micah credits Miriam with being part of the leadership team that brought the children of Israel out of Egypt: "I brought you up out of Egypt and redeemed you from the land of slavery. I sent Moses to lead you, also Aaron and Miriam" (Mic. 6:4, NIV). For people who tend to overlook or erase women's leadership in Scripture, Micah's aside here is significant to demonstrate women's leadership was legitimized in and for the ancient community.

Exodus 15:20–21 records a scene on the heels of the Red Sea miracle that brings Miriam's leadership into focus. "After such a great escape and mighty display of power, the people of God were finally free. Miriam took a tambourine in her hand and was inspired by God to lead the women in an exuberant and lively dance ritual, perhaps symbolizing the victory march of a conquering army."[10] Through movement and celebration, Miriam connected the women together to perform a ritualized victory dance.

Rituals help bring meaning to significant events, as well as mark points of transition. Miriam led the women in dance symbolizing the end of their slavery and the beginning of their freedom. Miriam led the women in dance marking the passage through the Red Sea as their identity transformation from slaves to God's liberated people. Spontaneous yet exuberant, Miriam choreographed freedom and victory into this dance, connecting the people to a new reality and to each other in new ways. Choreographic leaders connect us with each other, and they connect us with the purpose of God as seen in our own internal transformation toward the unified people of God.

The leader as choreographer tends to:

- Bring people of diverse backgrounds together by providing a unifying vision
- Be creative and develop routines for others to follow
- Show the significance of the steps or processes they manage
- Connect with other supporters
- Maintain their finger on the pulse of the organization

How to spot a choreographer

Choreographers are connectors and have the distinct ability to socialize in and span many different worlds. They are gifted at making acquaintances and friends and staying linked to them. Choreographers are connecting leaders who know people who know people. Yet, choreographic leaders know how to bring those people together for a connected cause. Look for the women in your church who are connected to multiple ministries and maintain a strong network inside and outside of your church. They can help build infrastructures of support.

Alison is such a leader. Alison's connections transcend her church but the gifts of connecting and choreography bless her church. For years, she taught Sunday school, but once she entered into formal leadership development classes, her gifts for connecting became evident. Alison now heads up an outreach program requiring her team to match families in the church with needy families and children in the community. Alison's extensive network never fails to come through for these programs that she has now led for five years. Like so many other women in churches, her gifts may have been overlooked, but instead she has been enabled to flourish in her leadership gift that blesses her church and the surrounding communities.

Conclusion

Women provide valuable leadership gifts that churches need now more than ever before. As you saw in this chapter, I have provided six images that can help you more readily recognize the latent leadership gifts of women in your church. Further, as you saw in this chapter, many women, though not all, need a little encouragement to assume leadership once roles are made clear.

Pastors, you hold the key to creating a church culture that is open to the leadership gifts of women. As a leader, you must provide diverse images, frameworks, and ways of talking about leadership that not only resonate with women but also provide a lens for leadership through which you can more readily recognize the gifts that already exist in the women of your church.

Broadening your models of church leadership will also help leaders create more inclusive images and models that welcome the gifts of women right alongside those of men. This chapter provides six images of leadership that can be a part of identifying and developing women for leadership and honoring women's ways of leading in the church. With these images, you hold the key to giving more women opportunities to lead.

Strategies for Coaching Women in Ministerial Leadership

ANTOINETTE G. ALVARADO, DMIN, THM

My relational experiences as an African American woman in ministry have been very affirming overall. These experiences have greatly enhanced my calling and have instilled within me confidence in my unique gifting. I practice ministry from an ethos of coaching relationships because of my life and leadership experiences. I strongly encourage pastors to develop coaching models in the local church to aid women toward a healthy sense of self-identity so that they can approach Christian living and the practice of ministry with a godly understanding of their unique identity, a positive attitude, and a clearer life focus.

Women's leadership and accomplishments are frequently highlighted today in articles, periodicals, documentaries, and books. Despite the strides that women have made, it is perplexing how so many women in the local church continue to search for significance. Women's involvement in the church community is marked by regular attendance, strong financial support, and dedicated ministry participation. Yet, many pursue life and ministry with little to no understanding of their unique story and experiences and how these relate to their gifting, purpose, and relationships within the community of faith.

So, why do so many women, who are significantly involved in the church, lack a clear understanding of their identity? What leadership coaching model would best address their needs? I identified several needs in the women who serve in leadership at Total Grace Christian Center. These needs include an understanding of God's sovereign work in their life experiences; authentic peer relationships; identification of values, personality characteristics, and gifting (both natural and spiritual); and a clear life focus. Although these women are contributors to the success of our local church, I presumed their effectiveness would increase significantly with a better understanding of self that included gifting and life purpose, thereby establishing a greater sense of community in our local church.

An Understanding of Helper as Leader

Susan Hunt and Peggy Hutcheson have an interesting approach to women and leadership in the church. Writing to help Christian men and women recognize and use the unique leadership talents of women, Hunt and Hutcheson suggest that the church is the most appropriate context for Christian women to be developed as leaders. According to them, women should fully embrace an expanded definition of the role of "helper," viewing it as a positive and powerful role.[1]

Traditionally, Western language has excluded women from the leadership conversation. However, transformative leadership models challenge the status quo and the pictures that come to mind when one speaks of a "leader."[2] Dr. Jeanne Porter King seeks to add female images to the language of leadership that empower and broaden our understanding of leadership. Whereas terms such as director, guide, pilot, shepherd, helmsman, father, or commander have been acceptable terms, new terms are being added to describe leadership such as coordinator, collaborative, support, team, and communicator, which are perceived to be feminine.

In ancient Greek, Roman, and Jewish societies women exercised leadership behaviors and responsibilities despite structures of oppression, silence, and seclusion.[3] Women in the early church served in liturgical settings, and we can identify when some of the oppression, silence, and seclusion of women began in the church. Feminist theologian Teresa Berger wrote a gender analysis of liturgical historiography where she discusses ways women have traditionally and historically worshipped. She states,

The earliest Christian communities grew in a cultural context where space was clearly gendered. Initially, Christian communities met in a space typically associated with women, that is in private homes, and they used that sphere's language, namely family-centered language, to describe themselves. "In church" was synonymous with "in the home."[4]

It seems that as the church began to organize in a more formal way, women were no longer welcomed to lead in the public setting. Women were distanced from the altar and prohibited from presiding in the celebrations. This move toward a male-dominated style of leadership resulted in a disadvantage for women in public worship spaces.[5]

Many women's liturgical movements emerged in the twentieth century that shifted the culture within the church. According to Teresa Berger, such movements typified the presence of women in liturgical practice and discourse.[6] Berger chose the term, "Women's Liturgical Movement"[7] over and against "Feminist Liturgical Movement," because she wanted to approach the subject from a broader perspective, including liturgies that focus on women specifically. These movements included men and women and advocate for liturgical gender justice.[8]

Through her preaching, leadership, and writings, Vashti McKenzie, the first female Presiding Bishop of the African American Episcopal Church, encourages African American women to explore freely their ancestry and rich heritage in leadership. She gives them no choice but to accept their leadership roles and to face the struggles and oppressive structures that women have faced since antiquity. One of the major ways to develop women in leadership, according to McKenzie, is to "help women develop strategies that are based on expressing their female strengths rather than denying their gender traits."[9] Coaching is an avenue for sharing power and information that will enhance women's self-worth and produce leaders who are confident and empowered.

When I reflect upon my foundational experiences, it was the significant relationships with men and women in my local church that shaped my early view of God, faith in Christ, and women in ministry. The church community where I belonged nurtured my leadership potential and afforded many opportunities to exercise my gifts of administration, leadership, and music.

Though I revered that church community, at age nineteen, I began to feel spiritually dissatisfied and began searching for what I sensed was missing. I visited mainline Pentecostal churches where I was trained to listen to the Spirit of God in new ways.

Many years later, after enrolling and dropping out of nursing school, relocating from Chicago to Atlanta, I understood God's call on my life more clearly. I gained an understanding of my unique gifting and leadership capacity and comprehended the vital role of the local church in the nurture, affirmation, and development of women in ministry. While the church in which I was raised served as the incubator for my ministry calling, I realized the church needed to develop an environment in which women could be coached in ministerial leadership.

Creating a Coaching Culture

Leadership studies have shown that God-ordered, foundational experiences in a future leader's life can be used as building blocks as he or she grows and matures. J. Robert Clinton refers to these life experiences in a leader's formative years as "Sovereign Foundations."[10] These "Sovereign Foundations" are factors over which the leader has no control such as, personality characteristics, parental love, birth order, childhood illness, prosperity or poverty, loss of loved ones, and stability versus constant upheaval.[11] How we respond to these factors will often determine our future leadership roles. Coaching can be an effective way to guide individuals as they build upon those foundational experiences.

Coaching relationships are very common in the business world. There is an increased number of top-level executives who are bringing in outside experts for one-on-one and group coaching. Because leadership is important to the life of any organization, these executives place high value, money, and training on optimizing the performance of those who are at the helm. Deborah Butler, Assistant Professor of Management at Georgia State University agrees, "I don't see it as a reactive measure as much as a proactive one. It says that this person is so valuable that important development dollars should be set aside for coaching."[12]

There are several partnerships and development programs designed to coach corporate executives and leaders throughout the United States and the world at large. It is interesting to note that books and professional articles on coaching often mention spirituality and values that are consistent with Christian principles. This shows that much of coaching in the secular arena has its roots embedded within the ethos of the Christian community. Therefore, the ministry of coaching is not a new concept to the Christian community but rather a revitalization of a relational practice that was common within Hebrew culture and the early Christian church.

The business world is realizing that a one-size-fits-all training and consulting program is ineffective for developing people and helping them reach their full potential as a leader.[13] Yet the church continues to place more emphasis on conferences, seminars, and training sessions for leadership development. Not that these vehicles for developing leaders are ineffective, but it is my hope that church leaders will view and value coaching as a way to develop leaders.

In their book, *Leadership for Women in The Church*, Hunt and Hutcheson report on the alarming drop-out rate of women who actively participate in the women's ministry of their local church. They suggest that churches develop ministries to address the challenges women face because the church has failed to invest in women's gifts, callings, and abilities.[14]

Further investigation of literature from the business, education, and psychology arenas concur that women maximize their leadership abilities when incubated in an environment that recognizes and honors the perspectives and experiences of women. Brenda McGlowan-Fellows, reflecting on corporate mentoring, states that "mental health executives, organizational psychologists, and policymakers have opportunities to play new roles to ease and shape a transition in corporate consciousness to achieve greater parity for all women."[15] I believe that coaching can fulfill one of these new roles by equipping women with the tools, confidence, self-development, and knowledge necessary for effective leadership.

To this end, I offer what Hunt and Hutcheson build as their argument for developing women for leadership. They suggest that such church leaders provide:

- A framework for growth and ministry within the context of the church
- A vehicle for women to develop and exercise leadership skills
- A means to unify the ministry of women
- A vehicle for women to support the total ministry of the church
- A safe place for women to cultivate nurturing relationships[16]

I suggest that the traditional ways of shaping and developing church leaders may also need to be reviewed and redesigned. According to Reggie McNeal, the spiritual formation of Christians includes personal spiritual disciplines, stewardship of relationships, work, and life mission.[17] If this is true, it is important to design programs that address such issues in a systematic way in order to develop leaders for twenty-first century life and ministry.

Edward H. Hammett suggests that coaching would aid church leaders in developing leaders in a secular age. Transformational coaching relationships can be "one of the most exciting and fruit-bearing modes of ministry" for women in the local church.[18]

In efforts to build leaders, Aubrey Malphurs suggests that leadership training programs target a limited number of maturing disciples. As these disciples grow and mature, experienced leaders should assess their gifts and abilities and assist in the development of their leadership skills.[19] Malphurs makes a strong statement and offers resources and tools for helping leaders clarify and articulate values; yet he does not outline for the reader a clear model of discipling in such manner. Therefore, I have taken the opportunity to explore further Malphurs' leadership principles by placing them in a context of women who had not pondered nor clarified their personal values. In leading these women through values discovery exercises, I found that stated values were a missing element in their leadership development and that any training of leaders must include values statements for various areas of their lives, work, and ministries.

A Case Study: Transformational Coaching Model for Women in Leadership

Among the most challenging aspects of church leadership is assessing the strengths and limitations of potential leaders and implementing the appropriate coaching strategies to improve their leadership effectiveness. In my tenure as co-pastor at Grace Church International (formerly Total Grace Christian Center), I have experienced successes and failures in the practice of leadership selection. Over the years, our pastoral team became increasingly aware of the importance of creating an environment that encourages members to explore and exercise their leadership skills.

In response to these concerns, I sought to provide a coaching program to train and develop women for leadership in the church, using models that have proven effective in many corporate settings. Administered in the local church context in the hope that it would be a viable tool to help women reach their maximum leadership potential, the program targeted identity formation, leadership development, and authentic relationships within the church community. As the women were motivated to discover a healthy sense of self in relationship to God, themselves, and the community of sisterhood, they were able to identify their unique gifts, values, personality traits, and life purpose.

Dr. Jeanne Porter King describes transformative leadership as "the movement of people toward collective and mutual goals of spiritual growth, higher purpose, and empowerment."[20] She further asserts that this type of leadership is about "freeing people to be who God called them to be and enabling them to lead according to their God-given gifts."[21] One key component is that transformative leaders "move people to places and accomplishments they dared not go or do on their own."[22] Hans Finzel picks up on this theme in his work, *Empowered Leaders*, listing various characteristics and contributions of transformational leaders beginning with the idea that these leaders are to remain open to God's transformational work in their own lives so they may, in turn, transform others, leading people to a closer, more intimate relationship with Jesus Christ.[23] This also includes inspiring others to excel and acting as a catalyst for change.

Throughout a twelve-month process, I implemented a series of coaching exercises that focused on: (1) the need for the women to see themselves as Christ sees them rather than be limited to the paradigms that have been prescribed by their environment; (2) the need to understand God's sovereign work in their life experiences; (3) an understanding of their unique identity as it relates to their personality characteristics and gift mix; (4) the need to make spiritual, personal, and professional decisions based upon identity, gifts, values, and life purpose; and (5) the need for authentic peer relationships for support, encouragement, and accountability. I was motivated by a desire to mobilize and develop women for leadership roles not only in the local church but to become a rallying point for women in my church who were leading in corporate, education, and community settings, as well.

Adopting the philosophy of transformative leadership, I served my pilot group as a leadership coach, remaining open and candidly discussing God's transformational work in my own life. In turn, God used me as an agent of transformation in the lives of the women of this focus group. Through the coaching relationship, these women were inspired to excel through their unique gifts and abilities and were anchored in their stated values as they were challenged to explore new paradigms for leadership in their lives and ministries.

Coaching is about asking, not telling. Begin by asking probing questions of your church culture and leadership milieu. Building upon the work of Hunt, Hutcheson, McKenzie, Berger, Porter King, and others, I offer the following questions as a guide for pastors and church leadership.[24] These questions serve as a framework for coaching and preparing women for ministerial leadership within the local church.

- Does your church offer women challenging, significant opportunities to serve?
- Is there a place in your local church for women who have gifts, training, and experience as executives, planners, implementers, etc.?
- Is your church an appropriate place for women to develop and exercise leadership skills?
- How does your church build upon the gifts of stay-at-home moms, empty nesters, and grandmothers, encouraging these women to exercise and value their leadership skills?
- How are women in various seasons and circumstances of life experiencing community as they grow and serve Christ together in your local church?
- What responsibility does your church leadership take in creatively developing women in ministerial leadership?[25]

Transformational coaching

Transformational coaching is a relational process that operates from the premise that change takes place primarily through experiences and relationships. Joseph Umidi asserts that the training programs and various programmed "experiences" in the church context offer limited effectiveness in developing leadership skills in people. It is, however, the relationships and experiences with God that spark significant long-term, lasting change and alter thoughts and behaviors. What makes the transformational moments in one's life memorable are the experiences with God and people.[26]

Transformational coaching is a form of "incarnation," argues Joseph Umidi.[27] Much like Jesus who left his frame of reference to relate to and serve humanity, transformational coaches serve others by leaving their own perspective or frame of reference to enter into the world of another. Therefore, the job of the coach is to engage the client and God in order to discern what God is actively doing in the client's life and situation.

Thomas Crane refers to transformational coaching as "applied leadership" whereby coaches bring their leadership to their life's work and relationships.[28] Transformational coaches are constantly aware of the effects their behavior has on the lives of the people around them. Through effective modeling of behavior and values, they build integrity in their lives and encourage a commitment to personal and organizational growth among coaches.

A transformational coach is a gift to the body of Christ. This type of coaching exists to aid people in knowing their true identity and destiny in Christ. They have the ability, through the Holy Spirit, to see the client's potential even when it is not apparent to the client. Joseph Umidi states, "The heart of a transformational coach is the heart of God: loving before changing, accepting before fixing, believing with unconditional love instead of judging according to religious conditions."[29]

The coach is not there to give advice or counsel. The coach enables the person being coached to transform their way of looking at their life, engaging God while connecting the dots to see the whole world. Coaching is helping people articulate the answers that already reside within them. In contrast to mentoring, where the mentor imparts to the mentee what God has invested in them, coaching draws out what God has invested in the person by way of gifting and life purpose.

"I don't think executive coaches change the culture of a company, but they can certainly help top-level team members work better with one another through a variety of mechanisms," says Sam Williams, president of the Metro Atlanta Chamber of Commerce.[30] This may be true of coaching in the secular and business world; however, Christian coaches have the power and ability through the application of biblical principles and values, prayer, and the work of the Spirit of God, to change the culture of their world and any world they have the privilege of engaging.

Coaching Techniques and Strategies

Leading in the twenty-first century requires that we develop techniques and strategies for reaching adults whose lives are very different than in previous eras. In his book, Hammett addresses the challenges of discipling busy adults in today's culture. He suggests that, with the advent and rise of single family homes, dual-career marriages, homeschooling movements, and increased community leadership and involvement, churches must make shifts away from the traditional models of discipling toward models that assist in filling the void of authentic relationships that our society desperately needs.[31] I believe the church is uniquely positioned to fill the relationship gap while providing ministries that will assist people in their efforts to rebuild their lives and recreate communities that offer wisdom, knowledge, support, and accountability. Therefore, Christian coaching is listed among a variety of ideas that Hammett and so many others believe would help churches create discipling relationships and structures to transform the lives of busy adults.

Coaching and mentoring can take place in a variety of situations and settings. These settings include one-on-one conversations, conferences, and classroom and group environments. The coaching milieu requires that coaches create an atmosphere where learning and growing can take place through active reflection and dialogue between the coach and the client. The following are some of the strategies and techniques I found as I researched and reviewed coaching methods that are being used in business, education, and corporate arenas.

Peer relationships

A key factor in the growth and development of emerging and established leaders is a network of significant relationships. In fact, some would suggest that it is the absence of authentic relationships that often contributes to the downfall and failure of leaders who succumb to the misuse of power, sex, and money. Paul D. Stanley and J. Robert Clinton offer a solution in their "constellation model" which provides leaders with a circle of accountability that will lead to their success and their ability to "finish well."[32]

The model includes a range of relationships that provide *upward mentoring* from mature leaders who provide wisdom, guidance, and insight that stem from the wealth of their experiences. It also includes *lateral relationships*, or co-mentoring with peers. These are relationships that we are naturally inclined toward because of commonalities such as age, gender, family, and work circumstances. Because these relationships are based upon shared experiences and familiar situations, they produce feelings of comfort and relaxation that create authenticity at a greater level. Finally, the model allows for *downward mentoring*, the developing of people who are following. Stanley and Clinton view this as the primary means for helping leaders develop their capacity to lead and a greater commitment to serve God and their communities.[33]

Diane M. Ruebling, president of The Ruebling Group LLC, a company that provides executive coaching, business planning, and performance systems, leverages peer relationships in her efforts to assist organizations. She states, "peer accountability is often an organization's untapped mine of transformational possibilities."[34] Ruebling refers to peer coaches as *action learning*.[35] This learning is facilitated through a structured process whereby peers make inquiries regarding specific goals, commitments, and actions that produce results, execution of commitments, and reflective learning. Follow-up on commitments are critical to the process because they produce increased awareness, alignment, action, and accountability among the peers.[36] In her study and work with peer groups, Ruebling has discovered that peers are more apt to break commitments made to themselves and their superiors, but they rarely break commitments to their peers.

Ruebling further suggests "the capacity of peers to coach peers and to hold each other accountable can literally transform individuals, teams, and organizations."[37] I have witnessed firsthand the power of peer relationships as a result of this ministry project. Each woman who participated spoke of the value of these relationships and the key role they each played in the success of the program and their ability to accomplish goals and gain a greater awareness of themselves and their unique gifts and life purpose.

Goal setting

A great deal of coaching centers around goals that the client has set coupled with desired outcomes for the coaching relationship. Setting a goal involves visualizing the final objective. It is making a decisive choice to reach a certain end.[38] Coaching is a goal-driven process that leads to clarity, motivation, and action in a client's life. The client sets the agenda and the coach assists the client is achieving goals that are specific, measurable, attainable, realistic, and timely (SMART).[39]

Robert Fashano reveals that goal setting begins with the ability of the coach to ask questions that will lead the client to clarifying and identifying obstacles, skills, strengths, and activities that will assist or hinder their ability to reach stated goals.[40] It is important to note that the responsibility for reaching goals is always placed on the client and is never assumed by the coach. The coach is most effective when guiding the client through a process that points out specific talents, skills, attitudes, and knowledge that is either present or needs to be developed for the client to reach their goal. Coaches play a vital role in expressing potential growth opportunities, support, and accountability toward set goals.

Assessments

Assessment tools provide coaches and clients with insight regarding the client's strengths, inclinations, actions, and reactions in certain situations or in relationships.[41] These are often used in the initial discovery phase of the coaching process. They are extremely valuable in revealing critical information about the client, establishing benchmarks for the clients' progress, and evaluating the effectiveness of the coach/client relationship.

The following lists some of the assessment tools used by many professional business and life coaches:

1. Personality assessment: The Myers-Briggs Type Indicator (MBTI) identifies where people prefer to focus their attention and get energy (Extroversion or Introversion). This also includes the way people prefer to take in information (Sensing or Intuition), make decisions (Thinking or Feeling), and how they orient themselves to the external world (Judging or Perceiving). The DiSC and StrengthsFinder assessments are widely used as well as assessments from Kolbe and MAPP.[42]

2. Aptitude and special interest inventories focus on specific leadership skills and strengths. The Strong Interest Inventory and Birkman inventory are commonly used among coaches.

3. Values assessments identifies values and behavior that produce alignment and results. As leaders are coached effectively, their sense of congruence with their values will increase.[43] The TLC Values Inventory and Values Statement exercises were used with the women in this ministry project.

Although assessments are valuable in gaining insight and direction in the coaching relationship, coaches are advised against an overuse of assessment tools. Assessments must be weighed properly for comfort level in both the client and coach. They must also be considered for their ability to provide the information necessary for effective coaching.

Weekly and quarterly coaching sessions

Many coaches conduct sessions on a weekly, monthly, or quarterly basis. The coaching session or meeting is designed to receive feedback on past and present goals and tasks and to reflect upon situations in the client's life and work relationships.[44] Obstacles that affect the client's potential for growth and development are explored during these sessions. This is also where accountability is forged, and the coach is afforded the most opportunity to gain relationship capital with the client.

Electronic coaching

Peg Boyle and Carol B. Miller report that the use of the internet and e-mail is providing "unprecedented opportunities for establishing mentoring relationships."[45] E-mentoring, as they coin it, is the merging of mentoring and coaching principles and techniques with electronic communications. It links mentors with protégés irrespective of geographic location and scheduling constraints.

There are advantages and drawbacks to e-mentoring discussed in their work. Some advantages are the increased ability of the coach or mentor to reach a broader population of women than face-to-face opportunities provide. Yet, the electronic medium of communication creates a greater need for a more structured program of coaching and mentoring and must rely upon evaluations to determine its impact on participants. For the purpose of this study, e-mail and conference calls proved valuable and necessary in order to communicate effectively with the participants.

Asking powerful questions

One of the most critical skills a coach must possess is the art of listening and asking powerful questions. Robert Fashano suggests that the art of developing people is allowing them to discover answers for themselves.[46] True transformation comes from the internal world and rarely from external or ethereal places in people's lives. Joseph Umidi presses this point when he suggests that transformation occurs when a person hears the voice of God and discovers their own voice and destiny amid circumstances beyond their control.[47] Many coaches agree that this is best done with powerful questions.

The temptation for most leaders and coaches is to tell, give advice, and even preach to their followers. Effective coaching conversations involve active listening skills. These skills include maintaining good eye contact, appropriate smiling and facial gestures, avoidance of internal and external distractions, note-taking when necessary, sensitivity to body language, restraint from interruptions, and occasional repeating of what the client says.

It is also important to note that active listening requires that the coach resist the judgmental and internal dialogue that will ultimately hinder the flow of the conversation. Transformational coaches must not allow their personal values, attitudes, belief systems, and experiences to interfere with their ability to listen effectively and facilitate growth and development in the client. The desire is to focus on the core dreams in another and serve as an advocate to call them forth into faithful stewardship of their own lives. Coaches can focus the conversation around the "5WH basic interrogatives": who, what, why, when, where, and how.[48] This line of questioning leads the client down a road that unearths true goals, desires, objectives, obstacles, and progresses that are often unknown to the client themselves.

Machen MacDonald outlines categories of questions that range from those that clarify and bring understanding for the coach and client to those that bring increased perspective and insight.[49] Transformational coaches must be creative, intuitive, and courageous enough to ask poignant questions. These powerful questions will ultimately reveal strategy for continued growth and development and produce the awareness that results in the client's alignment with their values, gifts, skills, and life purpose.

Summary

There have been increased efforts to mobilize and develop women for leadership roles in corporate, education, community, and church settings. The literary resources on this topic, as it pertains to the local church, seem to underscore the necessity for specific development of women to reach their full potential. Coaching is a tool that is useful and needed in the development of women.

Christian formation and discipleship can be linear at times, focusing primarily on the component of spiritual maturation to the exclusion of practical skill enhancement.

I suggest pastors observe women who exhibit leadership in the church, home, and marketplace. Once identified, a representative focus group of these women should be invited into an exploration process that confirms their leadership abilities, gifts, and skills. Each woman in the focus group I chose displayed consistent participation in the active life of the congregation and a willingness to participate in a leadership coaching program.

Focus groups should be demographically diverse. For example, my original focus group was comprised of both single and married women ranging from age twenty-seven to forty-five. Forty percent of the participants were married with children. Fifteen percent of the women were divorced with at least one child. The remaining forty-five percent of the women were single, having never been married and had no children. All of the women had some specialized skill or employment, and sixty percent of the women possessed at least a bachelor's degree.

This quasi-quantitative approach provides an environment for a leadership coaching model to be tested on a group of women measuring the growth of their knowledge and understanding of God's sovereign work in their lives, spiritual and natural gifting, personality characteristics, values, peer relationships, and life focus. A representative group of women among a congregation of any size can be assisted in a self-discovery process through a series of coaching exercises aimed at improving their self-image as they engage with a transformational coach, themselves, and a community of women.

The coaching program can be facilitated during a nine to twelve-month time frame and include group and one-one sessions with a trained leadership coach. A variety of reflective coaching and peer mentoring exercises can be implemented to reflect the core values of the program such as self-identity, life focus, life stewardship, peer mentoring, and community connectedness. Monthly group sessions can address such topics as authentic relationships, gifting, self-awareness, values-driven leadership, and purpose/destiny.

Each participant should be given the opportunity to work one-on-one in a coaching relationship that targets areas of potential growth related to character formation, relationships, and overall life-focus issues. The coaching sessions can be conducted via telephone or in person as the needs dictate, with additional correspondence via e-mail for support, encouragement, and accountability.

Paul Stanley and J. Robert Clinton's constellation model served as a framework for the relationships in the coaching program at Total Grace Christian Center.[50] This model included upward mentoring in which women interacted with the coach who then provided resources and experiences to foster what each client needed. The constellation model supports the idea of lateral relationships or "co-mentoring" with peers.[51]

The women of our focus group are exemplars of the values of coaching relationships. The group sessions, coaching sessions, peer and homework assignments provided them with a plethora of experiential knowledge. They continued to learn by listening to themselves and to others within the group. The most interesting aspect of their journey was their ability to exegete and gain knowledge from their life experiences and current cultural, work, and worship contexts. They readily exercise the power of their voice in the relationships they built with me as their pastor/coach and among their ministerial colleagues. Finally, near the conclusion of the coaching program, each woman was expected to identify another woman for which she could provide coaching to perpetuate the values of this program within the larger church context or community of women.

Case Studies in Church Abuse and Cover-Ups and How We Can Prevent Them

ASHLEY EASTER

The #MeToo abuse survivor movement hit mainstream media in late 2017, and quickly thereafter #ChurchToo and #SilenceIsNotSpiritual were born, spotlighting the abuses in the church.[1] But long before any of these abuse survivor hashtags were created, abuse was happening in our faith communities. In fact, there is documentation from the eleventh century of abuse and cover-ups in the church.[2] For as long as the church has been established there have been those who abused and covered up abuse and those who suffered at the hands of abusers.

The birth of the #MeToo movement gave a long overdue platform for survivors to share their stories. The extent and breadth of this new information makes it clear that the public, and certainly the church, has no excuse but to confront the issue of abuse. For years, the church has pointed out sin and abuse in secular realms while simultaneously forsaking its sacred duty to root out abuse among itself. The media highlights of #MeToo, and the like, only exemplified what was already there and brushed under the holy rug.

For years, many in the church have insisted on looking down at the so-often-called crumbling morals of the world. But with so many sexual abuse cases and cover-ups coming to light now, the church's integrity is being questioned in a significant way. In many instances, this is rightly so. How can we expect those who are not Christians to listen to what the church has to say when the church is neck deep in its own abuse scandals and crimes? It's time that we stop our hypocrisy, take a good look at ourselves in the mirror, and truly repent of our collective sin of abuse, cover-ups, and crimes. No more excuses. We have to get our moral act together on this issue, or others will continue to suffer just as we will lose credibility.

In my opinion, the greatest threat to the church is not outside forces, but our own failure to address the evils we have done. Young people are walking away from some of our churches in droves. I believe this is not solely because they are being "seduced by worldliness," as my childhood community feared, but because they will no longer tolerate the injustices their forebearers did. I say this as an ordained minister, a millennial, and a survivor of abuse and attempted cover-up.

If we want to reestablish the church as a moral authority, it is essential for us to care well for the people in our churches. We've got to put massive efforts toward creating safer faith communities. And this begins with you and me. In this chapter I want to look at two instances of church abuse scandals as case studies. We will examine the failures enacted in these cases and how churches can do better in the future. In order to care for people and represent God's people well, we must do better.

A Case Study in Church Child Safety Gone Tragically Wrong: Jules Woodson's Story

Jules Woodson is perhaps the most joyful person I have ever met. Her smile lights up the room, and she instantly makes you feel like a long-lost friend when she hugs you. Warm and bright doesn't come close to fully describing the energy she brings to a room. But despite her joyous constitution, Jules has been saddled with one of the most painful experiences known to humanity. She was selected, groomed, and eventually sexually preyed upon by a man who dozens of people, from parents to pastors, had placed their trust in—her youth pastor Andy Savage.

On January 5, 2018, Jules publicly shared her story of abuse perpetrated by then Memphis megachurch pastor Andy Savage when he was her youth leader.[3] The impact of the trauma greatly distressed Jules. It affected everything from her sleeping to her performance at school.

Twenty years before her public exposé, Jules gathered the courage to report the abuse to Larry Cotton, another pastor on staff, trusting that he would do the right thing and help her navigate the traumatic experience. When she reported the abuse to pastor Cotton, he seemed more concerned with whether or not she had "participated" than with Savage's actual behavior. He went on to encourage her not to speak about the event to anyone and told her that he would handle it. What followed was a gentle removal of Savage from staff without alerting the congregation or her parents about what had happened.[4] Jules tried to move forward and work toward her healing. Andy Savage moved on to become a pastor of a new megachurch.

Shortly after Jules came forward with her story on a survivor advocate blog, *The Wartburg Watch*,[5] mainstream media caught wind of it and suddenly it was in every major newspaper from *The New York Times*[6] to *The Washington Post*.[7]

When Andy Savage's new church heard about Jules's story, the pastoral staff responded to the public outcry. Andy Savage gave an apology, admitting to a "sexual incident" and reminding people over and over again that it happened twenty years ago.[8] In the apology, Savage continued to distance himself from the abuse and externalize the event rather than taking personal responsibility for the damage he caused. In the presentation to the church, Jules was painted as a person who just hadn't gotten over it.[9]

In summary, at no point did any of the pastors at his old or new church report the sexual assault to the police. It appears that none of the pastors felt the congregation should be warned until the story hit the mainstream news cycle, and none of the pastors seemed to feel sexual assault was a disqualifier from pastoral ministry. As the story of abuse and pastoral cover-up played out in the media, Savage's church seemed more interested in restoring his career than in the restoration and healing of his victim.

A few months later, Andy Savage issued a statement in March announcing his resignation from his position as teaching pastor at Highpoint Church. However, just 19 months later he filed paperwork with the state to start his own church.[10] In a letter to church members, Savage, referring to the sexual assault of Woodson in Texas twenty years earlier, said he "has come to understand he was wrong to make the story about him[self]."[11] Larry Cotton, the pastor to whom Jules first reported the abuse, also resigned saying he failed to protect her and should have reported the abuse.[12]

Six Failures the Church Can Learn From

The abuse of Jules Woodson is a tragic and detailed story that occurred over a number of years, so I cannot cover each and every misstep that occurred. But I would like to bring attention to six significant failures made by the church and then discuss how we can do better.

Failure to follow the two-deep policy

The two-deep policy is a firm rule that no minor in the church is to be left alone with one adult caregiver. There must always be two unrelated adults supervising a minor in the care of the church. When combined with other protection practices, this is a vitally important rule in child protection. While it will not protect in every case, the two-deep policy allows for additional accountability and a greater chance for another adult to be alerted to predation.

Predators are more likely to be detected if there is another responsible adult in the same vicinity, such as in Andy Savage's vehicle that night. While predators are extremely creative and will always look for loopholes, implementing the two-deep policy likely would have saved Jules from a world of pain.

Failure to report to police

Once abuse has occurred, many survivors like Jules bravely report their abuse to another leader or pastor, trusting them to know what to do. We must do more to train pastors and insist that when this happens, their first action step must be to immediately report the incident to the police. Attempting to investigate the report internally without contacting the police is a significant failure churches and faith communities make and one that furthers the impunity of predators. What is more, their failure to report the abuse can mean that survivors may not have criminal recourse when the statute of limitations expires.

Pastors are not usually qualified to address abuse on their own and doing so can have devastating effects for both survivors and the church as a whole. In addition to many states legally requiring clergy to report allegations of abuse to police, clergy are also morally required to report. Look at it this way: it would be morally unconscionable for a pastor who is not also a licensed medical doctor to try to diagnose and treat a congregant who came into their office with a medical emergency. In the same way, it is immoral and dangerous for a pastor who is not also law enforcement or a licensed trauma therapist to try to diagnose or treat a person with abuse allegations. Pastors simply are not trained, licensed, or qualified to address abuse on their own. When abuse is disclosed, no matter how farfetched it may seem, no matter how much you like or know the accused, no matter how much the accused denies the abuse or apologizes for it, reporting the allegation to the police and referring the victim to a licensed therapist must happen immediately.

Failure to support the victim

When Jules reported the abuse to pastor Larry Cotton, he asked what her involvement was. Minors cannot consent to sexual conduct with an adult because there is a power differential. Minors do not have all the legal privileges of an adult and therefore they cannot engage in equal power and decision making in determining participation in a sexual relationship. Nor can a congregant consent to sexual conduct with their spiritual leader due to the inherent power difference between them.[13] This is true from both a moral and a legal standpoint in many states including Texas, the state where Jules Woodson was abused.

When the abuse was brought to light years later, the pastors at Andy Savage's new church focused their support on Savage to the point that he received a standing ovation from the congregation and was permitted to keep his pastoral position. No effort was invested into seeking justice or healing for Jules, and she and the advocates supporting her felt shamed and demonized.

Victim blaming, shaming, or silencing is the complete opposite of a Christlike response to abuse. Celebrating predators, even those who publicly "repent," is incredibly damaging to the survivors and to the reputation of the church. The church's role is to support the victim first and foremost, to help them seek justice through the proper authorities, find healing through care from licensed professionals, and to place their priority on compassion and protection of the victim. This would have characterized a true Christlike response.

Failure to warn others

When Andy was asked to leave his first church, the leadership failed to let the congregation know what had happened so congregants could check with their own children to see if they had likewise been affected.[14] In fact, Savage was given a celebratory going away party, which surely gave parents and teens the impression that he was still a safe individual. Savage's new church only alerted their congregation when Savage had been publicly outed, and they had no choice but to address the situation.

Failure to warn others about predators puts vulnerable people in harm's way and is a serious safety violation. Covering for abusers, even those who are friends, makes many complicit in abuse.

Failure to call abuse by its name

During Andy Savages apology he admitted to a sexual incident but failed to call it by its name, a crime of sexual assault. The pastors he worked under in his old and new churches failed to do the same.

Referring to abuse as an incident—like Savage did—a mistake, a relationship, or a mere sin, detracts from the seriousness of the exploitation. Calling it what it is—abuse, sexual assault, a crime—is the only way to truly address the root of the issue at stake.

Failure to remove wrongdoers

Christians talk about repentance, but true repentance is not saying you are sorry or even shedding a few tears. True repentance means calling abuse "abuse," submitting fully to the authorities, and stepping down from positions of power. Church leaders and Christians need to recognize that a predator is not qualified to care for the souls of others. Repentance does not demand or assume forgiveness must be given from the victim because this is a deeply personal choice. True repentance willingly submits to the victim's choices for physical and emotional boundaries without guilting or pressing for reconciliation.

Only when the mainstream media held him accountable and there was a strong public outcry, did Savage step down from his position of power over vulnerable people. This does not represent true repentance on his or the church's part. It is merely a reaction to being caught. The fact that his pastor friends allowed this to happen places many innocent individuals at risk for abuse.

Jules Woodson is a hero. She not only suffered greatly during her abuse, but she bravely came forward with her story and is an inspiration to thousands across the globe. Without her grit and determination, Savage may never have been exposed. Truly she exemplified Jesus as she laid down her life and risked public ridicule, re-victimization, and persecution to tell her story so others might find hope and healing, and to protect others like her.

A Case Study in Egalitarian Church Abuse Failings: The Women of Willow Creek Community Church

I work full time in victim advocacy, focusing much of my attention on those who have been abused in church or faith contexts.[15] The great majority of victims I work with who have experienced abuse or cover-up have come from patriarchal churches where women are not allowed in upper-level leadership in the home or church.

I see a distinct connection between patriarchy and abuse.[16] In short, abuse is always motivated by power and control. Patriarchy is a system centered on power and control of males over females, and while I believe that not everyone who believes in patriarchal teaching is abusive, the system in and of itself is abusive in nature. Generally speaking, I hold a belief that where patriarchy is, there abuse will be also.

It's easy to point a finger at complementarian churches when you come from an egalitarian perspective, but patriarchy with its potential for abuse of power creeps into egalitarian churches, too. Thus, I want to make a point of doing a case study of a large egalitarian church abuse scandal.

For years Willow Creek Community Church, founded by Pastor Bill Hybels, was presented as a shining example of an evangelical egalitarian church. Hybels marketed his faith community as one that empowered female leaders, and indeed women were in high levels of leadership. Willow Creek was even slated to promote a woman, Heather Larson, as lead pastor upon Hybels's retirement, which seemed to display the ultimate show of equality-based leadership principles.

Despite their egalitarian exterior, equality-based relationships were far from reality behind the scenes.

In 2018 news broke that Hybels was stepping down from his position as lead pastor of Willow Creek amid allegations of inappropriate behavior, which included allegations of suggestive comments, extended hugs, an unwanted kiss, invitations to hotel rooms, and an affair with a married woman who later said her claims were untrue.[17] Allegations came from women who were working alongside Hybels in church ministry. Hybels denied or downplayed their accusations.

Despite requests by victims and some elders for an independent investigation, the church first did an internal investigation, eventually hiring a law firm to look into the allegations.[18] Both the church staff investigation and the law firm concluded that the allegations were not credible. Several church meetings were held in which the victims were made out to be liars "colluding" to destroy Hybels and Willow Creek.[19]

Public pressure forced the church to form an independent advisory panel to investigate the allegations. The independent advisory group concluded the allegations were credible.[20] As a result, the church leadership had to come back and apologize for the accusations of lying and collusion against the victims.[21] Bill Hybels denied the allegations and resigned in April 2018.[22]

Six Major Failures of an Egalitarian Church and How We Can Do Better

Failure to root out patriarchy

We must never be lulled to sleep in our egalitarian churches by thinking that because we believe in women in leadership, we don't have abuses of power, dominance patriarchal biases, and hidden agendas in our midst. Just as a person who says they believe in patriarchal theology can operate as a functional egalitarian in their relationships, a person who says they believe in equality theology can functionally operate with patriarchal practices. This subtle danger may be more frightening in some cases because the deception causes us to let our guards down.

Safeguarding egalitarian churches will necessarily include a robust look at the church leaders' practices, not just their theology. We must never assume a silver tongue is representative of a heart of gold. Egalitarian churches should undergo abuse prevention and response training led by qualified professionals. They should also create a safe reporting system, complete with third-party investigators, that is well known, easily accessible, and understood by the congregation at large.

Failure to acknowledge grooming

Grooming is the act of subtly, over a period of time, desensitizing a victim to abuse through words and actions. As reported in the *Chicago Tribune*, Bill Hybels nurtured relationships with women slowly by introducing sexualized language and touch.[23] He would slip this in naturally during normal conversation, which caused his victim to question whether it was an accident, or they were overreacting. Pairing this process with the fact that Hybels was their pastor, their boss, and the gatekeeper to their career advancement—a distinct position of power over these women—this manipulative behavior was nothing short of an abuse of power.

I spoke to a woman who experienced a similar abuse of power perpetrated by her trusted pastor. This woman was going through a spiritually and emotionally painful life event, and she reached out to her pastor for support and counseling. During their counseling sessions this pastor used her dependence on his spiritual guidance as an opportunity to groom and violate her while she was vulnerable. Counseling sessions slowly changed from spiritual guidance to conversation around sexuality and romance. These conversations turned into inappropriate emails and text messages from the pastor to the woman. Eventually the pastor physically and sexually exploited this woman. In addition to being extremely confused about the pastor's advances, the woman felt she had no recourse because of his position of power over her and her family. When the abuse was finally brought before the other church leaders, instead of acknowledging the grooming and coercion in this power-laden relationship, the other church leaders blamed the victim. They treated the situation like a consensual affair instead of abuse perpetrated by a pastor who had wielded his power over a woman in his care.

Every church should develop a safety and ethics policy through the guidance of a third-party professional abuse prevention service. These policies should make it crystal clear that any grooming techniques such as romantic and emotional conversations, calls, text messages, or emails are strictly prohibited on the part of the pastoral staff. And of course, all romantic relationships with congregants, including intimate and sexual touch or behaviors, are off limits as well. A pastor's failure to comply should be grounds for immediate removal and disqualification from leadership and ministry of any kind. The remaining church staff should protect the victim's identity while making a public announcement to the congregation about the abuse so other potential victims can come forward as well. Law enforcement should be involved immediately. All congregants should be made aware of the specifics of these policies and how to make a safe report if any boundaries are crossed.

According to the *Chicago Tribune*, complaints had been made against Hybels over the years, but it seems the staff pastors failed to see how this subtle sexualization was in fact serious grooming techniques that needed swift intervention.[24] When any sexual harassment is reported it must be taken seriously, no exceptions.

Failure to take women's voices seriously

Over and over again, women reported abuse or harassment by Hybels. Over and over again, they were disbelieved, discounted, and accused of seeking to collude against this powerful male pastor. For a church that claimed to value women's voices, they failed when the rubber hit the road.

We live in a patriarchal society and church culture. Both have taught men and women from birth that women are easily deceived, untrustworthy, and prone to cause men to stumble. Women's voices are routinely discounted. Patriarchy has been so ingrained in us that we have to fight extra hard to eliminate its ideology from our thoughts and actions.

When we experience fear—fear of church scandal or fear that a beloved spiritual leader might not be as they seem—we can slip into old patterns of silencing women out of self-protection. But we mustn't let our fear get in the way of our biblical values. When fear and uncertainty set in, we need to be extra vigilant that we are not slipping back into old patriarchal ways that demean and silence women for the protection of men.

One way we check our biases is by having a preset agreement that when allegations are made, the one making the accusations will be treated kindly and respectfully, and a third-party independent team will be brought in to lead the investigation. This helps us remove our own biases from the process while still taking appropriate actions.

Failure to have proper accountability

As far as I can tell, Hybels's elder board was mainly composed of friends, and Hybels remained largely in control of the pastoral team. His church is nondenominational, so they answer to no one outside of their staff. This lack of substantive accountability made it easy for abuse to be covered up and discounted.

Each church denomination has different structures, so there is no one-size-fits-all model for accountability, but accountability must exist in some shape or fashion. Who does a victim go to if the elder board or other church leaders refuse to hear their story of abuse? What is their next step if their local congregation will not take action? Every church must answer these questions and empower their congregants with the information they need to protect themselves. The best and perhaps only form of accountability available in the Willow Creek Community Church case was for the victims to go public with their painful stories and pray that others outside of the protectionist church leadership would hold Hybels accountable. The victims never should have been forced into a position where this was their only option.

As mentioned above, an official policy should have been in place where the victim was treated with respect and dignity and immediately put in contact with police and a victim-centered, third-party investigation team. Church leaders and elder boards should not be the gatekeepers to whether or not the victim receives proper care and justice. Formal policies should be in place that create a direct pipeline from victims to third-party investigators.

Failure to embrace an independent investigation

Not only did Willow Creek not have an adequate accountability structure, but they also thought they could handle investigations on their own. Instead of seeking an independent investigation, they initially chose an internal investigation that was led by Willow Creek's own law firm. This kind of investigation tends to be fairly unreliable in providing objective information.

Expert Boz Tchividjian explains the qualities of a truly independent investigation like this:

> When a practicing attorney or law firm is hired to conduct the investigation, the institution is in the driver's seat and the process is not independent. An independent investigator has a fiduciary duty to the truth, regardless of where it may be found. . . .
> An investigation that is legitimately independent means that the institution being investigated is not in the driver's seat when it comes to controlling the investigator.[25]

Police are the first line for independent investigation, but when an abuse claim is made where police are unable to investigate due to expiration of the statute of limitations, a truly independent investigation is needed. GRACE (Godly Response to Abuse in the Christian Environment) is one such resource for both church safety training and independent investigations.[26] Not only does GRACE teach about practical safety policies, but they also evaluate and make recommendations based on the individual culture of the church being trained so that they can help a church reach the maximum level of safety for their individual congregation.

Failure to create a space where victims feel safe coming forward

When the women came forward about the abuse they had experienced, one woman was fired from her church position shortly thereafter.[27] This left her wondering whether this was due to her decision to report the abuse. Credible women banded together to tell their stories in a reputable publication, the *Chicago Tribune*, and the church ridiculed them as "colluding" to take down Bill Hybels before an independent investigation took place. Disconcertingly, Bill Hybels was given a platform at the Willow Creek's "family meetings" to call these women liars, again without proper investigation of the matter.

Not only did these behaviors affect the group of women reporting, but one could conclude it created a culture of fear for other victims who might have considered coming forward. This climate of fear not only damages a victim's sense of self-worth and pursuit of justice, but it signals to predators that they are safe to abuse women in this church because it is not safe for victims to report what is happening to them.

Instead, Willow Creek should have immediately involved law enforcement and a third-party investigation team, and taken the church "family meetings" as an opportunity to affirm the women who came forward and encourage other potential victims to come forward and speak to the professionals.

A word for church leaders on behalf of survivors

I've spoken with hundreds of survivors and the common thread I hear from them is that they do not feel safe in the church. From pastor-predators to church abuse cover-ups, they don't find it safe to step inside the doors of a church building. Many of them tell me they still love Jesus, but would never consider entrusting themselves or their children to a church again.

I'd like to spend some time speaking about a vision of a safe church community, but before I do, I want to say a word about those who have left the church.

Leaving the church is a huge step for most survivors. It can feel like losing a family or even an entire social community. This often leaves the survivor feeling a great sense of grief and loss. The survivor knows that to many, they will be seen as an outcast, a backslider, or even a target for evangelism. But they may no longer feel safe inside church walls and have made the brave decision to prioritize their healing journey. As an ordained minister I beseech fellow clergy to refrain from judgement and shaming of those who choose to leave the church. Stop the blanket characterizations of sinfulness and backsliding and instead tap into your empathy.

Teach your congregation that God is not angry at those who choose to exit the church. After all, the true church is made up of all those who follow Christ, not a brick-and-mortar building. Prioritize safety and compassion for those who leave. Educate yourself on trauma to gain an understanding of the triggers and grief survivors face when abused within a faith context. Encourage survivors to pursue safety and healing, even if that means walking away from your congregation.

A vision of safety in the church

The church itself was founded on the story of an abuse survivor. In his time on earth, Jesus endured and overcame physical, emotional, spiritual, institutional, mental, and even sexual abuse (when he was forced to be publicly stripped before being lifted onto the cross). It's notable that Jesus was not ashamed or embarrassed to speak openly about his abuse.

Jesus understands abuse; he understands PTSD; he understands depression, which he experienced in the garden of Gethsemane; he understands feeling forsaken, crying out on the cross, "my God, my God, why have you forsaken me;" he even understands people not believing his story.

If Jesus understood and cares about these things, should not the church also seek to understand and care?

Our vision of a safe church is not complete without a clear image of Jesus. To walk in the footsteps of Jesus, we too must seek to bring the way of love and light here on earth as he did. In the very words of Jesus, love and light look like this:

> The Spirit of the Lord is on me, because he has anointed me to proclaim good news to the poor.
> He has sent me to proclaim freedom for the prisoners and recovery of sight for the blind, to set the oppressed free, to proclaim the year of the Lord's favor. (Luke 4:18–19, NIV)

Are we creating churches' environments that would welcome the beaten and abused Jesus if he walked through our doors? How would we respond if Jesus came to share his abuse story? Would we believe him? What if the survivor, Jesus, wanted to talk about his depression or feelings of being forsaken by God? Would our churches even welcome him?

The true answer lies in our churches' treatment of the abuse survivors and victims among us. As Jesus said, "I tell you the truth, when you did it to one of the least of these my brothers and sisters, you were doing it to me!" (Matt. 25:40, NLT). The way we treat survivors is a reflection of the way we are treating Jesus. If our message to survivors is not that of freedom, practical good news, recovery, and favor, we are not only disrespecting survivors but Christ himself.

Recommended Resources

When churches ask me for more information on how to keep their ministries safe, I provide them with the following resources:

1. Ashley Easter's Resources

Ashley provides custom abuse prevention and response training for church and ministry staff, and speaks about abuse and healing at both faith and secular events. She is a mindset life coach for survivors of abuse and those who wish to step into the role of social justice advocate, helping them break free from limiting beliefs, walk in peace and freedom, and find their true calling and potential. Ashley is the founder of Courage 365, home of The Courage Conference, a yearly event that exists to be a refuge for survivors, educate and empower advocates, and create the conditions where this movement for change can raise a justice generation that recognizes and resists abuse everywhere. Learn more at www.AshleyEaster.com and www.Courage365.org.

2. GRACE (Godly Response to Abuse in the Christian Environment)

GRACE provides top quality training, independent investigations, organizational assessments, safeguarding certifications, videos, articles, and more—all with the goal of safeguarding churches and Christian ministries. Learn more at www.netGrace.org.

3. For Such A Time As This Rally

For Such A Time as This Rally is an organization named after Queen Esther's bold words in the face of possible death. This organization is a group of concerned Christians standing for change in the church's treatment of women and all abuse survivors. Find resource lists, rallies, activism opportunities, and more at www.ForSuchATimeAs ThisRally.com.

4. SNAP (Survivors Network of Those Abused by Priests)

SNAP is an independent, peer network of survivors of institutional sexual abuse and their supporters. They host national conferences, local peer support groups, and hotlines. SNAP is on the forefront of creating legislative change on behalf of survivors. Learn more at www.SNAPNetwork.org.

5. Jimmy Hinton Ministries

Pastor and son of a convicted sexual predator, Jimmy Hinton educates churches on abuse prevention through speaking, consulting, educational podcasts, videos, and more. Learn more at his website, www.JimmyHinton.org.

Developing a Code of Conduct: Ensuring Protection of Women, Children, and Vulnerable People

NICOLA LOCK

You are the light of the world. A town built on a hill cannot be hidden. Neither do people light a lamp and put it under a bowl. Instead they put it on its stand, and it gives light to everyone in the house. In the same way, let your light shine before others, that they may see your good deeds and glorify your Father in heaven. (Matt. 5:14-16, NIV)

Matthew 5 exhorts us to bring glory to God through our good works, living our Christian lives, following God's teachings as set out for us in scripture, and being an example and witness to those around us. The violence against women, children, and vulnerable people that has occurred in Christian churches and homes does not hold up the Christian community as "the light of the world." Faith leaders are uniquely positioned to influence their communities regarding cultural values related to the protection of women and children.

Faith leaders can speak with a unique moral authority and credibility and represent often very large numbers of people. At community and congregation level, where they have a permanent presence, and often at national and even international levels as well, they hold respected positions; they are listened to.[1]

This chapter seeks to inform and resource church leaders in the matter of creating a safe environment for women, children, and vulnerable people in a context of gender equality. Through development and implementation of clear and simple policies on professional standards that give guidelines for godly behavior—codes of conduct[2]—the church can model to the surrounding world how all whom God created can be treated equally, remain safe, and be protected.

Introduction

I have been involved in the work of professional standards for over twenty years in a variety of roles: seeing victims of clergy abuse in my counseling practice, working as a contact person for those coming forward with complaints of sexual misconduct in the church, and consulting for the Anglican Church in Australia to develop policy in the area of professional standards and safeguarding.[3]

Guidelines and standards for conduct in the Anglican Church of Australia were first introduced in 1999, when the Anglican Diocese of Sydney established their fledgling professional standards unit to deal with sexual misconduct by the clergy in response to criticisms that followed the Wood Royal Commission. This commission examined corruption within the New South Wales police force and the existence of criminal gangs abusing children sexually. One shameful outcome of that commission was the statement in the final report that

> [M]any churches, educational bodies, and other government and non-government organizations had adopted practices which were better designed to protect themselves and offenders, than to expose the latter.[4]

To counter these sad accusations, the Anglican Church in Sydney set up a formal process for handling allegations of abuse. This process would support victims with trained counselors and financial assistance, while also providing accountability and disciplinary measures for perpetrators.

In my role as contact person, I would meet with people coming forward with stories of sexual misconduct, document the story, and then send my report into the professional standards unit. The first story I heard was from Alisha (name has been changed), a young woman in her early twenties who had been abused by the youth minister in her church about five years previously. Despite knowing about sexual abuse occurring, it was shocking to me that this was happening in my church denomination in a very ordinary suburban church. Generously Alisha has allowed me to tell her story to assist others in understanding how this can occur (details have been changed to protect her identity).

Alisha was the third child in a family of four children; she had two older sisters and one younger brother. After a three-year long struggle with cancer, her mother died when she was fourteen. During that time the children largely looked after themselves and each other, as their father was busy working, bringing in the money that paid for their housing, food, and medical costs. It was a very stressful time, but Alisha found friendship and meaning through her local church. Alisha was a quiet, shy girl who loved small children and was keen to volunteer for the Sunday school when the youth minister put out a notice that he was looking for volunteers.

Soon after her mother died, the youth minister started paying special attention to Alisha, inviting her to his house next to the church for one-on-one Bible study to help her with her work in the Sunday school. Alisha was a little uncertain about going, but his wife was usually at home, busy with their small children in the room next to where she met with the youth minister. After some months, something changed with these meetings: often the wife was not home, and the youth minister insisted on sitting very close to her when they prayed at the end of their study. Again, Alisha was not comfortable, but she thought she had to obey what the minister asked of her.

She got tense and uncomfortable sitting next to him, and after a few of these meetings the minister commented on her not being relaxed. He suggested that he could help her get relaxed so they could pray together well and their prayers would be more effective for the children in Sunday school. What happened next was a complete shock for Alisha and she froze: the youth minister put his hands under her blouse and massaged her breasts, inviting her to relax. Eventually their prayer time was over and Alisha was able to leave.

Alisha was in such a state that she didn't know what to do. She felt dirty and disgusted and ashamed of herself. She felt there was no one she could tell—her sisters were very busy with their schoolwork and housework, and it didn't feel like the sort of thing she could tell her father. Also, she was terrified about meeting with the youth minister the following week to plan Sunday school. In the end she didn't tell anyone, and she felt she had to meet with him again.

Sadly, when she did meet with him again the same thing happened. After a few weeks, she tried to talk with the senior minister, saying she was having some difficulties with the youth minister and wondering whether he could help her. The senior minister told her that she would have to meet with the youth minister herself and explain what those difficulties were. She knew she couldn't do that, so the only thing she felt she could do was to stop being a Sunday school teacher, which was a great loss for her. Here was a desperate young girl, recently having lost her mother, who had been abused by the youth minister and now had to give up her ministry to children whom she loved so much. Alisha didn't say anything to anyone about what happened for over five years.

Then she attended child protection training run by her church. At once she realized that she had been a victim of abuse and that what had happened was not her fault. She found the courage to tell the mother of a good friend who reported it to the professional standards unit, where she was able to speak with a contact person.

When the report was made, it was discovered that other complaints had come in about this man: he had abused several young women in several different churches. Alisha sought counseling and began to feel better about herself, but it took years for her to fully recover. Eventually a disciplinary process took place, and the youth minister was fired from the Anglican Church and his name was placed on a register of offenders so that he could not get work in another church. He never really admitted that what he did was wrong.

Sadly, this is not an isolated story. Embedded within it are all the hallmarks of an abuser, but also the ways in which a structured church process both brought the perpetrator to justice and provided a pathway for healing for Alisha. Alisha's story highlights how the dynamics of power and spiritual authority can fuel and provide cover for a perpetrator, but also how a structured program within the institution of the church allowed for a way forward from a terrible situation.

Why Should Churches Develop Codes of Conduct—Isn't the Bible Enough?

On one level it is disturbing to believe that codes of conduct are necessary in church communities, particularly for those who are ordained by their religious community to be a priest, minister, or pastor. It could be assumed that the formation process and vows taken at a clergyperson's ordination would indicate that they are "fit for office" and understand the standards required of them.

In the ordination service in *A Prayer Book for Australia*, the bishop asks those who are presenting persons for ordination whether those presented are "suited by their godly living and learning" and have been "examined" and "found fit for office."[5] The ordinands themselves vow that they "accept the canonical scriptures of the Old and New Testaments," that they "will take part in the reading of the Holy Scriptures," and that they will "strive to shape their own life according to the way of Christ."[6] Yet it is patently clear from the scandal of childhood sexual abuse in all denominations worldwide that these vows in and of themselves are insufficient to ensure godly behavior among our ordained clergy. Furthermore, there is widespread evidence that when those who have been abused in church contexts come forward with their reports, they have not been responded to well. The Project Anna, a research project established in Melbourne, Australia, to gather the stories of Christian women who had experienced violence, outlined how abused women did not come forward with reports to those in authority in the church because they feared an inadequate response.[7] More recently, an Australian investigation by the Australian Broadcasting Association (ABC) unearthed accounts from women who had experienced violence from their Christian husbands that showed them still receiving the very same responses from the church hierarchy that had been outlined in the earlier study.[8]

Provide Guidelines for Appropriate Behaviors

In his examination of the development of the code of conduct for the Anglican Church in Australia, "Faithfulness in Service: A National Code for Personal Behaviour and the Practice of Pastoral Ministry by Clergy and Church Workers," Garth Blake explains:

> In the majority of cases, abuse within the Church had occurred through the ignorance
> or confusion of leaders as to appropriate personal and professional boundaries in

their relationships. When coupled with loneliness, depression, and/or marriage difficulties this failure of understanding had led to the incremental crossing of these boundaries and had resulted in abuse.[9]

In addition to ignorance, Blake alludes to another contributing factor to the crossing of appropriate personal and professional boundaries in pastoral relationships—the unhealthy psychological and mental state of the church leader, which can include depression, loneliness, burnout, and marriage difficulties. This is supported by those who note that there are two types of offenders: those whose character is disordered, and the situational offender who may only have one victim or offend at a time of extreme stress in their ministry as described by Marie Fortune:

> At the time of the sexual activity with the parishioner, this minister is not functioning well personally or professionally. . . . This clergyperson takes little care of himself or herself and is easily overcome by stress. Thus, the opportunity to "fall" into a relationship with someone who is emotionally vulnerable and who holds the pastor in total positive regard to the point of adoration is a temptation to which the wanderer responds.[10]

My own research into clergy who access professional supervision for their personal wellbeing and the wellbeing of their ministry discovered that they valued supervision because of the accountability. "It gives permission to a discerning person to raise issues that they see I need to address because as it says in Jeremiah 17:9, 'the heart is more deceitful than all else.' Good supervision is essential to expose these things."[11]

Statistics of Abuse Against Women, Children and Vulnerable Persons in the Church

The World Health Organization (WHO) has been gathering statistics concerning violence against women and children for over 100 years. Their 2017 report outlines the following:[12]

• Violence against women—particularly intimate partner violence and sexual violence—is a major public health problem and a violation of women's human rights.

- Global estimates published by WHO indicate that about one in three (35 percent) women worldwide have experienced either physical and/or sexual intimate partner violence or non-partner sexual violence in their lifetime.
- Most of this violence is intimate partner violence. Worldwide, almost one-third (30 percent) of women who have been in a relationship report that they have experienced some form of physical and/or sexual violence by their intimate partner in their lifetime.

Along with their data gathering of the prevalence of violence against women, the WHO has examined what factors are either causative or preventative for this violence. Primary among the causative factors is unhelpful gender norms.

- Men are more likely to perpetrate violence if they have . . . unequal gender norms, including attitudes accepting of violence and a sense of entitlement over women.
- Women are more likely to experience intimate partner violence if they have . . . attitudes accepting of violence, male privilege, and women's subordinate status.[13]

These two factors point to the need for the church to be clear in pointing out unhelpful and wrong attitudes about gender relations. This means teaching that gender norms which promote men's privileged status and women's subordinate status and accept violence are wrong and harmful to women. It also means empowering women through education about what is acceptable behavior.

Violence against women and children in the church has been less systematically researched; however, there are recent studies on family violence in the Christian community coming out of the UK and US. Three major studies conducted in the UK in 2002, 2012, and 2013 uncovered disturbingly high levels of physical, sexual, and emotionally abusive behaviors among church attenders. Among Methodist church attenders, there was a reported level of 17 percent of respondents having experienced intimate partner violence. The main perpetrators of intimate partner violence were husbands and partners.[14] In a survey of UK evangelical Christians[15], nearly 10 percent of respondents had experienced physical violence or abuse at least once in their relationship, a figure not inconsistent with recent data drawn from Australian women and men in the wider population, (17 percent of all women and 6 percent of men).[16] A phone survey among church attenders revealed 19 percent being coerced into sex by their partner and nearly one-third being emotionally abused by their partner. A large-scale study in the US among conservative Christian couples demonstrated a 29 percent prevalence of sexual violence, with women being at greater risk of sexual victimization.[17] Another US study which examined the impact of women's religious beliefs and practices on their experience of abuse in relationships demonstrated that women who attended churches that did not accept divorce in cases of domestic abuse were more likely to be victims of abuse.[18]

For children, government figures in Australia put the overall risk of the four types of abuse (emotional, physical, sexual, and neglect) at 3.8 per 1,000 children in 2015–2016.[19] Worldwide figures are difficult to ascertain with accuracy; however, a 2018 study in South Africa reported the following prevalence of sexual violence against children:

> 9.99% of boys and 14.61% of girls reported some lifetime sexual victimisation. Physical abuse, emotional abuse, neglect, family violence, and other victimisations were all strongly associated with sexual victimisation.[20]

Following the Royal Commission into Institutional Responses to Childhood Sexual Abuse, we have comprehensive figures about childhood sexual abuse in churches in Australia. Nearly 7,000 survivors came forward and made reports to the Royal Commission. Of these, 58.6 percent of survivors were sexually abused in an institution managed by a religious organization, including places of worship, schools, and children's homes. In the US, while there are no complete figures, studies completed in the Catholic church indicate that sexual abuse of minors took place in 95 percent of Catholic dioceses between 1950 and 2002 involving 4,392 priests, resulting from 10,667 total allegations[21]. Of all survivors, 36.2 percent were abused in Roman Catholic institutional settings; 14.7 percent told of abuse in Anglican institutions. The majority of those abused in Anglican settings were male (76.4 percent).

Navigate the Dynamics of Power

The presence and necessary existence of power is a basic fact of human life. Daniel Migliori describes it thus:

> Experiences of both power and weakness . . . are woven into the fabric of life. Every human being indeed every living creature, possesses and exercises power to some degree. . . . To be human is to have some power, to be able to do something, to reach a goal, to make a difference in the world. There is no life where there is no power.[22]

Hence, we all need others in positions of power at times, but there are dangers when power is misused. When we use our power for our own benefit at the expense of those whom we are serving or ministering to, when we exercise power oppressively rather than cooperatively, we threaten to bring unhappiness and destruction to those around us and ultimately to the whole of creation.

Many pastors—under the pressure of being under-resourced, underpaid, and finding their congregations less than cooperative with their vision for the parish—may not recognize the inherent power they have in their position as pastor. The usual sources of power for someone in leadership (power based on their role in society, personal power supported by their education and expertise, and any cultural power they have by virtue of education, gender, etc.) are heightened by their spiritual authority (or role power), which is of particular significance for those who are ordained or in some way commissioned by their church institution.[23]

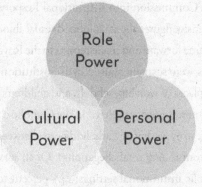

In these circumstances, the trio of role power, cultural power, and personal power can result in having a level of power that lends itself to abuses. The less empowered person may allow an abusive situation to occur because they give referent power to the leader due to of their level of education and position.

As in Alisha's story at the beginning of this chapter, it would be reasonable for a staff member of a church to be mentoring or praying with a volunteer in ministry. However in this case, the staff member made a number of serious boundary violations when he met with her. A code of conduct could have provided him with some useful guidelines about meeting with a younger woman, and assisted him to recognize his inherent power as a youth pastor, power which prevented Alisha from protesting about his behavior. The challenge to those in ministry is to be constantly self-examining our behavior to protect against abuses of power by naming our sources of power:

> One of the most important self-examinations we can do is to name our sources of power, for we are most at risk of ethical misconduct when we minimise or ignore our power[24]

Voice for the Voiceless

Research demonstrates that only about 30 percent of sexual abuse victims talk about what happened to them.[25] For 43 percent of survivors, the revelation of their abuse is accidental, often only revealed by eyewitnesses either at the time of the incident or later, or their stories are inferred from subtle remarks made over a period of time. There are a range of issues which prevent victims from being open either informally with friends or family, or more formally through a reporting process. These include their inability to understand what happened, shame, loyalty conflicts, fear of retaliation, and their belief that they are in some way to blame for what happened.

Many adult survivors have an ongoing fear of reprisal, or wish to protect their church or their families, or may feel stigmatized by revealing their history. Additionally, many have attempted to disclose but have received negative responses that make them reluctant to attempt to disclose again.[26] Alisha had made an attempt to tell her senior minister that "something awful" had happened but did not disclose the full details and was horrified when her senior minister suggested that she meet in a closed room with her attacker to "try to sort things out."

However, being exposed to a clear code of conduct is often the first time a survivor begins to recognize that what happened to them was abuse, was not their fault, and that their perpetrator is fully responsible for what happened. A code of conduct may give the survivor the language, understanding, and the courage to tell their story to an appropriate person, either a friend, family member, or person in authority. This is what happened for Alisha when she attended child protection training at her church. Finally, she could tell someone what had happened to her.

Failing to report abuse is not limited to reporting childhood sexual abuse. It is common knowledge that many affected by domestic violence do not report the abuse to authorities or tell their friends and family. People don't report domestic abuse for similar reasons as those who don't report childhood sexual abuse: confusion about what is happening, shame, fear of harm to the family unit, etc.

However, women still turn to the church for help with the problem of intimate partner violence. A US study details that 60 percent of persons who experience intimate partner violence will turn to their pastor for assistance.[27] An Australian study explored the responses women received when they reported domestic abuse to their senior pastor or minister. Of the women who reported abuse to their faith leaders, many were fearful of the response they would receive. And of those who did report, a large number received unhelpful or inadequate responses such as being told to "accept God's will," "suffer gladly," "keep praying for healing," or "be more faithful and the violence will stop."[28]

These inadequate responses emphasize the need for careful and dedicated attention to ensure that proper transformative policies and training procedures are put in place to guard against a continuation of violence against women and children in the home. Further, being trained in what is acceptable behavior in ministry circumstances often gives the abuse survivor the language and clarity they need to be able to name what happened to them as abuse.

Removes Blindness

It is clear in some cases of boundary violations that the offender was "confused or uncertain" about what appropriate boundaries were. There can be further confusion where surrounding cultural norms do not support the protection of women and children. When the Church of England wrote the first "Guidelines for Professional Conduct of the Clergy" in the UK, it was noted that the written guidelines would "alert trusted leaders to their responsibilities and increase the safety of vulnerable individuals within congregations. Such standards can serve also to guide pastoral accountability."[25] So the guidelines assist in both raising awareness about what is proper behavior and providing procedures for victim safety and holding perpetrators accountable.[29]

What Is a Code of Conduct?

When the Hippocratic oath first developed between the fifth and third centuries BCE, it was the first code for ethical conduct for a profession, with its emphasis on ensuring good and avoiding harm among those practicing medicine. The power of this code is demonstrated in its longevity; it's still the cornerstone for medical ethics in the twenty-first century and is still being sworn by those entering the field of medicine.

Developing and adopting a code of conduct has become the standard practice for many churches, institutions, corporations, and nongovernment organizations. They became particularly important in the corporate sector in the majority world when the drive to follow market policies with less government intervention gave much greater freedom to large corporations and businesses.[30] There is a challenge though to ensure the effectiveness of such codes of conduct: this can only be demonstrated when there is a concerted plan of consultation in the development of the code of conduct, and when there is ongoing investment of time, money, and resources into their implementation and continuing review.[31]

Furthermore, codes of conduct need to be backed up by legislative and disciplinary frameworks that ensure consequences for those who breach the code. It is of no benefit to have a code of conduct that is not used and cannot be enforced through any corrective action for those who break it.

Development of the Australian Anglican National Code of Conduct

The Anglican Church in Australia's code of conduct, "Faithfulness in Service: A National Code for Personal Behaviour and the Practice of Pastoral Ministry by Clergy and Church Workers," came about at a time when crimes of sexual violence against women, children, and other vulnerable people were being brought to the attention of church authorities in the early 1990s. It was apparent that simply expecting church workers to understand correct behavior was not enough to protect women and children. Hence, a code of conduct was developed that (a) was based on biblical principles, (b) sets limits that assist both the victim and the perpetrators, (c) teaches correct and incorrect behaviors, and (d) provides justice after a breach of the code.

It was first implemented by the National Synod in 2003. In 2017, in response to the Royal Commission investigation into sexual abuse of children in the church, this code was adopted by all Anglican dioceses in Australia.

Anglican Communion Safe Church Commission

In 2017, the worldwide Anglican Communion Safe Church Commission (ACSCC) met in South Africa to draft a policy for developing codes of conduct. The policy requires all dioceses within the Anglican Communion to develop a code of conduct describing standards of practice for ministry and providing support and help for churches in that development.[32] The ACSCC's hope is that the production and implementation of codes of conduct will lead to greater safety in the church.

Developing a Code of Conduct

This leads to the question of how to develop a code of conduct. The ACSCC report was adopted by the Anglican Communion in 2019 and the document "Guidelines to enhance the safety of all persons—especially children, young people and vulnerable adults—within the provinces of the Anglican Communion" (available in English, French, Spanish, and Portuguese) was accepted.[33] Other codes of conduct that may be suitable to adapt for your setting can also be sourced. (See the list of sample codes in the Additional Resources section at the end of this chapter.)

Process for Developing a Code of Conduct

The first step is to get commitment from leadership at all levels within your church, from the congregational leadership through any denominational or institutional leadership. Church leaders are those who can champion the establishment of a code of conduct within your churches and denominations. And leaders together can establish what the code of conduct should contain within the guidelines of the essential areas listed below.

Next, a sample or foundational code can be accessed that will give some guidance to the shape of any code of conduct you develop. From the samples, leadership at the regional or national level can draft a code of conduct that is suitable for a congregation.

The next key stage is to preview the draft code with stakeholders in your church community, both clergy and lay people, who can submit feedback. It is important to include victims of violence in these discussions, since they have personal experience with the ways abuse can be hidden and hard to see.

Once the code is finalized, develop a plan for implementation that involves an education process throughout your church. It is at this stage that resistance is often discovered. Any difficulties with a code of conduct, especially those dealing with local cultural issues, will need to be readdressed when introducing the code to a new community or region.

Finally, there needs to be an ongoing process of reviewing the code of conduct. This provides the opportunity to evaluate its effectiveness and allows the church to make any necessary changes in response to the review process.

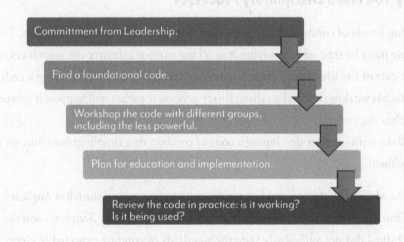

The code of conduct should address the following areas:

1. *Pastoral relationships*: (any relationship between clergy or church workers, and any person for the purposes of pastoral ministry) the nature of these relationships and how they can safeguard the best interests of those being ministered to
2. *Personal relationships*: define appropriate boundaries in ministry relationships including emotional, financial, physical, and sexual boundaries and the misuse of power
3. *Ministry to children*, including provisions for avoiding adults working alone or in isolation with children

4. *Ministry to vulnerable adults*

5. *Financial integrity*

6. *Confidentiality*: define how the confidentiality of information received in ministry is maintained and any limits to such confidentiality (such as where disclosure is required by law, especially for minors)

7. *Communications in ministry*, including the use of language and images, the use of technology, and the location and conduct of meetings, interviews, and conversations

8. *Reporting known or suspected abuse* by another church worker to the church authority, and relevant civil authorities such as the police and child protection agencies

9. *Responding to breaches of behavioral standards*: outline a fair process for victims and anyone accused of such a breach

Why You Need Disciplinary Processes

Having a code of conduct that is agreed upon is the most important first step. Then, people must be trained in applying it in all the various ministry circumstances that form part of the life of your church. Another crucial aspect of developing a code of conduct is working out a clear disciplinary process for what will happen if someone breaches the code.

Blake warns against developing a code of conduct that simply gathers dust on the office shelf:

> The adoption of the code marked a major cultural shift in the [Australian Anglican] Church by the recognition at the national level that the Holy Scriptures and the Ordinal did not sufficiently state the standards of conduct expected of clergy and church workers. At a more fundamental level it remains to be seen whether *Faithfulness in Service* gathers dust on the shelves of clergy and church workers or becomes an instrument to help change the culture of the Church so that it becomes a safe place for everyone.[34]

It is generally recommended that a panel of people are appointed to administer breaches of the code, people who are not in direct leadership positions. For example, the bishop in a diocese should not be involved in the process of dealing with those who break the code of conduct, even though the bishop may be the person who finally assents to any recommendation made by the panel. In some places these committees are called "Safeguarding Committees" or "Professional Standards Committees."

One detailed piece of church legislation from the Australian Anglican Church outlines the following as possible outcomes for the person breaching the code of conduct:[35]

(a) Making an apology

(b) Making of reparation

(c) Undertake training or retraining

(d) Counselling

(e) Resigning from their position, office, or position of employment

(f) Agreeing not to accept nomination or appointment to any specified position, office, or any specified employment

(g) Relinquishment of holy orders or request voluntary deposition from holy orders

(h) Exclusion from entry or access to specified church premises or activities

(i) That no further action be taken with respect to the complaint

Toward *Shalom*

Shalom is a rich concept that English cannot convey adequately in a single word, but which encompasses ideas of rest, peace, flourishing, and reconciliation. In his work on missional work and *shalom*, Tim Harris reminds us that in the Bible, "creation is depicted as an ongoing project in which order is imposed on chaos where God acts to bring light and order."[36]

Developing and implementing a code of conduct is concerned with imposing order on some of the chaos that can occur when human beings do not behave in godly and respectful ways to those in their care. This is going to take hard work and determination. I began this chapter with the illustration from Matthew 5 about being a light to the world, hence bringing glory to God. When violence is perpetrated against women, children, and vulnerable people in the church, we are not bringing glory to God but rather dishonor. Working on developing codes of conduct for your church is one step in the fight against gender inequality, shining a clear light on what is right and proper conduct for clergy and church workers and contributing toward the safety of women, children, and the vulnerable.

Harris challenges the Church to not limit the mission of God solely to personal salvation, but rather to ensure that we retain an emphasis on the mission of the Church which includes the flourishing of God's creational purposes.[37] Keeping an eye on the end point of *shalom*, we need to retain an equal focus on salvation and a redemptive mission for life on earth presently. By attending to matters of injustice on earth and working to reverse injustice and redeem victims of that injustice, we are equally working toward *shalom*, the way things ought to be. By shining a light on the issue of misconduct in the church which results in various forms of violence against women and children, the church is bringing order out of the current chaos. Harris challenges us thus:

> If we are to be true to the scope of the biblical narrative, then the mission of
> God is understood as the bringing of order out of chaos, of light prevailing
> over darkness, and in the fulfillment of the creation project manifest in the
> flourishing of all creation. Within this wider working of God, and into which
> all humanity is called to participate, the mission of God in redemption in
> Christ and through the Spirit brings personal and global salvation, wholeness
> and healing to all creation.[38]

Additional Resource List

1. Introduction to the Anglican Communion Safe Church Commission
    (International)

https://www.youtube.com/watch?time_continue=66&v=dh2w9j3cQV4

2. Anglican Communion Safe Church Commission "Guidelines to enhance the
    safety of all persons—especially children, young people and vulnerable adults—
    within the provinces of the Anglican Communion"

These international guidelines to protect the safety of children, women and vulnerable persons were approved by the Anglican Communion Safe Church Commission in 2019. https://www.anglicancommunion.org/community/commissions/the-anglican-communion-safe-church-commission.aspx

3. Guidelines for the Professional Conduct of Clergy (UK)

This code has been developed in the UK for the Church of England. In the foreword by the Archbishops of York and Canterbury, this code of conduct is called "a source of counsel, advice and comfort." They emphasize that the code should not be seen as something that is impossible to live up to or to implement. https://www.churchofengland. org/more/policy-and-thinking/guidelines-professional-conduct-clergy/guidelines -professional-conduct

4. Safe Ministry in the Anglican Church of Australia

https://www.anglican.org.au/professional-standards-commission

5. Ethical Standards and Standards of Practice for Ministry Personnel (United Church Canada)

This code of conduct was developed so that "ministry personnel may commit to agreed-upon standards of conduct that will guide their practice and behaviour." https://www.united-church.ca/sites/default/files/resources/ethical-standards -practice-ministry-personnel.pdf

6. UMSexualEthics from the United Methodist Church (US)

The United Methodist Church (US) has a website dedicated to "preventing misconduct and addressing it when it occurs."

   http://umsexualethics.org/

7. A sample code of conduct agreement from the Australian National Council of Churches can be downloaded here: https://www.ncca.org.au/safe-church -training-agreement/228...code-of-conduct/file

8. The US National Association of Evangelicals developed the "Code of Ethics for Pastors," designed to provide a consistent code of ethics that crosses denominational lines: https://www.nae.net/code-of-ethics-for-pastors/

9. The Australian Anglican Church's national code of conduct, "Faithfulness in Service," can be found here: https://safeministry.org.au/faithfulness-in-service -code-of-conduct/

10. A "Faithfulness in Service" video resource has been developed for use with rural and indigenous pastors: https://www.youtube.com/playlist?list=PLTj4KeEVypf D3QhiNDnphpYslSLo83WLr

11. The Baptist Church of Victoria, Australia, has a clear guide on developing a code of conduct: https://www.buv.com.au/documents/item/189

Appendix: Additional Resources on Abuse

Abuse

Why do women stay?

"She Didn't Realize She Was Living in an Abusive Relationship." *MJB Productions: A Woman's Place*, 2016. https://youtu.be/xwQDKjJZDN8.

Sanchez, Crystal. "8 Steps that Explain Why Women Stay in Abusive Relationships." *Ms Magazine*, May 11 2016. https://msmagazine.com/2016/05/11/8-steps-that -explain-why-women-stay-in-abusive-relationships/.

"Why Do Victims Stay?" *National Coalition Against Domestic Violence*. https://ncadv.org /why-do-victims-stay.

Types of abuse

"Emotional and Verbal Abuse." *US Department of Health and Human Services Office on Women's Health*, 2018. https://www.womenshealth.gov/relationships -and-safety/other-types/emotional-and-verbal-abuse.

Lamothe, Cindy. "Coercive Control: 12 Signs and How to Get Out." *Healthline*, Oct 10 2019. https://www.healthline.com/health/coercive-control.

"Power and Control Wheel." *National Center on Domestic and Sexual Violence*. http://www .ncdsv.org/images/PowerControlwheelNOSHADING.pdf.

"Six Different Types of Abuse." *REACH Beyond Domestic Violence*, Mar 23 2017. https:// reachma.org/6-different-types-abuse/.

Warford, Patricia. "Facing Nabal: Working with Men who Abuse." *Priscilla Papers* 28, no. 1 (2014): 11–13. https://www.cbeinternational.org/resource/article/priscilla-papers -academic-journal/facing-nabal.

Health effects of abuse

"Effects of Violence against Women." *US Department of Health and Human Services Office on Women's Health*, 2019. https://www.womenshealth.gov/relationships-and-safety/effects-violence-against-women.

Gluck, Samantha. "Effects of Domestic Violence, Domestic Abuse on Women and Children." *HealthyPlace*, May 3 2019. https://www.healthyplace.com/abuse/domestic-violence/effects-of-domestic-violence-domestic-abuse-on-women-and-children.

Sexual assault and rape

Hopper, Jim. "Sexual Assault and the Brain in 6 Minutes." *Youtube*, Mar 16 2018. https://www.youtube.com/watch?v=7G8weF4jsZw.

Mitsutomi, Marjo. "I Was Sexually Abused in the Church and I Thought I Was the Problem." *Mutuality*, Jan 15 2019. https://www.cbeinternational.org/resource/article/mutuality-blog-magazine/i-was-sexually-abused-church-and-i-thought-i-was-problem.

Moniz, Erin. "A Tale of Two Rapes: What Tamar and Bathsheba Teach Us about Power, Consent, and Sexual Violence." *Mutuality*, June 4 2019. https://www.cbeinternational.org/resource/article/mutuality-blog-magazine/tale-two-rapes-what-tamar-and-bathsheba-teach-us-about.

Randall, Mitch. "Theological Malpractice Stands Culpable in Sexual Abuse." Conference presentation, "Created to Thrive" conference, Houston, TX, Aug 3 2019. https://www.cbeinternational.org/resource/audio/theological-malpractice-stands-culpable-sexual-abuse.

Woolgar, Christine. "What I Wish the Church Had Told My Husband and Me about Sex and Consent." *Mutuality*, Nov 4 2018. https://www.cbeinternational.org/resource/article/mutuality-blog-magazine/what-i-wish-church-had-told-my-husband-and-me-about-sex.

Secondary abuse

Oltmans, Annette. "Understanding Double Abuse® and Its Consequences." Conference presentation, "Created to Thrive" conference, Houston, TX, Aug 3 2019. https://www.cbeinternational.org/resource/audio/understanding-double-abuser-and-its-consequences.

Yang, Amanda. "When Churches Don't Believe Victims, They Commit Abuse." *Mutuality*, Jul 2 2019. https://www.cbeinternational.org/resource/article/mutuality-blog-magazine /when-churches-dont-believe-victims-they-commit-abuse.

Christianity and violence

Baird, Julia and Hayley Gleeson. "'Submit to Your Husbands': Women Told to Endure Domestic Violence in the Name of God." *Australian Broadcasting Corporation*, Jul 17 2017. https://www.abc.net.au/news/2017-07-18/domestic-violence-church-submit-to -husbands/8652028?nw=0.

Fortune, Marie M. and Cindy G. Enger. "Violence against Women and the Role of Religion." *National Online Research Center on Violence against Women*, 2005. https:// vawnet.org/material/violence-against-women-and-role-religion.

Glassborow, Paula. "Unconscious Incompetence: Domestic Violence and the Church." *Common Grace*, 2018. https://www.commongrace.org.au/unconscious_incompetence _domestic_violence_and_the_church.

Hoppe, Steve. "I'm a Marriage Counselor. Here's what I Want Christians to Know about Domestic Spiritual Abuse." *Sojourners*, Apr 26 2018. https://sojo.net/articles/im -marriage-counselor-heres-what-i-want-christians-know-about-domestic-spiritual-abuse.

Luimes, Wilma. "Love and Power or a Powerful Love? Submission, Headship, and Abuse." *Mutuality*, Summer 2016. https://www.cbeinternational.org/resource/article/mutuality -blog-magazine/love-and-power-or-powerful-love.

Resources for Congregations

Asproth, Rachel. "30 Strategies for Fighting Abuse in the Church." *Mutuality*, Summer 2017. https://www.cbeinternational.org/resource/article/mutuality-blog-magazine/30 -strategies-fighting-abuse-church.

Easter, Ashley. "5 Steps for Churches When Abuse Happens." *Mutuality*, Mar 27 2018. https://www.cbeinternational.org/resource/article/mutuality-blog-magazine/5-steps -churches-when-abuse-happens.

"Know Your A to Z: Preventing Violence against Women Poster" (free downloadable resource). *OurWatch*. https://www.ourwatch.org.au/resource/know-your-a-z-preventing -violence-against-women-poster/.

"Make Your Church a SAFER Space." *SAFER*. https://www.saferresource.org.au/make
_your_church_a_safer_space#.

Medina, Gricel. "6 Principles for Guarding Churches against Predators." *Mutuality*, Spring
2018. https://www.cbeinternational.org/resource/article/mutuality-blog-magazine/6
-principles-guarding-churches-against-predators.

Pastoral response and prevention

Collins, Natalie. "Five Ways Pastors Unconsciously Reinforce Abuse, and How to Do
Better." *Mutuality*, Sep 4 2017. https://www.cbeinternational.org/resource/article
/mutuality-blog-magazine/five-ways-pastors-unconsciously-reinforce-abuse-and-how-do.

Huffine, Chris. "12 Reasons Why Couples Counseling Is Not Recommended when
Domestic Violence Is Present." *Allies in Change Counseling Center*, 1998. https://www
.co.washington.or.us/CommunityCorrections/VictimServices/Services/upload/12
-Reasons-Why-Couples-DV.pdf.

"Safety First: Responding." *SAFER*. https://www.saferresource.org.au/safety_first#.

Smietana, Bob. "How Pastors Perceive Domestic Violence Differently." *Christianity Today*,
Feb 20 2017. https://www.christianitytoday.com/news/2017/february/how-pastors
-perceive-domestic-violence-lifeway-autumn-miles.html.

Tracy, Steven R. "Clergy Response to Domestic Violence." *Priscilla Papers* 21, no. 2 (2007): 9–16.
https://www.cbeinternational.org/resource/article/priscilla-papers-academic-journal
/clergy-responses-domestic-violence.

Patriarchy

Scripture

Heath, Elaine. "The Levite's Concubine." *Priscilla Papers*, 1999. https://www.cbeinternational
.org/resource/article/priscilla-papers-academic-journal/levites-concubine.

Hinkley, Chesna. "What to Say when Someone Says that Wives Should Stay with Abusive
Husbands." *Mutuality*, Sept 17 2019. https://www.cbeinternational.org/resource/article
/mutuality-blog-magazine/what-say-when-someone-says-wives-should-stay-abusive.

Kroeger, Catherine Clark. "The Biblical Option of Divorce." *Priscilla Papers*, 1999. https://
www.cbeinternational.org/resource/article/priscilla-papers-academic-journal/biblical
-option-divorce.

Miller, Becky Castle. "Misinterpreting 'Head' Can Perpetuate Abuse." *Mutuality*, Winter 2017. https://www.cbeinternational.org/resource/article/mutuality-blog-magazine /misinterpreting-head-can-perpetuate-abuse.

Timm, Allyson McKinney. "When There Is No Justice in Scripture: The Rape of Tamar." *Sojourners*, Oct 12 2015. https://sojo.net/articles/troubling-texts-domestic-violence-bible /when-there-no-justice-scripture-rape-tamar.

Theology and culture

Asproth, Rachel. "Speaking of Justice: Ten Terms Christian Justice Advocates Should Know." *Mutuality*, Summer 2016. https://www.cbeinternational.org/resource/article /mutuality-blog-magazine/speaking-justice.

Haddad, Mimi. "How American Evangelicalism Has Been Weaponized against Women." *Mutuality*, Nov 13 2018. https://www.cbeinternational.org/resource/article/mutuality -blog-magazine/how-american-evangelicalism-has-been-weaponized-against.

Krueger, Tim. "If Anyone Can Abuse, Why Are We Still Talking Gender Roles? It's about Power." *Mutuality*, Jun 4 2018. https://www.cbeinternational.org/resource/article /mutuality-blog-magazine/if-anyone-can-abuse-why-are-we-still-talking-gender-roles.

Krueger, Tim. "Love and Respect: A Better Way." *Mutuality*, Spring 2016. https://www .cbeinternational.org/resource/article/mutuality-blog-magazine/love-and-respect -better-way.

Wartick, J.W. "Jesus Christ: God in Male-Human Flesh?" *Mutuality*, Fall 2015. https:// www.cbeinternational.org/resource/article/mutuality-blog-magazine/jesus-christ-god -male-human-flesh.

Preventing Sexism and Misogyny

Gender-accurate language

Ago, Sarah. "Why Using Gender-Accurate Language in Worship Is Important." *Mutuality*, Jan 30 2018. https://www.cbeinternational.org/resource/article/mutuality-blog-magazine /why-using-gender-accurate-language-worship-important.

Krueger, Tim. "Why We Need to Correct for Patriarchal Bias in Bible Translations." *Mutuality*, Dec 4 2017. https://www.cbeinternational.org/resource/article/mutuality -blog-magazine/why-we-need-correct-patriarchal-bias-bible-translations.

Wallace, Gail. "4 Reasons to Use a Gender-Accurate Bible Translation." *Mutuality*, Dec 4 2017. https://www.cbeinternational.org/resource/article/mutuality-blog-magazine/4-reasons-use-gender-accurate-bible-translation.

Mentoring

Weber, Leanne. "Moving beyond the Billy Graham Rule." *Mutuality*, Jan 29 2020. https://www.cbeinternational.org/resource/article/mutuality-blog-magazine/moving-beyond-billy-graham-rule.

Williams, Patricia. "Reforming Mentor Relationships by Rereading Genesis 1-3." *Mutuality*, May 20 2020. https://www.cbeinternational.org/resource/article/mutuality-blog-magazine/reforming-mentor-relationships-rereading-genesis-1-3.

Women in leadership

Cho, Theresa. "Mary and Martha: Women in Ministry in the 21st Century." *Sojourners*, Feb 1 2011. https://sojo.net/articles/mary-and-martha-women-ministry-21st-century.

Richardson, Jill. "The Subtle Hazing of Women in Ministry." *Mutuality*, Nov 6 2019. https://www.cbeinternational.org/resource/article/mutuality-blog-magazine/subtle-hazing-women-ministry.

Winslow, Karen Strand. "Women Priests and the Image of God." *Priscilla Papers* 34, no. 2 (2020): 23–30. https://www.cbeinternational.org/resource/article/priscilla-papers-academic-journal/women-priests-and-image-god.

BOOKS

Heath, Elaine. *We Were the Least of These: Reading the Bible with Survivors of Sexual Abuse*. Brazos Press, 2011.

Instone-Brewer, David. *Divorce and Remarriage in the Church*. Intervarsity Press, 2006.

Kroeger, Catherine Clark and Nancy Nason-Clark. *No Place for Abuse: Biblical and Practical Resources to Counteract Domestic Violence*. Intervarsity Press, 2010.

Miles, Al. *Domestic Violence: What Every Pastor Needs to Know*. Fortress Press, 2011.

Morris, Susan Yarrow. *Opening the Door: A Pastor's Guide to Addressing Domestic Violence in Premarital Counseling*. FaithTrust Institute, 2006.

Nason-Clark, Nancy, Barbara Fisher-Townsend, Catherine Holtmann, and Stephen McMullin. *Religion and Intimate Partner Violence: Understanding the Challenges and Proposing Solutions*. Oxford University Press, 2017.

Tucker, Ruth. *Black and White Bible, Black and Blue Wife: My Story of Finding Hope after Domestic Abuse*. Zondervan, 2016.

CONTRIBUTORS' WEBSITES

Antoinette Alverado: https://www.drtonialvarado.com/

Natalie Collins: https://www.nataliecollins.info/

Chuck Derry, Gender Violence Institute: https://www.genderviolenceinstitute.org/

Ashley Easter: https://www.ashleyeaster.com/

Mimi Haddad, CBE International: https://www.cbeinternational.org/

Jeanne Porter King: https://jeanneporterking.com/

Rebecca Kotz: http://www.rebeccakotz.com/

Annette Oltmans, The M3ND Project: https://themendproject.com/

DOMESTIC VIOLENCE HOTLINES BY STATE

In an emergency, call 911

United States National Domestic Violence Hotline: 1-800-799-SAFE (7233)

TTY: 1-800-787-3224

Videophone for the Deaf: 1-855-812-1001

Live Chat: https://www.thehotline.org/help/

United States National Sexual Assault Hotline: 1-800-656-HOPE (4673)

United States National Teen Dating Abuse Hotline: 1-800-331-9474

StrongHearts Native Helpline: 1-844-762-8483

Americans Overseas Domestic Violence Crisis Center: 1-866-USWOMEN (879-6636)

National Coalition against Domestic Violence: http://ncadv.org/

Alabama

1-800-650-6522

Alabama Coalition against Domestic Violence: http://www.acadv.org/

Alaska

CARELINE for Crisis Help: 1-877-266-4357

Alaska Network on Domestic Violence and Sexual Assault: https://andvsa.org/

Arizona

1-800-799-7233

TTY: 1-800-787-3224

Arizona Coalition to End Sexual & Domestic Violence: https://www.acesdv.org/

Arkansas

1-800-269-4668

Arkansas Coalition against Domestic Violence: https://www.domesticpeace.com/

California

Local Hotlines; see website below

California Partnership to End Domestic Violence: https://www.cpedv.org/

Colorado

National Hotline

Violence Free Colorado: https://www.violencefreecolorado.org/

Connecticut

English: 1-888-774-2900

Spanish: 1-844-831-9200

Connecticut Coalition against Domestic Violence: http://www.ctcadv.org/

Delaware

New Castle County: 1-302-762-6110

Northern Kent County: 1-302-678-3886

Kent and Sussex Counties: 1-302-422-8058

TTY: 1-800-232-5460

Delaware Coalition against Domestic Violence: https://dcadv.org/

District of Columbia

Police Headquarters Domestic Violence Coordinator: 1-202-727-7137

DC Coalition against Domestic Violence: https://dccadv.org/

Florida

1-800-500-1119

TTY: 1-800-621-4202

Florida Coalition against Domestic Violence: https://www.fcadv.org/

Georgia

1-800-33-HAVEN (42836)

Georgia Coalition against Domestic Violence: https://gcadv.org/

Hawaii

Kaua'i County: 1-808-245-6362

Honolulu County: 1-808-841-0822

Maui County (Maui): 1-808-579-9581

Maui County (Lana'i): 1-808-563-0216

Hawai'i County (Hilo): 1-808-959-8864

Hawai'i County (Kona): 1-808-322-7233

Hawaii State Coalition against Domestic Violence: https://www.hscadv.org/

Idaho

1-800-669-3176

Idaho Council on Domestic Violence and Victim Assistance: https://icdv.idaho.gov/

Illinois

1-877-TO END DV (863-6338)

TTY: 1-877-863-6339

Illinois Coalition against Domestic Violence: https://www.ilcadv.org/

Indiana

National Hotline

Indiana Coalition against Domestic Violence: https://icadvinc.org/

Iowa

1-800-770-1650

Iowa Coalition against Domestic Violence: https://www.icadv.org/

Kansas

1-888-END-ABUSE (363-2287)

Kansas Coalition against Sexual & Domestic Violence: https://www.kcsdv.org/

Kentucky

National Hotline

Kentucky Coalition against Domestic Violence: https://kcadv.org/

Louisiana

1-888-411-1333

Louisiana Coalition against Domestic Violence: http://lcadv.org/

Maine

1-866-834-HELP (4357)

Maine Coalition to End Domestic Violence: https://www.mcedv.org/

Maryland

National Hotline

Helpline (business hours): 1-800-MD-HELPS

Maryland Network against Domestic Violence: https://mnadv.org/

Massachusetts

(877) 785-2020

TTY: (877) 521-2601

Casa Myrna: https://casamyrna.org/

Our Deaf Survivors: https://www.odscunity.org/

Michigan

Helpline: 1-800-799-7233

Michigan Coalition to End Domestic & Sexual Violence: https://mcedsv.org/

Minnesota

Day One Crisis Hotline: 1-866-223-1111

Violence Free Minnesota: https://www.vfmn.org/

Asian Women United of Minnesota: https://www.awum.org/

Mississippi

1-800-898-3234

Mississippi Coalition against Domestic Violence: https://mcadv.org/

Missouri

National Hotline

Missouri Coalition against Domestic and Sexual Violence: https://www.mocadsv.org/

Montana

National Hotline

Montana Coalition against Domestic and Sexual Violence: https://mcadsv.com/

Nebraska

National Hotline

Nebraska Coalition to End Sexual and Domestic Violence: https://www.nebraskacoalition.org/

Nevada

Crisis Support Services Hotline: 1-800-273-8255

Nevada Coalition to End Domestic and Sexual Violence: https://www.ncedsv.org/

New Hampshire

1-866-644-3574

New Hampshire Coalition against Domestic & Sexual Violence: https://www.nhcadsv.org/

New Jersey

1-800-572-SAFE (7233)

New Jersey Coalition to End Domestic Violence: https://njcedv.org/

New Mexico

Legal Aid Domestic Violence, Sexual Assault, and Stalking Helpline (business hours):
   1-877-974-3400

New Mexico Coalition against Domestic Violence: https://www.nmcadv.org/

New York

Statewide: 1-800-942-6906

Text: 1-844-997-2121

New York City: 1-800-621-HOPE (4673)

New York City TTY: 1-800-810-7444

Ayaan Hirsi Ali Foundation Forced Marriage Textline: 741-741

New York State Coalition against Domestic Violence: https://www.nyscadv.org/

New York City Safe Horizon: https://www.safehorizon.org/

North Carolina

National Hotline

North Carolina Coalition against Domestic Violence: https://nccadv.org/

North Dakota

National Hotline

CAWS North Dakota: https://www.cawsnorthdakota.org/

Ohio

1-800-934-9840

Ohio Domestic Violence Network: https://www.odvn.org/

Oklahoma

1-800-522-SAFE (7233)

Oklahoma Coalition against Domestic Violence & Sexual Assault: https://www
.ocadvsa.org/

Oregon

Call to Safety Crisis Line: 1-888-235-5333
Oregon Coalition against Domestic & Sexual Violence: https://www.ocadsv.org/

Pennsylvania

National Hotline
Philadelphia: 1-866-723-3014
Pittsburgh: 1-412-687-8005
Pennsylvania Coalition against Domestic Violence: https://www.pcadv.org/

Rhode Island

1-800-494-8100
Rhode Island Coalition against Domestic Violence: http://www.ricadv.org/en/

South Carolina

National Hotline
South Carolina Coalition against Domestic Violence and Sexual Assault: https://www
.sccadvasa.org/

South Dakota

1-800-430-SAFE (7233)
South Dakota Coalition Ending Domestic & Sexual Violence: https://www.sdcedsv.org/

Tennessee

National Hotline
Tennessee Coalition to End Domestic and Sexual Violence: https://www.tncoalition.org/

Texas

National Hotline
Texas Council on Family Violence: https://tcfv.org/

Utah

1-800-897-LINK (5465)

Utah Domestic Violence Coalition: https://www.udvc.org/

Vermont

1-800-228-7395

Vermont Network against Domestic and Sexual Violence: https://vtnetwork.org/

Virginia

1-800-838-8238

Text: 1-804-793-9999

Virginia Sexual & Domestic Violence Action Alliance: http://www.vsdvalliance.org/

Washington

National Hotline

Washington State Coalition against Domestic Violence: https://wscadv.org/

West Virginia

National Hotline

West Virginia Coalition against Domestic Violence: http://wvcadv.org/

Wisconsin

National Hotline

End Domestic Abuse Wisconsin: https://www.endabusewi.org/

Wyoming

1-307-755-5481

Wyoming Coalition against Domestic Violence and Sexual Assault: https://www.wyomingdvsa .org/

Contributors

Dr. Antoinette Alvarado is the Co-Pastor of Grace Church International, Founder and Executive Director of My Sister's Keeper Foundation for Women and President of Targeted Living Coaching & Consulting, LLC. A dynamic preacher, teacher, and workshop presenter, she is also author of *Run and Not be Weary: The Pursuit of Purpose and Destiny*, *Stoking the Fire of Your Dreams*, *Harmonize Your Life: A Journey Toward Self-Care*, and co-author of *Let's Stay Together: Relationship Strategies for Successful Marriages*.

Natalie Collins is a Gender Justice Specialist. She is the author of *Out of Control: couples, Conflict and the capacity for change* and the Interim CEO of The Women's Liberation Collective. She set up *Spark* and works to enable individuals and organizations to prevent and respond to male violence against women. She is the Creator and Director of the DAY Programme, an innovative youth domestic abuse and exploitation education programme and of the *Own My Life* course for women who have been subjected to abuse. She organizes Project 3:28 (www.project328.info), co-founded the UK Christian Feminist Network (www.christianfeministnetwork.com), and has written a short book, *Gender Aware Youth Work*. She speaks and writes on understanding and ending gender injustice nationally and internationally.

Chuck Derry has worked to end men's violence against women since 1983. From 1983 to 1993, he worked with male offenders in St. Cloud, Minnesota, and was the men's program coordinator for six of those years. In 1994 he co-founded the Gender Violence Institute in Clearwater, Minnesota, and through that organization provides training and technical assistance nationally and internationally on the dynamics of domestic violence, criminal justice system reform, effective coordinated community responses to domestic violence, law enforcement investigations, rehabilitative programs for men who batter, and engaging men and communities in primary prevention. Throughout his career, Chuck has worked to develop and implement strategies and community initiatives for involving men and male leaders in the primary prevention of sexual and domestic violence, including commercial sexual exploitation, to stop it before it starts.

Ashley Easter is a Christian feminist, writer, speaker, TV producer, news pundit, ordained reverend, and abuse-victim advocate who educates churches and secular communities on abuse. She is the founder of The Courage Conference for survivors of abuse and those who love them.

Dr. Mimi Haddad is president and CEO of CBE International. She is a graduate of the University of Colorado and Gordon Conwell Theological Seminary (Summa Cum Laude). She holds a PhD in historical theology from the University of Durham, England. Palmer Theological Seminary of Eastern University awarded Mimi an Honorary Doctorate of Divinity in 2013. Haddad is part of the leadership of Evangelicals for Justice. She is a founding member and leader of the Evangelicals and Gender Study Group at the Evangelical Theological Society. She was a convener of the Issue Group 24 for the 2004 Lausanne III Committee for World Evangelization. She is an award-winning author and has written more than one hundred academic and popular articles and blogs. She has contributed to twelve books, and is author of *Is Women's Equality a Biblical Ideal?* with Sean Callaghan. Haddad is an adjunct assistant professor of historical theology at Fuller Theological Seminary and Zinzendorf School of Doctoral Studies. Mimi has taught for colleges and seminaries around the world. She currently serves as a gender consultant for World Vision International, World Relief, and Beyond Borders. She has appeared on podcasts with Daniel Fick; Fuller Theological Seminary's president, Mark Labberton; G.L.O.B.A.L. Justice; and Red Letter Christians. Mimi and her husband, Dale, live in Minneapolis/St. Paul, Minnesota.

Edith Johnson has served for more than forty years in global missions, both overseas as well as here in the US. She worked with world travelers in Amsterdam in the 1970s and then began working with international students in various universities, offering hospitality, and discipling young people. For twenty-five years she served as Advisor to Cornell International Christian Fellowship. Twenty years ago she returned to school to get a master's degree in counseling. Edith now works as a licensed marriage and family therapist, in addition to her ministry among international students. More recently she has begun working with refugees, and has been sponsor to one large Kar'en Burmese refugee family. Edith is a member of Global Member Care Network serving missionaries around the world. Edith has a passion for helping people heal and find wholeness in

Jesus, and for helping people grow in cross-cultural awareness and sensitivity as they understand God's love and plan for all peoples.

Rebecca Kotz is an advocate, speaker, community organizer, activist, liberation educator, consultant, and writer on sexual politics and feminism. She has worked at various social change and anti-violence organizations in Minnesota. She founded and facilitates a program for convicted male offenders, Men Accountable for Sexual Exploitation. She is currently finishing her master's degree in Social Justice at Prescott College in Arizona. Find more of her work at www.rebeccakotz.com

Nicola Lock (B.Sc, Grad Dip EFT, MMin, MAPC, AAOS, PACFA Reg Clinical) is course Coordinator and Lecturer in Pastoral Counselling at St. Mark's National Theological Centre. She was the founding Director of The Cottage and has over 25 years' experience as a counsellor, therapist, supervisor, and counselling educator and serves on a number of Anglican Church professional practice bodies.

Min. Johnrice Newton was born and raised in Lubbock, TX and is a 1979 graduate of Texas Tech University, Lubbock, Texas, with a BA in Social Welfare. She graduated from Methodist Hospital School of Nursing and has been a Registered Nurse since 1988. Relocating to Dallas in 1992 she received her Parish Nurse (Faith Community Nurse) training in 1998. She became a licensed minister in 2005 and went on to earn her master of divinity at Brite Divinity School-Texas Christian University Ft. Worth, TX in December 2014, and also received chaplain training. Min. Newton currently works as the Community Health Nurse for CitySquare Dallas, TX. Since 2000 Min. Newton has been president and founder of Tapestry Ministries, Inc. (a 501c3 non-profit organization) which hosts the YES (Youth Expecting Success) Program that provides SAT/ACT prep and Life Skills classes to at-risk teens, and Tapestry Women Ministry that provides emergency resources for women affected by domestic abuse. In May 2016 Min. Newton published her book, *Healing Voices: Women of Faith Who Survived Abuse Speak Out, Volume 1*, a collection of 11 women's stories that attributed their survival of domestic abuse to their faith in God. Min. Newton is the proud mother of four children: Johnice (Jerry), Dwayne (Ashley), Marcus (Jessica), and Veronica. She has three grandsons, Joshua, Axel, and Tyson, and one great-granddaughter, Elowyn. Her stance in ministry and in life is, "I work for God, and I am never unemployed." Tapestry Ministries: www.tapestrycare.org

Annette Oltmans (Founder and chairman of the board of directors of the Mend Project) is a philanthropist and passionate human rights advocate. She is a survivor. Annette's personal experiences of recovery and extensive field research into the topics of Original Abuse and Double Abuse® ignited Annette's passion to found The M3ND Project in 2016. Her discoveries and writings provide an array of instruction and knowledge to individuals and religious, institutional, and support communities regarding the correlation between unconscious and conscious abusive behaviors, the trauma they foster, and the generational liability they create. She conceptualized the term Double Abuse® naming the behaviors causing complex trauma (C-PTSD) to victim survivors. In working to prevent and remediate such harm, Annette developed protocoled models that are now being taught and implemented in churches and professional organizations across the United States. In addition to this work, she serves on the Board of Pepperdine University's Boone Center for the Family and is a Trustee of Northrise University in Zambia. Her writing on the topics of abuse, domestic violence and bullying, has been published in AACC, *Teen Vogue*, *OC Register*, and other publications.

Dr. Jeanne Porter King is the Founder and President of TransPorter Group Inc., a consulting practice that specializes in leadership development, diversity and inclusion training, process facilitation, and influence coaching. Dr. Jeanne has developed global leadership programs and has trained and coached leaders on every continent (except Antarctica!). She is passionate about coaching and developing executive and emerging leaders to be their best and reach their highest aspirations. Dr. Jeanne received both Bachelor and Master of Science degrees from The Ohio State University, a master of arts in Theological Studies from McCormick Theological Seminary and a doctor of philosophy in Organizational Communication from Ohio University. She has over 30 years of consulting and training experience in a variety of industries including manufacturing, telecommunications, financial services, as well as with community groups, governmental agencies, churches, and other faith-based institutions.

Endnotes

Foreword

1. President of World Relief, Scott Arbeiter's proven marketplace skills, pastoral experience, passion for mission, and history with World Relief uniquely equip him for his role. Scott was a partner at Arthur Andersen serving in a variety of functions over his seventeen-year marketplace career. In 2001, Scott resigned from the partnership to serve at Elmbrook Church in Milwaukee, where he became Lead Pastor. Scott has also served on World Relief's Board of Directors for nearly a decade, including three years as Chairman. Scott has been married to Jewel for thirty-three years and together they have raised three daughters, Kelsey, Jacquelyn, and Karis, all of whom have grown to love and serve Christ in their own remarkable ways.

Introduction

1. M. C. Black et al., "The National Intimate Partner and Sexual Violence Survey (NISVS): 2010 Summary Report" (Atlanta, GA: National Center for Injury Prevention and Control, Centers for Disease Control and Prevention, 2011), https://www.cdc.gov/violenceprevention/pdf/nisvs_report2010-a.pdf.

2. Sharon G. Smith et al., "National Intimate Partner and Sexual Violence Survey: 2015 Data Brief—Updated Release" (Atlanta, GA: National Center for Injury Prevention and Control, Centers for Disease Control and Prevention, 2018), https://www.cdc.gov/violenceprevention/pdf/2015data-brief508.pdf, 7.

3. Black et al., "The National Intimate Partner and Sexual Violence Survey (NISVS)," 46.

4. Smith et al., "National Intimate Partner and Sexual Violence Survey: 2015 Data Brief—Updated Release," 10.

5. Jennifer L. Truman and Rachel E. Morgan, "Nonfatal Domestic Violence, 2003–2013," U. S. Department of Justice, April 2014, https://www.bjs.gov/content/pub/pdf/ndv0312.pdf, 1.

6. "Domestic violence Counts National Summary," National Network to End domestic Violence, 2017, https://nnedv.org/wp-content/uploads/2019/10/NNEDV-2017-Census-Report-National-Summary-FINAL.pdf.

7. Truman and Morgan, "Nonfatal Domestic Violence," 1.

8. "When Men Murder Women: An Analysis of 2018 Homicide Data," Violence Policy Center, September 2020, https://vpc.org/studies/wmmw2020.pdf.

9. Emiko Petrosky et al., "Racial and Ethnic Differences in Homicides of Adult Women and the Role of Intimate Partner Violence—United States, 2003–2014," Center for Disease Control, July 21, 2017, https://www.cdc.gov/mmwr/volumes/66/wr/mm6628a1.htm?s_cid=mm6628a1_w.

10. "2017 NCVRW Resource Guide: Intimate Partner Violence Fact Sheet," National Criminal Justice Refernce Service (NCJRS), https://www.ncjrs.gov/ovc_archives/ncvrw/2017/images/en_artwork/Fact_Sheets/2017NCVRW_IPV_508.pdf.

11. Matthew J. Breiding and Brian S. Armour, "The Association between Disability and Intimate Partner Violence in the United States," *Annals of Epidemiology* 25, no. 6 (June 2015): 455–457

12. "Domestic Violence: The High Cost to Your Community," RAVE Mobile Safety, https://www.ravemobilesafety.com/hubfs/Resource%20Center/Domestic_Violence_Infographic_General_Final.pdf.

Chapter 1: Words Make Worlds: How We Speak About Abuse

1. Lauren Eichler Berkun, "Words Create Worlds," *JTS* (November 9, 2002) http://www.jtsa.edu/words-create-worlds.

2. Natalie Collins, *Out of Control: Couples, Conflict and the Capacity for Change* (London, SPCK, 2019), 57.

3. Stassa Edwards, "Philosopher Kate Manne on 'Himpathy,' Donald Trump, and Rethinking the Logic of Misogyny," *Jezebel,* (August 2, 2018) https://jezebel.com/philosopher-kate-manne-on-himpathy-donald-trump-and-r-1822639677.

4. U.S. Department of Justice, "Family Violence Statistics; Including Statistics on Strangers and Acquaintances," *Bureau of Justice Statistics,* (June, 2005), https://www.bjs.gov/content/pub/pdf/fvs.pdf, 13, 11.

5. Crown Prosecution Service, "Violence Against Women and Girls: Crime report 2015/16," *Crown Prosecution Service* (September, 2016) https://www.cps.gov.uk/sites/default/files/documents/publications/cps_vawg_report_2016.pdf.

6. The Guardian, "Women Three Times More Likely to Be Arrested for Domestic Violence," *The Guardian* (August 28, 2009) https://www.theguardian.com/society/2009/aug/28/women-arrested -domestic-violence.

7. Office for National Statistics, "Homicide," *Office for National Statistics* (February 11, 2016) https://www.ons.gov.uk/peoplepopulationandcommunity/crimeandjustice/compendium /focusonviolentcrimeandsexualoffences/yearendingmarch2015/chapter2homicide.

8. Judith Herman, *Trauma and Recovery: The Aftermath of Violence—from Domestic Abuse to Political Terror* (New York, BasicBooks, 1992), 72.

9. NICE, "Costing Statement: Domestic Violence and Abuse," *National Institute for Health and Care Excellency*, (February, 2014), https://www.nice.org.uk/guidance/ph50/resources/costing -statement-pdf-69194701. CDC, "Preventing Intimate Partner Violence", National Center for Injury Prevention and Control, Division of Violence Prevention, October 9, 2020, https://www.cdc.gov /violenceprevention/intimatepartnerviolence/fastfact.html.

10. Judith Herman, *Trauma and Recovery*, 21.

11. May Bulman, "Most Women Murdered by Men are Killed by Current or Former Partner, Figures Show," *Independent*, (December 10, 2017), https://www.independent.co.uk/news/uk/home -news/women-murdered-men-mostly-current-former-partner-kill-uk-figures-femicide-census -womens-aid-a8099991.html.

12. Zoe Lodrick, *Sexualized and Relational Trauma*, (May 16, 2010), https://docs.google.com /viewer?a=v&pid=sites&srcid=ZGVmYXVsdGRvbWFpbnx6b2Vsb2RyaWNNrfGd4OjE4Mm YyN2ZjZTkyYWJlMA, 19.

13. Natalie Collins, *Out of Control*, 114–118.

14. Glynn Harrison, *A Better Story: God, Sex and Human Flourishing*, (London, IVP, 2017), 121.

15. Lundy Bancroft, *Why Does He Do That? Inside the Minds of Angry and Controlling Men*, (London, Berkley Books), 47.

16. Lundy Bancroft, *Why Does He Do That?*, 25.

17. Joanna Cook and Susan Bewley, "Acknowledging a Persistent Truth: Domestic Violence in Pregnancy," *Journal of the Royal Society of Medicine*, 101(7), (July 1, 2008): 358–363, https://www.ncbi .nlm.nih.gov/pmc/articles/PMC2442136/.

18. Playmobible, "The Four Causes of Biblical Divorce by Dr David Instone-Brewer in Playmobil," *YouTube*, (November 15, 2012), https://www.youtube.com/watch?v=lRiCoLEoDaM.

19. UNICEF, "Behind Closed Doors; The Impact of Domestic Violence on Children," *UNICEF*, (2006), https://www.unicef.org/media/files/BehindClosedDoors.pdf.

20. Glynn Harrison, *A Better Story*, 109.

21. Douglas A. Brownridge, "Partner Violence Against Women With Disabilities: Prevalence, Risk, and Explanations," *Violence Against Women*, 12(9), (September 1, 2006), 805-822, http://journals.sagepub.com/doi/abs/10.1177/1077801206292681.

22. Stassa Edwards, "Philosopher Kate Manne on 'Himpathy'" *Jezebel* (August 2, 2018) https://jezebel.com/philosopher-kate-manne-on-himpathy-donald-trump-and-r-1822639677.

Chapter 2: Why Men Batter

1. Domestic Abuse Intervention Programs (DAIP), "FAQs About the Wheel," accessed August 14, 2020, https://www.theduluthmodel.org/wheels/faqs-about-the-wheels/.

2. M. L. Walters, J. Chen, & M. J. Breiding, "The National Intimate Partner and Sexual Violence Survey (NISVS): 2010 Findings on Victimization by Sexual Orientation" (Atlanta, GA: National Center for Injury Prevention and Control, Centers for Disease Control and Prevention,2013).

3. Wlaters, Chen, Breiding, "The National Intimate Partner and Sexual violence Survey," 2013

4. Andrew R. Klein, *Practical Implications of Current Domestic Violence Research: For Law Enforcement, Prosecutors, and Judges* 4, (US Dep't of Justice, Nat'l Institute of Justice, 2009), 52.

5. Chuck Derry, "MN Clean Hotels Initiative," Gender Violence Institute, accessed August 13, 2020, https://www.genderviolenceinstitute.org/mn-clean-hotels-initiative.

6. Ana J. Bridges, Robert Wosnitzer, Erica Scharrer, Chyng Sun, Rachael Liberman., "Aggression and Sexual Behavior in Best-Selling Pornography videos: A Content Analysis Update," *Violence Against Women Vol 16 Iss. 10*, October 1, 2010, https://journals.sagepub.com/doi/abs/10.1177/1077801210382866, first published online October 26, 2020.

Chapter 3: Sexual Abuse in Dating and Marriage Relationships

1. David Finkelhor, "Marital Rape: The Misunderstood Crime," South Eastern CASA. PDF. 209. https://www.secasa.com.au/assets/Documents/Marital-rape-The-misunderstood-crime.pdf.

2. Lili Loofbourow, "The Female Price of Male Pleasure," The Week. January 25, 2018. https://theweek.com/articles/749978/female-price-male-pleasure.

3. Kris Vallotton, "4 Reasons Men Really Delay Marriage (And How to Step it Up)," Kris Vallotton, December 20, 2018. https://krisvallotton.com/4-reasons-men-really-delay-marriage-and-how-to-step-it-up/.

4. Chuck Derry, "Abusive Men Describe the Benefits of Violence," Voice Male Magazine, October 14, 2015. https://voicemalemagazine.org/abusive-men-describe-the-benefits-of-violence/.

5. David Tombs, "Crucifixion, State Terror, and Sexual Abuse," Union Seminary Quarterly Review 53:1-2 (1999): 89–109. https://www.koreannewsletter.org/uploads/7/0/4/0/7040474/tombs_1999_-_usqr_-_crucifixion__state_terror__and_sexual_abuse.pdf.

6. David Tombs, "Crucifixion, Sate Terror, and Sexual Abuse."

7. Nate Pyle, "Seeing a Woman: A Conversation Between a Father and Son," Nate Pyle, August 13, 2014. https://www.natepyle.com/blog/2019/3/5/seeing-a-woman-a-conversation-between-a-father-and-son.

8. Douglas Wilson, *Fidelity: What it Means to be a One-Woman Man* (Moscow, Idaho: Canon Press, 1999), 86-87.

9. C. K. Egbert, "Why consent is not enough," *Feminist Current*, June 23, 2104 https://www.feministcurrent.com/2014/06/25/why-consent-is-not-enough/.

10. Rebecca Bratten Weiss, "Yes, There is an Institutional Problem: Power," *Patheos*, August 16, 2018. https://www.patheos.com/blogs/suspendedinherjar/2018/08/on-the-abuse-scandal-the-problem-is-power/?fbclid=IwAR1HvbyFQl3Y5AOEhqzUM-k5-gQs3P8XkZYGBIIF_HmcIxLAceBgzQMnfJc.

11. Andrea Dworkin, Pornography: Men Possessing Women, (New York: Penguin Books, 1989), xxxix.

12. Josh McDowell, "The Porn Phenomenon: The Impact of Pornography in the Digital Age," Barna, 2016. http://www.cbcrh.com/home/180005292/180009741/docs/The-Porn-Phenomenon.pdf?sec_id=180009741.

Chapter 4: Covert Emotional Abuse

1. StrongHearts Native Helpline, "Why Do People Abuse?", accessed May 7, 2019, https://strongheartshelpline.org/abuse/why-do-people-abuse.

2. Jennifer Williams-Fields, "You Can Get PTSD From Staying In An Emotionally Abusive Relationship," PTSD Journal, last modified Feb 25, 2016, https://www.ptsdjournal.com/posts/you-can-get-ptsd-from-staying-in-an-emotionally-abusive-relationship/.

3. Centers for Disease Control and Prevention, "Intimate Partner Violence," CDC, last reviewed 23 Oct. 2018, accessed July 6, 2020. www.cdc.gov/violenceprevention/intimatepartnerviolence /index.html.

4. Matthew J. Breiding and Brian S. Armour, "The Association between Disability and Intimate Partner Violence in the United States," *Annals of Epidemiology* 25 (2015): 457.

5. Gwyneth Kerr Erwin (PH.D., PSY.D, training and supervising psychoanalyst in private practice) discussion with Annette Oltmans, 2016.

6. David Hawkins, "When Coping is Killing You," Marriage Recovery Center. Marriage Recovery Center, Inc., April 19, 2020, https://marriagerecoverycenter.com/when-coping-is -killing-you/.

7. Jim Merriam, "Shunning is one way to express political opinions," *Wiarton Echo*, July 18, 2018,

8. Peter Salovey, John D. Mayer, "Emotional Intelligence," *Imagination, Cognition and Personality*, vol. 9, iss.3, (1990) 189.

9. Daniel Goleman. *Emotional Intelligence: Why it Can Matter More Than IQ.* (New York: Bantam Books, 1995), 43, 80, 83, 97, 259.

10. Goleman, *Emotional Intelligence*, 42.

11. Goleman, *Emotional Intelligence*, 42.

12. Goleman, *Emotional Intelligence*, 42.

13. Howard Gardner, *Frames of Mind: The Theory of Multiple Intelligences* (New York: Basic Books, 2011), 239.

14. Gardner, *Frames of Mind*, 79, 119, 159, 187, 206, 240.

15. Gardner, *Frames of Mind*, 4.

16. Gardner, *Frames of Mind*, 311.

17. Kimberly A. Lonsway et al. "False Reports: Moving Beyond the Issue to Successfully Investigate and Prosecute Non-Stranger Sexual Assault," *National Sexual Violence Resource Center* (2009): 2,

18. Henry Cloud. Necessary Endings: The Employees, Businesses, and Relationships that All of Us Have to Give Up in Order to Move Forward (New York: HarperCollins, 2011), 21

19. Belleruth Naparstek, *Invisible Heroes: Survivors of Trauma and How They Heal* (New York: Bantam Books, 2004), 68-73.

20. Leslie Vernick, *The Emotionally Destructive Relationship-Seeing It, Stopping It, Surviving It*, (Eugene, OR, Harvest House Publishers, 2007), 239.

Chapter 5: Double Abuse?

1. Double Abuse is a registered trademark of Annette Oltmans. All rights reserved.

2. Judith Lewis Herman, *Trauma and Recovery: The Aftermath of Violence—From Domestic Abuse to Political Terror* (New York: Basic Books, 1992), 58, 158.

3. Erwin, Gwyneth Kerr. (PH.D., PSY.D., training and supervising psychoanalyst in private practice), discussion with Annette Oltmans, 2016.

4. Belleruth Naparstek, *Invisible Heroes: Survivors of Trauma and How They Heal* (New York: Bantam Books, 2004), 59-60.

5. Naparstek, *Invisible Heroes*, 80.

6. Bessel van der Kolk, "Developmental Trauma Disorder: Toward a rational diagnosis for children with complex trauma histories," *Psychiatric Annals* 35, no. 5 (2005): 6.

7. Belleruth Naparstek, *Invisible Heroes*, 80.

8. *Diagnostic and Statistical Manual of Mental Disorders: DSM-5* (Arlington, VA: American Psychiatric Association, 2013).

9. *International Classification of Diseases Eleventh Edition: ICD-11* (Geneva, Switzerland: World Health Organization, 2018).

10. Theresa Walker, "2 Orange County women reaching church leaders and others on how to help when abusive treatment," *Orange County Register* (Orange County, CA), Dec. 26, 2017.

11. Lundy Bancroft, *Why Does He Do That?: Inside the Minds of Angry and Controlling Men* (New York: G.P. Putnam's Sons, 2002), 149; Erwin, Gwyneth Kerr, (PH.D., PSY.D., training and supervising psychoanalyst in private practice), discussion with Annette Oltmans, 2018.

12. Herman, *Trauma and Recovery*, 7.

13. Susan M. Johnson, *The Practice of Emotionally Focused Couple Therapy: Creating Connection* (New York: Brunner-Routledge, 2004), 17.

14. Susan M. Johnson, *The Practice of Emotionally Focused Couple Therapy*, 17.

15. Judith Herman, *Trauma and Recovery*, 135.

Chapter 6: How Abuse Impacts Health

1. Kyle Benson, "The Magic Relationship Ratio According to Science," The Gottman Institute, Oct. 4, 2017, https://www.gottman.com/blog/the-magic-relationship-ratio-according-science/.

2. Anna Aslanian, "Betrayal Trauma in Addiction," The Gottman Institute, Oct. 21, 2019, https://www.gottman.com/blog/betrayal-trauma-in-addiction/.

3. Beth Daley, "Domestic Violence: the psychology of coercive control remains a legal battlefield," The Conversation, Mar. 20, 2019, https://theconversation.com/domestic-abuse-the-psychology-of-coercive-control-remains-a-legal-battlefield-113053.

4. Louise Chang, MD, "Unhappy Marriage: Bad for your Health," webmd.com, Dec. 5, 2005, https://www.webmd.com/sex-relationships/news/20051205/unhappy-marriage-bad-for-your-health.

5. Janice K Kiecolt-Glaser & Stephanie J Wilson, "Lovesick: How Couples' Relationships Influence Health", ncbi.clm.nih.gov, Nov. 8, 2017, https://www.ncbi.nlm.nih.gov/pmc/articles/PMC5549103/.

6. Domesticshelters.org, "The Link Between Abuse, Chronic Fatigue and Fibromyalgia, domeslticshelters.org, Oct. 18, 2017, https://www.domesticshelters.org/articles/health/the-link-between-abuse-chronic-fatigue-and-fibromyalgia.

7. Evan Stark & Anne Flitcraft, *Women at Risk: Domestic Violence and Women's Health* (London: Sage Publications, 1996), 165.

8. Michele C Black, "Intimate Partner Violence and Adverse Health Consequences: Implications for Clinicians", *American Journal of Lifestyle Medicine,* June 2011, 430, http://ajl.sagepub.com/content/5/5/428.

9. Anne C. Petersen, Joshua Joseph, and Monica Feit, eds., *New Directions in Child Abuse and Neglect Research* (Washington, DC: The National Academies Press, 2014), https://www.nap.edu/read/18331/chapter/1, 117-118.

10. Steven Ertelt, "Their 'Rescuing Hug Stunned' the World, Now the Twins are All Grown Up", lifenews.com, (Washington, DC, 06/20/2014), https://www.lifenews.com/2014/06/20/their-rescuing-hug-stunned-the-world-now-the-twins-are-all-grown-up/.

11. Jennifer Sweeton "Here's Your Brain on Trauma", jennifersweeton.com, 03/14/2017,https://www.jennifersweeton.com/blog/2017/3/14/heres-your-brain-on-trauma.

12. Bessel Van der Kolk, *The Body Keeps the Score: Brain, Mind, and Body in the Healing of Trauma: Brain, Mind, and Body in the Healing of Trauma,* (New York, Penguin Books, 2015), 159.

13. Jacqui L. Plumb, Kelly A. Bush, and Sonia E. Kersevich, "Trauma Sensitive Schools: An Evidence Based Approach", *School Social Work Journal,* Vol. 40, No. 2, (Spring 2016), 40, http://www.communityschools.org/assets/1/AssetManager/TSS.pdf.

14. Van der Kolk, *The Body Keeps the Score*, 158–159. (quoted from American Psychiatric Association. *Desk reference to the diagnostic criteria from DSM-5®*. American Psychiatric Pub, 2014, 143–145.)

15. Van der Kolk, The body Keeps the Score, 161. (Criteria submitted to the American Psychiatric Association for inclusion in the DSM-5).

16. Van der Kolk, *The Body Keeps the Score*, 160.

17. Joseph Feit Petersen, eds., *New Directions in Child Abuse and Neglect Research*, 112-113.

18. Jane Ellen Stevens, "The Adverse Childhood Experiences Study—the largest most important public health study you never heard of—began in an obesity clinic", acestoohigh.com, 10/03/2012, https://acestoohigh.com/2012/10/03/the-adverse-childhood-experiences-study-the-largest-most -important-public-health-study-you-never-heard-of-began-in-an-obesity-clinic/.

19. Stevens, "Adverse Childhood Experiences Study."

20. Stevens, "The Adverse Childhood Experiences Study."

21. Donna Jackson Nakazawa, *Childhood Disrupted: How your biography becomes your biology, and how you can heal,* (New York, Atria Books, 2015), 13.

22. Nakazawa, *Childhood Disrupted*, 11.

23. Nakazawa, *Childhood Disrupted*, 11.

24. Stevens, "The Adverse Childhood Experiences Study."

25. Nakazawa, *Childhood Disrupted*, 16; I. Shalev, S. Entringer, P.D. Wadhwa, et al., "Stress and Telomere Biology: A Lifespan Perspective," *Psychoneuroendocrinology* 38, no. 9 (September 2013), 835-42; L.H. Price, H.T. Kao, D.E. Burgers, et al, "Telomeres and Early Life Stress: An Overview," *Biological Psychiatry* 73, no. 1 (January 2013), 15-23.

26. Nakazawa, *Childhood Disrupted*, 15.

27. Nakazawa, *Childhood Disrupted*, 14-15.

28. Nakazawa, *Childhood Disrupted*, p. 96; V.J. Felitti and R.F. Anda, "The Relationship of Adverse Childhood Experiences to Adult Medical Disease, Psychiatric Disorders, and Sexual Behavior: Implications for Healthcare," in *The Effects of Early Life Trauma on Health and Disease: The Hidden Epidemic,* edited by R. Lanius, E Vermetten, C. Pain (New York: Cambridge University Press. 2010), 77.

29. Nakazawa, *Childhood Disrupted*, 97.

30. Claudia Garcia-Moreno, Alessandra Guedes and Wendy Knerr, World Health Organization, "Understanding and Addressing Violence Against Women", apps.who.int, 2010, 1. https://apps.who .int/iris/bitstream/handle/10665/77431/WHO_RHR_12.43_eng.pdf;jsessionid=E65137C650E7 99FE166796B0E20CCC86?sequence=1.

31. Garcia-Moreno, Guedes and Knerr, "Understanding and Addressing Violence Against Women."

32. Shukla Jyoti & Singh Neetu, "Atrocity against Women at Their Own Homes and its Implications on Their Health Status," *International Journal of Humanities and Social Science Invention* Vol 2, Iss 9, September 2013, 27–30, https://www.scribd.com/document/179129033/International-Journal-of-Humanities-and-Social-Science-Invention-IJHSSI.

33. Garcia-Moreno, Guedes and Knerr, "Understanding and Addressing Violence Against Women."

34. Garcia-Moreno, Guedes and Knerr, "Understanding and Addressing Violence Against Women,"apps.who.int, 2010, 2. Heise L, Garcia Moreno C. "Violence by intimate partners," In: Krug EG et al., eds. *World report on violence and health,* Geneva, World Health Organization, 2002:87– 121.

35. Garcia-Moreno, Guedes and Knerr, "Understanding and Addressing Violence Against Women," apps.who.int, 2010, 3. (WHO Study Group on Female Genital Mutilation and Obstetric Outcome, "Female genital mutilation and obstetric outcome: WHO collaborative prospective study in six African countries," *Lancet*, 2006, 367(9525):1835–41.

36. Garcia-Moreno, Guedes and Knerr, "Understanding and Addressing Violence Against Women", 3.

37. Claudia Garcia-Moreno, Alessandra Guedes and Wendy Knerr, World Health Organization, "Understanding and Addressing Violence Against Women", apps.who.int, 2010, 3. https://apps.who.int/iris/bitstream/handle/10665/77431/WHO_RHR_12.43_eng.pdf;jsessionid=E65137C650E799FE166796B0E20CCC86?sequence=1; WHO Department of Gender, Women and Health, Global Coalition on Women and AIDS. "Intimate partner violence and HIV/AIDS: information sheet. Violence against women and HIV/AIDS–critical intersections," Geneva, World Health Organization, 2004.

38. Claudia Garcia-Moreno, Alessandra Guedes and Wendy Knerr, World Health Organization, "Understanding and Addressing Violence Against Women", apps.who.int, 2010, 4. https://apps.who.int/iris/bitstream/handle/10665/77431/WHO_RHR_12.43_eng.pdf;jsessionid=E65137C650E799FE166796B0E20CCC86?sequence=1; JC Campbell, "Health consequences of intimate partner violence," *Lancet*, 2002, 359(9314):1331–36; SR Dube et al. "Long-term consequences of childhood sexual abuse by gender of victim," *American Journal of Preventive Medicine*, 2005, 28(5):430–38; C. Pallitto, "Domestic violence and maternal, infant, and reproductive health: a critical review of the literature," Paper submitted to the Pan-American Health Organization, Washington, DC, 2004.

39. Garcia-Moreno, Guedes and Knerr, "Understanding and Addressing Violence Against Women," apps.who.int, 2010, 4. https://apps.who.int/iris/bitstream/handle/10665/77431/WHO_RHR_12.43_eng.pdf;jsessionid=E65137C650E799FE166796B0E20CCC86?sequence=1; V. Fauveau et al., "Causes of maternal mortality in rural Bangladesh, 1976–85," Bulletin of the World Health Organization, 1988, 66(5):643–51.

40. Vincent T. Cunliffe, "The epigenetic impacts of social stress: how does social adversity become biologically embedded?" Epigenomics, Vol. 8, No. 12, (2016), 1655, https://www.futuremedicine.com/doi/full/10.2217/epi-2016-0075.

41. Michigan State University. "Domestic abuse may affect children in womb." ScienceDaily. www.sciencedaily.com/releases/2014/12/141216100628.htm (accessed July 9, 2020).

42. National Scientific Council on the Developing Child, *Excessive Stress Disrupts the Architecture of the Developing Brain: Working Paper 3*, Updated Edition, https://developingchild.harvard.edu, (2005/2014) 3. https://developingchild.harvard.edu/wp-content/uploads/2005/05/Stress_Disrupts_Architecture_Developing_Brain-1.pdf (Sapolsky, R. M., Romero, L.M., & Munck, A. (2000). How do glucocorticoids influence stress responses? [21(1), 55–89.)

43. National Scientific Council on the Developing Child, *Excessive Stress*, 3.

44. Heal for Life Staff, "Cortisol, Trauma, Stress & Memory", (2017). (Abercrombie, H. C., Kalin, N. H., Thurow, M. E., Rosenkranz, M. A. & Davidson, R. J. (2003). Cortisol variation in humans affects memory for emotionally laden and neutral information. *Behavioural Neuroscience*, 117, 305-516.), http://healforlife.com.au/cortisol-trauma-stress-memory/.

45. Van der Kolk, *The Body Keeps the Score*, 206.

46. Van der Kolk, *The Body Keeps the Score*, p. 24; G. Ross Baker, et al., "The Canadian Adverse Events Study: The Incidence of Adverse Events Among Hospital Patients in Canada," *Canadian Medical Association Journal* 170, no. 11 (2004): 1678-86; A. C. McFarlane, et al., "Posttraumatic Stress Disorder in a General Psychiatric Inpatient Population," *Journal of Traumatic Stress* 14, no. 4 (2001): 633-45; Kim T Mueser, et al., "Trauma and Posttraumatic Stress Disorder in Severe Mental Illness,: *Journal of Consulting and Clinical Psychology* 66, no. 3 (1998): 493; National Trauma Consortium, www.national traumaconsortium.org.

47. Heal for Life Staff, "Cortisol, Trauma, Stress & Memory."

48. Rachel Yehuda, MD, "How Trauma and Resilience Cross Generations", onbeing.org, (2017), https://onbeing.org/programs/rachel-yehuda-how-trauma-and-resilience-cross-generations-nov2017/.

49. Mark Wolynn, *It Didn't Start With You: How Inherited Family Trauma Shapes Who We Are and How to End the Cycle.* (New York, Penguin, 2017), 19. (R. Yehuda and J. Seckl, "Minireview: Stress-Related Psychiatric Disorders with Low Cortisol Levels: A Metabolic Hypothesis," *Endocrinology,* October 4, 2011, http://press.endocrine.org/doi/full/10.1210/en.2011-1218.)

50. Wolynn, *It Didn't Start with You,* 20.

51. Wolynn, *It Didn't Start with You,* 31; David Samuels, "Do Jews Carry Trauma in Our Genes? A Conversation with Rachel Yehuda," *Tablet Magazine,* December 11, 2014, http://tabletmag.com /jewish-arts-and-culture/books/187555/trauma-genes-q-a-rachel-yehuda.

52. Wolynn, *It Didn't Start with You,* p. 27. (Bruce H. Lipton, "Maternal Emotions and Human Development," *Birth Psychology,* https://birthpsychology.com/free-article/maternal-emotions-and -human-development.)

53. Wolynn, *It Didn't Start with You,* p. 27. (Bruce H. Lipton, PhD, *The Wisdom of Your Cells: How Your Beliefs Control Your Biology* (Louisville, CO: Sounds True, Inc., 2006), audiobook, Part 3.)

54. Wolynn, *It Didn't Start with You,* p. 31. (Rachel Yehuda, et al., "Holocaust Exposure Induced Intergenerational Effects on FKBP5 Methylation," *Biological Psychiatry,* August 12, 2015, www .biologicalpsychiatryjournal.com/article/S0006-3223(15)00652-6/abstract/ doi:10/1016/j .biopsych.2015.08.005.)

55. Van der Kolk, *The Body Keeps the Score,*151. (Martin Teicher, MD, PhD, Scientific American)

Chapter 7: Ideas Have Consequences

1. The term the girl effect is used by Nicholas D. Kristof and Sheryl WuDunn in *Half the Sky* (New York, NY: Vintage, 2009).

2. R. David Freedman, "Woman, a Power Equal to a Man," *Archaeology Review 9* (1983): 56–58.

3. Aristotle, *Politica* 1.5.B4v, trans. Bejamin Jowett, vol. 10 in *The Works of Aristotle Translated into English under the Editorship of W. D. Ross* (Oxford: Clarendon, 1921).

4. Plato, *Laws* 6.781a, b, trans. A. E. Taylor, in *The Collected Dialogues of Plato: Including the Letters,* Bollingen Series LXXI, ed. Edith Hamilton and Huntington Cairns (Princeton, NJ: Princeton University Press, 1963), 1356.

5. See *Ancient History & Civilization, Ancient Greece and Rome: An Encyclopedia for Students,* "Marriage and Divorce," https://erenow.net/ancient/ancient-greece-and-rome-an-encyclopedia-for -students-4-volume-set/274.php accessed 7/24/2020.

6. Menahoth 43b–44a; Talmud; Shabbath 86a–86b.

7. Gordon Fee, *Listening to the Spirit in the Text* (Grand Rapids, MI: Eerdmans, 2000), 58ff.

8. See Gordon Fee, *Commentary on Galatians* (Blandford Forum, UK: Deo, 2007) and Ben Witherington, *Grace in Galatia: Paul's Letter to the Galatians* (Grand Rapids, MI: Eerdmans, 1998.

9. See *Discovering Biblical Equality: Complementarity without Hierarchy*, ed. Ronald Pierce, Rebecca Merrill Groothuis, and Gordon Fee (Carol Stream, IL: InterVarsity, 2004), see also Christine Schenk, *Crispina and her Sisters: Women and Authority in the Early Church*. (Minneapolis, MN: Fortress Press, 2017).

10. "Our Battle against Judah," German Propaganda Archive, Calvin College Web site, http://www.calvin.edu/academic/cas/gpa/rim3.htm.

11. Comte Agenor de Gasparin, *The Uprising of a Great People*, trans. Mary Booth (New York, NY: Scribners, 1862), 103–04.

12. Irenaeus, fragment 32, in *The Ante-Nicene Fathers*, ed. Philip Schaff (Grand Rapids, MI: Eerdmans, 2001), 1:573. Emphasis mine.

13. Augustine, *On Marriage and Concupiscence* 1.10, trans. Robert Ernest Wallis, in *Nicene and Post-Nicene Fathers*, Series 1, ed. Philip Schaff [hereafter NPNF] (Grand Rapids, MI: Eerdmans, 1886), 5:267. Emphasis mine.

14. John Chrysostom, "Homily IX," in *Homilies on 1 Timothy*, NPNF 13:436. Emphasis mine.

15. John Calvin, *Commentaries on the Epistle to Timothy, Titus, and Philemon*, in *Calvin's Commentaries*, trans. William Pringle (Edinburgh: Calvin Translation Society, 1856) 37. Emphasis mine.

16. John Knox, "The First Blast of the Trumpet against the Monstrous Regiment of Women 1558," in *The Political Writings of John Knox*, ed. Marvin A. Breslow (Cranbury, NY: Associate University Presses, 1985), 43. Emphasis mine.

17. Mark Driscoll, Mars Hill Church, Seattle, WA. Quoted at http://www.dennyburk.com /mark-driscoll-on-women-in-ministry-2, accessed March 24, 2010.

18. Dana L. Robert, *American Women in Mission: A Social History of their Thought and Practice* (Macon: GA: Mercer University Press, 2005), ix.

19. Katharine Bushnell, *Dr. Katharine Bushnell: A Brief Sketch of Her Life Work* (Hertford, UK: Rose and Sons, Salisbury Square, 1930).

20. Charles O. Knowles, *Let Her Be: Right Relationships and the Southern Baptist Conundrum over Woman's Role* (Columbia, MO: KnoWell Publishing, 2002), 85.

21. Katharine Bushnell, *God's Word to Women: One Hundred Bible Studies on Woman's Place in the Church and Home* (Minneapolis, MN: Christians for Biblical Equality, 2003), 9.

22. Bushnell, *God's Word to Women*, 10.

23. Bushnell, *God's Word to Women*, 37–42.

24. Bushnell, *God's Word to Women*, 43–46.

25. Bushnell, *God's Word to Women*, Ibid. n

26. Bushnell, *God's Word to Women*, 66–70.

27. Bushnell, *God's Word to Women*, 169.

28. Bushnell, *God's Word to Women*, Ibid.

29. Bushnell, *Dr. Katharine Bushnell*, 13.

30. Bushnell, *Dr. Katharine Bushnell*, 13–14.

31. Kristoff and WuDunn, *Half the Sky*, 198.

32. Shuji G. Asai and David H. Olson, "Spouse Abuse and Marital System Based on ENRICH," University of Minnesota, https://www.prepare-enrich.com/pe_main_site_content /pdf/research/abuse.pdf.

33. Asai and Olson, "Spouse Abuse," Ibid.

34. Kristoff and WuDunn, Half the Sky, xiv–xv.

35. Kristoff and WuDunn, *Half the Sky*, Ibid.

36. "Gendercide," *The Economist*, March 2010, 13.

37. For a complete discussion on gender equality as a reform movement, see chapter 1 in *Global Voices on Biblical Equality: Women and Men Serving Together in the Church*, ed. Aída Besançon Spencer, William David Spencer, and Mimi Haddad (Eugene, OR: Wipf & Stock, 2008).

38. Much of what follows in this section can be found in Willard Swartley's excellent book, *Slavery, Sabbath, War, and Women* (Scottdale, PA: Herald Press, 1983).

39. The interpretive methods provided here are carefully noted in Swartley, *Slavery, Sabbath, War, and Women*, 58ff.

40. W. B. Sloan, *These Sixty Years: The Story of the Keswick Convention* (London: Pickering & Inglis, 1935), 91.

41. Sloan, *These Sixty Years*, 91.

42. See Mimi Haddad's chapter, "Reading the Apostle Paul through Galatians 3:28," in *Coming Together in the 21st Century: The Bible's Message in an Age of Diversity*, ed. Curtiss Paul DeYoung (Valley Forge, PA: Judson, 2009), 73–93.

43. Fee, *Listening to the Spirit in the Text*, 59.

44. In a second-century document, Ignatius of Antioch cites Onesimus, a bishop of Ephesus, who offered him hospitality. See chapter 1, Praise of the Ephesians, at http://www.newadvent.org/fathers/0104.htm, accessed Jan. 5, 2012.

45. Linda Belleville, "Teaching and Usurping Authority," in *Discovering Biblical Equality: Complementarity without Hierarchy*, ed. Rebecca Merrill Groothuis, Ronald Pierce, and Gordon Fee (Downers Grove, IL: InterVarsity, 2005), 205–24.

Chapter 8: Sexual Integrity and Consent

1. Catharine A. MacKinnon, "Liberalism and the Death of Feminism," The Sexual Liberals and the Attack on Feminism, (New York, Pergamon Press, 1990) 4.

2. Andrea Dworkin. Letters from a Warzone (Brooklyn: Lawrence Hill Books, 1993), 266-267.

3. RAINN, "The Criminal Justice System: Statistics," RAINN. https://www.rainn.org/statistics/criminal-justice-system.

4. Tim Krueger, "Love and Respect: A Better Way," CBE International, 2016. https://www.cbeinternational.org/resource/article/mutuality-blog-magazine/love-and-respect-better-way.

5. Jone Johnson Lewis, "24 Andrea Dworkin Quotes," Thought Co., February 17, 2019. https://www.thoughtco.com/andrea-dworkin-quotes-3530027.

6. "What Does it Mean to Ask for Consent?," Teensource.org, accessed August 22, 2020, https://www.teensource.org/hookup/what-does-it-mean-ask-consent.

7. Tina Schermer Sellers. Sex, God, and the Conservative Church Erasing Shame from Sexual Intimacy. (Milton: Taylor and Francis, 2017).

8. Domestic Abuse Intervention Programs (DAIP), "Understanding the Power and Control Wheel," accessed August 22, 2020, https://www.theduluthmodel.org/wheels/.

Chapter 9: Teaching and Preaching about Domestic Violence

1. John S. McClure and Nancy J. Ramsay, eds., *Telling the Truth: Preaching about Sexual and Domestic Violence*, (Cleveland, OH, United Church Press, 1998), 2.

2. McClure and Ramsay, *Telling the Truth*, 2.

3. This statement was a comparison to modern day women that must depend on the system for survival (food, shelter, etc. In order to care for their children) such as was Hagar's situation. See: Phyllis Trible, *Text of Terror* (Philadelphia, PA, Fortress Press, 1984) Kindle Chapter 1, Hagar.

Chapter 10: Breaking Down Barriers for Women in Church Leadership

1. Mary Crawford, *Transformations: Women, Gender, and Psychology*, 2nd ed. (New York: McGraw-Hill, 2012), 28.

2. Jioni Lewis, "From Modern Sexism to Gender Microaggressions: Understanding Contemporary Forms of Sexism and Their Influence on Diverse Women," in *APA Handbook of the Psychology of Women*, vol. 1, *History, Theory, and Battlegrounds*, eds. C. B. Travis and J. W. White (Washington, DC: American Psychological Association, 2018), 381.

3. Lewis, "From Modern Sexism to Gender Microaggressions," 381.

4. Mahzarin R. Banaji and Anthony Greenwald, *Blindspot: The Hidden Biases of Good People* (New York: Random House, 2013), Kindle loc 64.

5. Lewis, "From Modern Sexism to Gender Microaggressions," 382–83.

6. Klyne Snodgrass, *The Covenant Quarterly*, 67.2 (May 2009): 26–44.

7. Elizabeth Hopper, "What Is a Microaggression? Everyday Insults With Harmful Effects," ThoughtCo., November 1, 2018, https://www.thoughtco.com/microaggression-definition-examples-4171853.

8. Lewis, "From Modern Sexism to Gender Microaggressions," 388.

9. Lewis, "From Modern Sexism to Gender Microaggressions," 388.

10. Kimberlé Crenshaw, "Demarginalizing the Intersection of Race and Sex: A Black Feminist Critique of Antidiscrimination Doctrine, Feminist Theory and Antiracist Politics," *University of Chicago Legal Forum* 1.8 (1989): http://chicagounbound.uchicago.edu/uclf/vol1989/iss1/8.

11. See the documentary *Miss Representation* as an example (Jennifer Siebel Newsom, *MISSRepresentation: A Documentary Film*, Virgil Films & Entertainment, 2012).

12. Jaimee Swift and Hannah Gould, "Not an Object: On Sexualization and Exploitation of Women and Girls," UNICEF, January 15, 2020, https://www.unicefusa.org/stories/not-object-sexualization-and-exploitation-women-and-girls/30366.

13. Swift and Gould, "Not an Object."

14. "Women 'Take Care' and Men 'Take Charge:' Stereotyping of U.S. Business Leaders Exposed," Catalyst, October 19, 2005, https://www.catalyst.org/research/women-take-care-men-take-charge-stereotyping-of-u-s-business-leaders-exposed/.

15. Stefanie Simon and Crystal Hoyt, "Exploring the Effect of Media Images on Women's Leadership Self-perceptions and Aspirations," in *Group Processes & Intergroup Relations* 16.2 (2013): 232–45.

16. Jeanne Porter King, *Building a Church Full of Leaders* (Chicago: Life2Legacy Publishers, 2014), Kindle loc 512.

Chapter 11: Women's Ways of Leading in the Church

1. Drorah O'Donnell Setel, "Exodus" in *Women's Bible Commentary*, ed. Carol A. Newsom and Sharon H. Ringe (Louisville: Westminster John Knox, 1992, 1998), 33.

2. Setel, "Exodus."

3. Setel, "Exodus."

4. Wanda is a pseudonym, as are all names used in this chapter.

5. Jeanne Porter, *Leading Lessons: Insights on Leadership from Women of the Bible* (Minneapolis: Augsburg Fortress, 2005), 111.

6. Porter, *Leading Lessons*, 112.

7. Danna Nolan Fewell, "Judges" in *Women's Bible Commentary*, 75.

8. Gail R. O'Day, "Acts," *Women's Bible Commentary*, 310.

9. Setel, "Exodus," 31.

10. Jeanne Porter, *Leading Ladies: Transformative Biblical Images for Women's Leadership* (Philadelphia: Innisfree Press, 2000), 67.

Chapter 12: Strategies for Coaching Women in Ministerial Leadership

1. Susan Hunt and Peggy Hutcheson, *Leadership For Women In The Church* (Grand Rapids: Zondervan, 1991), 10–11, 27.

2. Jeanne Porter, *Leading Ladies* (Philadelphia: Innisfree Press, 2000), 24–26.

3. Vashti M. McKenzie, *Not Without a Struggle* (Cleveland, OH: The Pilgrim Press, 1996), 1.

4. Teresa Berger, *Women's Ways of Worship* (Collegeville, MN: The Liturgical Press, 1999), 19.

5. Berger, *Women's Ways*.

6. Berger, *Women's Ways*, 109.

7. Berger, *Women's Ways*.

8. Berger, *Women's Ways*, 110.

9. McKenzie, Not Without a Struggle. 70.

10. Henry Blackaby and Richard Blackaby, *Spiritual Leadership* (Nashville: Broadman and Holman Publishers, 2001), 43.

11. Blackaby and Blackaby, *Spiritual Leadership*.

12. Barry, "Coaching to Win."

13. Barry, "Coaching to Win."

14. Hunt and Hutcheson, *Leadership*, 49.

15. Brenda McGlowan-Fellows, "Changing Roles: Corporate Mentoring of Black Women," *International Journal of Mental Health* 33.4 (2004): 3–18.

16. Hunt and Hutcheson, *Leadership*, 49–53.

17. Reggie McNeal, *The Present Future* (San Francisco: Josey-Bass, 2003), 73.

18. Edward H. Hammett, *Spiritual Leadership in a Secular Age* (St. Louis: Lake Hickory Resources, 2005) 113.

19. Aubrey Malphurs and Will Mancini, *Building Leaders* (Grand Rapids: Baker Books, 2004), 34.

20. Porter, *Leading Ladies*, 15.

21. Porter, *Leading Ladies*, 16.

22. Porter, *Leading Ladies*.

23. Hans Finzel, *Empowered Leaders* (Nashville: Word Publishing, 1998), 118–19.

24. Hunt and Hutcheson, *Leadership*, 20.

25. Hunt and Hutcheson, *Leadership*.

26. Joseph Umidi, *Transformational Coaching: Bridge Building That Impacts, Connects, Advances The Ministry And The Marketplace* (Virginia Beach, VA: Xulon Press, 2005), 74–75.

27. Umidi, *Transformational Coaching*, 78–79.

28. Thomas G. Crane, *The Heart of Coaching* (San Diego, CA: FTA Press, 2007), 199–200.

29. Crane, *Heart of Coaching*, 94.

30. Barry, "Coaching to Win," 6B.

31. Hammett, *Spiritual Leadership*, 108.

32. Paul D. Stanley and J. Robert Clinton, *Connecting: The Mentoring Relationships You Need to Succeed in Life* (Colorado Springs, CO: NavPress, 1992),157–59.

33. Stanley and Clinton, *Connecting*, 160–68.

34. Machen MacDonald, *The Power of Coaching: Engaging Excellence in Others* (Grass Valley, CA: PLI Publishing, 2007), 48–49.

35. MacDonald, *Power of Coaching*, 50.

36. MacDonald, *Power of Coaching*, 55.

37. MacDonald, *Power of Coaching*, 50.

38. Tony Stoltzfus, *Leadership Coaching: The Disciplines, Skills and Heart of a Coach* (Virginia Beach, VA: Booksurge, 2005), 128.

39. Stoltzfus, *Leadership Coaching*, 135–40.

40. MacDonald, *Power of Coaching*, 154–57.

41. Laura Whitworth, Karen Kimsey-House, Henry Kimsey-House, and Philip Sandahl, *Co-Active Coaching* (Mountain View, CA: Davies-Black Publishing, 2007), 218.

42. Whitworth et al., *Co-Active Coaching*, 218.

43. David Logan and John King, *The Coaching Revolution* (Avon, MA: Adams Media, 2004), 116.

44. MacDonald, *Power of Coaching*, 35–37.

45. Jack J. Phillips and Linda Kyle Stromei, *Creating Mentoring and Coaching Programs* (Alexandria, A: 2001), 107–19.

46. Phillips and Stomei, *Creating*, 159-160.

47. Umidi, *Transformational Coaching*, 24.

48. Robert R. Carkhuff, *The Art of Helping People* (Amherst, MA: Human Resource Development Press, 1993), 75.

49. MacDonald, 164-174.

50. Stanley and Clinton, *Connecting*, 157–67.

51. Stanley and Clinton, *Connecting*, 162.

Chapter 13: Case Studies in Church Abuse and Cover-Ups and How We Can Prevent Them

1. Abby Ohlheiser, "The woman behind 'Me Too' knew the power of the phrase when she created it—10 years ago," *The Washington Post*, Oct. 19, 2017, accessed August 6, 2020, https://www.washingtonpost.com/news/the-intersect/wp/2017/10/19/the-woman-behind-me-too-knew-the-power-of-the-phrase-when-she-created-it-10-years-ago/.

2. Peter Damian, *Liber Gomorrhianus*, AD 1051.

3. Dee Parsons, "I Thought He Was Taking Me for Ice Cream: One Woman's #MeToo Story of Molestation by Her Former Youth Pastor, Andy Savage," *The Wartburg Watch*, January 5, 2018, http://thewartburgwatch.com/2018/01/05/i-thought-he-was-taking-me-for-ice-cream-one-womans-metoo-story-of-molestation-by-her-former-youth-pastor-andy-savage/.

4. Parsons, "I Thought He Was Taking Me for Ice Cream: One Woman's #MeToo Story of Molestation by Her Former Youth Pastor, Andy Savage."

5. Parsons, "I Thought He Was Taking Me for Ice Cream: One Woman's #MeToo Story of Molestation by Her Former Youth Pastor, Andy Savage."

6. "I Was Assaulted. He Was Applauded," *The New York Times*, March 9, 2018, https://www.nytimes.com/2018/03/09/opinion/jules-woodson-andy-savage-assault.html.

7. Sarah Stankorb, "The Crusading Bloggers Exposing Abuse in Protestant Churches," *The Washington Post Magazine*, June 3, 2019, https://www.washingtonpost.com/news/magazine/wp/2019/06/03/feature/the-crusading-bloggers-exposing-sexual-assault-in-protestant-churches/.

8. Matthew Haag, "Memphis Pastor Admits 'Sexual Incident' With High School Student 20 Years Ago," *The New York Times*, January 9, 2018, https://www.nytimes.com/2018/01/09/us/memphis-megachurch-sex-assault.html?action=click&module=RelatedCoverage&pgtype=Article&region=Footer.

9. *New York Times*, "I Was Assaulted. He Was Applauded." Opinion, March 9, 2018, accessed August 7, 2020, https://www.nytimes.com/2018/03/09/opinion/jules-woodson-andy-savage-assault.html.

10. Katherine Burgess, "Andy Savage looks to launch new church in Memphis after sexual assault allegations, resignation," *Commercial Appeal*, October 28,2019, https://www.commercialappeal.com/story/news/2019/10/28/andy-savage-looks-launch-new-church-after-sexual-assault-allegations/2485740001/.

11. Ron Maxey, "Jules Woodson says Andy Savage resignation is only a step in fixing a systemic problem," *Commercial Appeal*, March 21, 2018, https://www.commercialappeal.com/story/news/2018/03/21/jules-woodson-says-andy-savage-resignation-first-step-fixing-systemic-problem/445251002/.

12. Dee Parsons, "Breaking News: Larry Cotton, Jules Woodson's Pastor to Whom She Reported Her Abuse, Has Resigned, Admitting He Should Have Reported," *The Wartburg Watch*, February 17, 2018, http://thewartburgwatch.com/2018/02/17/breaking-news-larry-cotton-jules-woodsons-pastor-to-whom-she-reported-her-abuse-has-stepped-down-admitting-he-should-have-reported/.

13. Ashley Easter, "Pastors Don't Have Affairs. . . . It's called Sexual Abuse," May 9, 2017, accessed August 6, 2020, https://www.ashleyeaster.com/blog/pastors-dont-have-affairs.

14. Parsons, "I Thought He Was Taking Me for Ice Cream: One Woman's #MeToo Story of Molestation by Her Former Youth Pastor, Andy Savage."

15. www.AshleyEaster.com.

16. Ashley Easter, "Why Patriarchy Is Abuse," March 20, 2017, accessed August 6, 2020, http://www.ashleyeaster.com/blog/why-patriarchy-is-abuse.

17. Manya Brachear Pashman, Jeff Coen, "After Years of Inquiries, Willow Creek Pastor Denies Misconduct Allegations," *Chicago Tribune*, March 23, 2018, https://www.chicagotribune.com/news/breaking/ct-met-willow-creek-pastor-20171220-story.html.

18. Pashman, Coen, "After Years of Inquiries, Willow Creek Pastor Denies Misconduct Allegations."

19. Laurie Goodstein, Willow Creek Church's Top Leadership Resigns Over Allegations Against Bill Hybels, *The New York Times*, August 8th, 2018, https://www.nytimes.com/2018/08/08/us/willow-creek-church-resignations-bill-hybels.html.

20. Jeremy Weber, "Here's Who Willow Creek Chose to Investigate Bill Hybels," *Christianity Today*, September 18, 2018, https://www.christianitytoday.com/news/2018/september/bill-hybels-willow-creek-investigation-advisors-iag.html; Kate Shellnutt, "Willow Creek Investigation: Allegations Against Bill Hybels are Credible," *Christianity Today*, February 28, 2019, https://www.christianitytoday.com/news/2019/february/willow-creek-bill-hybels-investigation-iag-report.html.

21. Megan Briggs, "Willow Creek: No Collusion in Bill Hybels Allegations," Church Leaders, May 10th, 2018, accessed August 6, 2020, hhttps://churchleaders.com/news/325250-willow-creek-no-collusion-in-bill-hybels-allegations.html.

22. Emily McFarlan Miller, "Misconduct Allegations Against Willow Creek Founder Bill Hybels are Credible, Independent Report Finds," *Religion News Service*, August 6, 2018, https://religionnews.com/2018/08/06/willow-creek-investigates-hybels-as-pastor-quits-over-new-allegations/.

23. Manya Brachear Pashman and Jeff Coen, "Hybels steps down from Willow Creek following allegations of misconduct," *Chicago Tribune*, April 11th, 2018, accessed August 6, 2020, https://www.chicagotribune.com/news/breaking/ct-met-hybels-willow-creek-resigns-20180410-story.html.

24. Pashman and Coen, "Hybels steps down from Willow Creek following allegations of misconduct."

25. Boz Tchividjian, "Are abuse survivors best served when institutions investigate themselves?", *Religion News Service*, October 16th, 2015, accessed August 6, 2020, https://religionnews.com/2015/10/16/are-abuse-survivors-best-served-when-institutions-investigate-themselves/.

26. https://www.netgrace.org/.

27. Vonda Dyer, "Vonda Dyer's Statement Re: *Chicago Tribune* and Bill Hybels," *Vonda Dyer*, April 4th, 2018, accessed August 6, 2020, https://vondadyer.weebly.com/blog/vonda-dyers-statement-re-chicago-tribune-and-bill-hybels.

Chapter 14: Developing an Organizational Code of Conduct

1. Solène Brabant and Jenny Brown, *Side by Side Advocacy Briefing: The Role of Faith Leaders in Achieving Gender Justice*, accessed March 23, 2020, https://jliflc.com/wp-content/uploads/2018/10 /SbSAdvocacyBrief_Final_2018English.pdf.

2. *Code of conduct* is the term used in this chapter, though it can be used interchangeably with the term *code of ethics*, which is used by several US denominations.

3. *Professional standards* and *safeguarding* are interchangeable terms relating to practices which protect vulnerable people by setting appropriate standards of behavior.

4. James Roland T. Wood, *Royal Commission into The New South Wales Police Service Final Report,* Sydney, N.S.W., 1997.

5. Anglican Church of Australia, *A Prayer Book for Australia,* Broughton Books, (Sydney, 1995), 784.

6. Anglican Church of Australia *A Prayer Book for Australia,* 784.

7. Anne Hall and Helen Last, "Violence Against Women in the Church Community: Project Anna," in *Without Consent: Confronting Adult Sexual Violence*, ed. Patricia Weiser Easteal (Australian Institute of Criminology, Canberra, 1993) 198.

8. Julia Baird and Hayley Gleeson, "'Submit to your husbands': Women told to endure domestic violence in the name of God," last updated October 21, 2018, accessed October 22, 2018, http://www .abc.net.au/news/2017-07-18/domestic-violence-church-submit-to-husbands/8652028.

9. Garth Blake, "Faithfulness in Service: The Development of a National Code of Conduct of the Anglican Church of Australia," *Ministry, Society, and Theology* vol. 18, 2004, 58ff.

10. Marie M. Fortune, *Is Nothing Sacred?: The Story of a Pastor, the Women He Sexually Abused, and the Congregation He Nearly Destroyed* (Cleveland: United Church Press, 1999), 152.

11. Nicola Lock, "An Exploration into the Nature of Reservations Concerning Professional Supervision Amongst Sydney Anglican Clergy" (unpublished master's thesis, Charles Sturt University, Canberra ACT, 2014).

12. World Health Organization, "Violence Against Women," November 29, 2017, accessed January 22, 2020, https://www.who.int/news-room/fact-sheets/detail/violence -against-women.

13. World Health Organization, "Violence Against Women," 2017.

14. Lorraine Radford and Cecilia Cappel, "Domestic Violence and the Methodist Church— The Way Forward," *Methodist Conference 2002 Report,* 2002, 2.

15. Evangelical Alliance. "How's the Family? A snapshot of the beliefs and habits of evangelical Christians." *21st Century Evangelicals*, Spring 2012, 5.

16. Australian Bureau of Statistics, "4906.0—Personal Safety, Australia, 2016," Canberra, Australia, 2016.

17. René Drumm et al., "Intimate Partner Violence in a Conservative Christian Denomination: Prevalence and Types," *Social Work & Christianity*, 2006: 233–251.

18. Mei-Chuan Wang, Sharon Horne, M. Levitt & Lisa Klesges. "Christian Women in IPV Relationships: An Exploratory Study of Religious Factors." *Journal of Psychology and Christianity*, 2009, Vol.28(3), pp.224–235.

19. Australian Institute of Family Studies, "Child Abuse and Neglect Statistics," accessed March 23, 2020, https://aifs.gov.au/cfca/publications/child-abuse-and-neglect-statistics.

20. Catherine Ward et al., "Sexual Violence Against Children in South Africa: A Nationally Representative Cross-sectional Study of Prevalence and Correlates," *Lance Global Health,* 6.4 (April 2018): e460–e468.

21. John Jay College of Criminal Justice, *The Nature and Scope of Sexual Abuse of Minors by Catholic Priests and Deacons in the United States 1950–2002* (Washington, D.C.: USCCB, 2004), http://www.bishop-accountability.org/reports/2004_02_27_JohnJay/.

22. Daniel L. Migliore, *The Power of God and the Gods of Power* (Louisville: Westminster John Knox, 2008), 3.

23. John R.P. French, Jr. and Bertram Raven, "The Bases of Social Power," in *Studies in Social Power*, ed. Dorwin Cartwright (Ann Arbor: University of Michigan Press, 1959), 150–67.

24. Richard M. Gula *Just Ministry: Professional Ethics for Pastoral Ministers.* (New York: Paulist Press, 2010), 123.

25. S. J. Collings, S. Griffiths, M. Kumalo, "Patterns of Disclosure in Child Sexual Abuse," *South African Journal of Psychology* 35 (2005): 270–85.

26. S. J. Collings et al., "Patterns of Disclosure in Child Sexual Abuse."

27. Nancy Nason-Clark, "Religion and Violence Against Women: Exploring the Rhetoric and the Response of Evangelical Churches in Canada," *Social Compass* (1996): 521.

28. Hall and Last, "Violence Against Women in the Church Community: Project Anna," 198.

29. Church of England, "Guidelines for the Professional Conduct of Clergy," accessed January 22, 2020, https://www.churchofengland.org/more/policy-and-thinking/guidelines-professional-conduct-clergy/guidelines-professional-conduct.

30. Shefali Virkar, "Can Codes of Conduct Work? Evaluating the Effectiveness of Privatised Corporate Governance," in *International Perspectives on Socio-Economic Development in the Era of Globalization,* eds. Saurabh Sen, Anshuman Battacharya, and Ruchi Sen (IGI Global, 2016), 67–95.

31. Virkar, "Can Codes of Conduct Work?," 86.

32. Garth Blake, personal communication concerning the *Anglican Communion Safe Church Commission Draft Report*, Appendix 4—Guidelines 2019.

33. "Anglican Communion Safe Church Commission," Anglican Communion, accessed January 23, 2020, https://www.anglicancommunion.org/community/commissions/the-anglican -communion-safe-church-commission.aspx.

34. Garth Blake, "Faithfulness in Service: The Development of a National Code of Conduct," 18:58ff.

35. Anglican Diocese of Sydney, "Ministry Standards Ordinance 2017," accessed March 23, 2020, https://www.sds.asn.au/ministry-standards-ordinance-2017.

36. Tim Harris, "Shalom, Gospel and the Mission of God," in *Flourishing in Faith: Theology Encountering Positive Psychology*, eds. Gillies Ambler et al. (Eugene, OR: Wipf and Stock Publishers, 2017), 68.

37. Tim Harris, "Shalom, Gospel and the Mission of God," 66.

38. Harris, "Shalom, Gospel and the Mission of God," 78.

CPSIA information can be obtained
at www.ICGtesting.com
Printed in the USA
LVHW031225030422
714886LV00002B/6